Palgrave Studies in Cybercrime and Cybersecurity

This book series addresses the urgent need to advance knowledge in the fields of cybercrime and cybersecurity. Because the exponential expansion of computer technologies and use of the Internet have greatly increased the access by criminals to people, institutions, and businesses around the globe, the series will be international in scope. It provides a home for cutting-edge long-form research. Further, the series seeks to spur conversation about how traditional criminological theories apply to the online environment. The series welcomes contributions from early career researchers as well as established scholars on a range of topics in the cybercrime and cybersecurity fields.

More information about this series at
http://www.palgrave.com/gp/series/14637

Vasileios Karagiannopoulos

Living With Hacktivism

From Conflict to Symbiosis

palgrave
macmillan

Vasileios Karagiannopoulos
Institute of Criminal Justice Studies
University of Portsmouth
Portsmouth, UK

Palgrave Studies in Cybercrime and Cybersecurity
ISBN 978-3-030-10106-0 ISBN 978-3-319-71758-6 (eBook)
https://doi.org/10.1007/978-3-319-71758-6

Cover credit: Raw Group / Alamy Stock Photo

Printed on acid-free paper

This Palgrave Macmillan imprint is published by Springer Nature
The registered company is Springer International Publishing AG
The registered company address is: Gewerbestrasse 11, 6330 Cham, Switzerland

To my parents

Preface

This book discusses one of the most ambiguous aspects of online political activity: the practice of transgressing, or at least challenging, cybercrime laws with the purpose of symbolically expressing dissent or facilitating political expression in cyberspace. Such activities have been dubbed hacktivism due to the use of software tools and computer modification and impairment techniques for realising their political symbolic expression online, usually through virtual sit-ins impairing the use of websites and unauthorised graffiti on web pages or the exposure of software weaknesses. The illegal nature of hacktivism has given rise to extensive discussions in relation to its moral and political usefulness as a form of online civil disobedience in conjunction with its potential for harmful effects on information networks and the interests of the networks' operators and users. This area of study is contested as will be seen throughout the book and both sides of the argument have their merits.

In recent years, these activities have proliferated, refuelling ongoing discussions regarding how they should be perceived and dealt with. Despite the existence of sociopolitical assessments of hacktivism, there has not been an extensive, more in-depth legal and regulatory analysis in relation to these political activities. Consequently, a motivating force for this book has been to provide such an analysis with a particular focus on the US and the UK, which have been two jurisdictions where there has been rich hacktivist activity and also legal developments in relation to the phenomenon of hacktivism. My aim will be to identify and highlight the potential problems of the existing approach that is followed when dealing with hacktivism and its impact on user rights, protesters, and overall cybersecurity. Having done that, I will eventually suggest an alternative rationale for responding to hacktivism, taking into account the potential sociopolitical importance of such practices, but also the risks that they can entail, shifting from conflict-based approaches to more symbiotic ones.

This work does not suggest a uniform and fail-proof way of dealing with hacktivism and does not aim to justify the existence and practices of particular groups, such as Anonymous. In fact, it defies the possibility of generalised solutions, since it acknowledges primarily that hacktivism by itself, as a movement and practice, defies uniformity and should not be defined through the groups that it is primarily associated with. On the contrary, it is a practice that is open to expressing political dissent in general and has been used by various groups that would not be characterised as hacktivist per se. It is exactly such generalisations that I would like to dispel. However, I also aim to show that the cases of hacktivism that have been dealt with have been done so in a manner that further reinforces all those conflicts, injustices, and power imbalances that give rise to hacktivism in the first place and try to deal with hacktivism in a very generalised manner.

Moreover, my aim is not to identify ways of eliminating hacktivism, as I do not believe that it would be feasible or positive to completely eliminate a phenomenon that has organically developed in our society as an expression of citizens' needs for political reaction. But I also do not generally glorify hacktivist actions as the reinvention of online politics and democratic deliberation, because its realisation can be far from the ideal portrayal of modern politics that proponents might think it is. A core part of the following discussion is the understanding that hacktivism is a diverse political practice and can be and has been abused, much like any other political practice, from parliamentary decision-making to legal striking and activist direct action.

Finding mitigating responses to the risks of hacktivism and nurturing any positive elements it might entail are all about admitting that these activities are part of the everyday life of cyberspace—which itself is part of our everyday lives. Dealing with hacktivism in ways that are educated, informed, and inclusive rather than reactionary and demonising and instead aiming at reducing its harms and reinforcing its positive aspects can be challenging, especially in the context of modern societies with the legal and practical tools at our disposal. After all, it needs to be understood that hacktivism is an activity that flows from conflict and expresses conflict. It is a response to perceived social problems and injustices. Consequently, trying to deal with it using more conflict-generating responses, as is the tendency today, can intensify the problems that caused hacktivism as well as the considerations hacktivist actions themselves entail, rather than abate them. How this happens will become more obvious throughout the analysis.

Essentially, hacktivism, as a novel form of politically motivated law-breaking, reframes the question of morality versus legality and the concept of social justice, democratic deliberation, and contestation in a new and challenging context in an era where preventing risk and achieving maximum security is a dominating rationale. Yet hacktivist practice with its novel reconfiguration of traditional protest methods induces, if not forces, us to rearticulate older discussions about justice and legitimate law-breaking as political expression as well as free expression and privacy in discussing how these are applied in the new cyberspace era. Our perceptions ought to be broadened and reconfigured in order to take into account different societal dimensions, reinvented communicational and behavioural norms, and tools created by novel communities supporting old and new sociopolitical causes. This will be a necessary step in our attempt to compromise the interpretation and enforcement processes of nascent criminal laws with activities that are purposefully designed to challenge them.

Essentially, this enquiry becomes an interesting example in the wider discussion regarding whether we, as a connected, networked society benefit from intensifying conflicts or by building on more understanding, symbiotic interplay; whether fragmentation and tension are better or whether learning from each other, even if we disagree, can be of more benefit from both a theoretical and a practical perspective. In social situations where conflict is default and is often the cause of the problem and also the problem itself, as in the case of hacktivists, perhaps a reconsideration of our established positions is needed. There will always be conflict-inducing situations, but it is how we understand these power conflicts and learn from the power and counterpower interactions that allows us to come up with ways that alleviate these tensions and lead to better, more just, and productive results.

This book and its rationale of symbiosis are not based on the naive premise that perceptions can so radically change from one day to the next. Instead, it works on the presumption that we will eventually realise that we want to mitigate the negative consequences of conflict-based approaches, rather than exacerbate them, and that, in principle, there are democratic values that should be safeguarded to an extent and that would essentially suggest these more symbiotic approaches. Therefore, it is better to actually try to understand how we can achieve our goals, from the perspective of state authorities, online corporations, political organisation, or user collective, without leading to situations that further negate the aims we are trying to achieve. Contrary to pure criminality, which generally derives from malign and personalised motivations, hacktivism also challenges the dipole between the socially considerate public authorities and socially inconsiderate criminals by putting forth motivations that also appear to promote socially considerate goals and even question the benign motivations on behalf of the authorities. That is why symbiosis is about configuring how power and counterpower can co-function, how their goals can best be achieved and compromised in situations where strong power tensions exist in order to ultimately facilitate these socially positive aims.

Some might find the discussion moot, arguing that there will always be conflict, which I do not deny. Eliminating conflict is not part of what this book is about. It is about learning where to use conflict and where and when it might be better to mitigate or promote tolerance and even collaboration in order to achieve the same or better results, depending on the balancing of different aims. Others might find it inspiring. Whatever the case, I would like this discussion to be viewed as something that has its roots in a reconfiguration of action and reaction based on a more holistic assessment of the different perspectives clashing and influencing each other. My goal is to generate more debate, and hopefully this book will attract the full spectrum of views. I do not plan to achieve an ultimate truth about how hacktivism should be viewed and treated and I accept that this cannot be attained anyway. Instead I aim to prove that there needs to be a more nuanced discussion about these activities and to help inform this discussion with some useful and interesting arguments. I hope you will enjoy the controversy and the intellectual challenge that hacktivism poses. For me, accepting the existence of such a challenge is the first step towards achieving symbiotic thinking and, consequently, relevant practices.

The book is split into seven chapters. Chapter 1 aims to provide the context within which hacktivism was born and developed and to demonstrate the organic nature of this type of political expression for information-based networked societies. This introductory chapter begins by explaining how the Internet came about and how it is revolutionising social relations, politics, and power conflicts. It highlights the rising importance of networks and information for contemporary societies and talks about the birth of hacktivism and its role as an inevitable hybridisation of political activism with hacking both in terms of rationales and also tactics. This chapter is a crucial step in familiarising the reader with the landscape within which hacktivism was born and develops and creates the necessary framework for the rest of the discussion.

Chapter 2 provides an analysis of the various groups and individuals that have contributed to the development of hacktivism from its birth in the early 1990s into what it is today. Although hacktivism can be seen as a continuum of action with varying groups and individuals being involved in it, this chapter will split the continuum into two eras. The first era discusses groups like the Critical Art Ensemble, the Electronic Disturbance Theater, and Hacktivismo, and provides information regarding their rationales, goals, and tactics. It then moves on to discuss the major contemporary hacktivist collective, Anonymous, with its diverse ideologies and tactics, as well as specific individuals, such as Aaron Swartz and Andrew Auernheimer, whose actions generated important discussions for the future of hacktivism and the impact of contemporary legislation and law-enforcement rationales on hacktivists. Although the book focuses on analysis of the practices rather than of particular groups, this chapter is crucial in providing a more holistic understanding of hacktivism as a movement, as well as a cluster of ideologies and practices, before moving on to discuss its positive and negative aspects and assess the ways it has been dealt with so far.

Chapter 3 moves the analysis into more depth by assessing the links of hacktivism to freedom of expression and civil disobedience. This is done with the aim of highlighting the main concerns behind hacktivist practices as a form of expressive law-breaking, but also in order to discuss the positive elements it entails as a novel political practice. It first reviews the links between symbolic law-breaking and free speech/expression and finds similarities and differences between hacktivist practices and protected speech conceptually and legally. Finding that a link between the two would be hard to establish in most cases, the analysis then moves on to review the links between hacktivist practices and civil disobedience, since hacktivism has been often characterised as electronic civil disobedience. The chapter discusses the value of civil disobedience and the moral and practical criteria that reinforce its positive elements, whilst mitigating its negative consequences. The chapter closes by analogising hacktivist tactics and practices to civil disobedience and translates the arguments regarding the positive and negative elements of civil disobedience into cyberspace situations.

Chapter 4 focuses on the sociopolitical norms and the legislation that relate to cybercrime and hacktivism more particularly and dictate how hacktivism is dealt with currently in the US and the UK. It discusses the predominance on command and control policies that prioritise security and risk-minimisation norms. Furthermore, it assesses how recent sociopolitical developments, media influences, and cybersecurity experts maintain and exacerbate such a framework and how this impacts on hacktivism as a cybercrime-related, contestational political practice. The discussion then moves on to analyse the current legislative framework regarding cybercrime and cyberterrorism in the US and the UK. It offers examples of how such legislation applies and has been applied to hacktivist actions and highlights the concerns that legislative broadness, vagueness, and punitiveness can entail for hacktivists. This chapter essentially provides a first-level critique of the current responses to hacktivist incidents in order to prepare the ground for offering an alternative rationale that moves away from the conflict-based model, which is currently predominant, to a more symbiotic framework.

Chapter 5 supplements and reinforces the discussion in Chapter 4. Essentially, it assesses the stakeholders and mechanisms facilitating the enforcement of the existing normative rationales and legal tools in relation to hacktivism. This section of the book essentially aims to analyse whether the enforcing actors mitigate or exacerbate the concerns expressed in the previous chapter regarding the legitimacy of the conflict-focused responses that dominant norms and cybercrime laws can generate. It looks into the function of prosecutorial discretion in conjunction with risk-averse and managerial mentalities that underlie it and also analyses the role of guilty pleas in dealing with crime and hacktivism in particular. It then discusses the importance of judicial decision-making and the stifling impact of sentencing guidelines as well as the influence judicial culture can have on decisions that involve politically contestational cyberdeviance. The role of juries within that system is also discussed. The chapter proceeds with a review of the role of large Internet corporations in collaborating with the authorities regarding surveillance and information sharing in relation to online deviance. The final part focuses on assessing the role of those information gatekeepers in safeguarding the diversity of expression online and the rights of their users, and how their policies and actions impact or could impact on hacktivism.

Chapter 6 follows and builds on the conclusions drawn from the previous chapters in finding a legitimacy deficit in the current rationales and actual responses to hacktivism. It highlights how responses that are based on conflict often prove counterproductive when applied to hacktivism, as an activity that itself flows from social conflict. The chapter then offers a theoretical and practical framework for responding to hacktivism that is based on more symbiotic rather than conflict-focused rationales and actions and suggests some ways symbiosis can be facilitated and promoted both from within and from outside the criminal justice system. It attempts to highlight the need for better understanding and interplay between all stakeholders involved and the requirement for everyone to attempt to act in ways that could reduce conflict and backlash effects and thus manage to more fully achieve the goals of crime prevention, proportionality and promotion of productive democratic deliberation. The chapter discusses responses relating to a reconsideration of the concepts of damage and loss and promoting technology-based, more relevant penalties when dealing with hacktivism. It also elaborates on the need for providing more inclusive processes and spaces for political deliberation and contestation to be realised and the ways the negative effects of protests could be mitigated through technology. Finally, it discusses the role of hacktivists in promoting symbiotic solutions and their responsibility to provide well-thought-out rhetoric and strategies and to try to maintain the standards of ethical protesting within their spaces and communities.

Finally, Chapter 7 closes the book by offering a summary of some of the major conclusions drawn throughout the book. It reminds the reader of the analysis regarding the positive and negative aspects of hacktivism and how this reinforces the need for more nuanced responses. It summarises the considerations that the current framework generates for producing such nuanced responses and how this leads to inefficacious and unjust results. It then proceeds to provide an overview of the main points relating to the suggested symbiotic framework and the various ways it could be practically applied. The chapter ends with a hope that this study will inform new discussions regarding hacktivism, but also cybercrime in general.

One of the basic premises of this book is that hacktivism is an organic development of the modern, network/information-based societies expressing both traditional and newly generated norms and power struggles. In order to get an initial idea of how hacktivism came about and where it fits into contemporary power struggles, it would be good to start by seeing how the Internet has developed and how power structures and conflicts have facilitated the natural transition of political contestation in the new arenas of cyberspace.

Portsmouth, UK Vasileios Karagiannopoulos

Acknowledgements

First, I would like to thank my parents, who have made my dreams possible, each in their own way.

A sincere thank you goes to my academic supervisors Professor Donald Nicolson, Dr Konstantinos Komaitis and Dr Benjamin Farrand. I will always be grateful for your support and guidance. I also thank my colleague and friend, Dr Jane Winstone, for her faith in me and my work.

Finally, a big thank you to all those who have stood by me all these years, when I was pleasant, but also when I was unbearable.

Contents

List of Abbreviations

ACTA	Anti-Counterfeiting Trade Agreement
AT&T	American Telecom and Telegraph
CAE	Critical Art Ensemble
CD	Civil Disobedience
cDc	Cult of the Dead Cow
CFAA	Computer Fraud and Abuse Act
CIA	Central Intelligence Agency
CMA	Computer Misuse Act
DDOS	Distributed Denial of Service
DEA	Digital Economy Act
DPP	Director of Public Prosecutions
DRM	Digital Rights Management
ECHR	European Convention on Human Rights
ECtHR	European Court of Human Rights
ECD	Electronic Civil Disobedience
EDT	Electronic Disturbance Theater
EU	European Union
FBI	Federal Bureau of Investigations
FCC	Federal Communications Commission
HADOPI	Haute Autorité pour la Diffusion des Oeuvres et la Protection des Droits sur Internet
HESSLA	Hacktivismo's Enhanced-Source Software License Agreement
ICANN	Internet Corporation for Assigned Names and Numbers

ICP	Internet Content Provider
IETF	Internet Engineering Task Force
IGF	Internet Governance Forum
IMF	International Monetary Fund
IP	Internet Protocol
iRC	Internet Relay Chat
IRS	Internal Revenue Service
ISOC	Internet Society
ISP	Internet Service Provider
IT	Information Technology
ITU	International Telecommunications Union
IWF	Internet Watch Foundation
LOIC	Low Orbit Ion Cannon
MPC	Model Penal Code
NGO	Non-Governmental Organisation
OS	Operating System
PET	Privacy-Enhancing Technologies
PJA	Police and Justice Act
SOPA	Stop Online Piracy Act
StGB	Strafgesetzbuch
TCP/IP	Transmission Control Protocol/Internet Protocol
UK	United Kingdom
URL	Universal Resource Locator
US	United States (of America)
USAPA	USA PATRIOT Act
WSIS	World Summit on the Information Society
WTO	World Trade Organization
WWW	World Wide Web

1

Introduction: The Birth of Cyberspace and the Development of Hacktivism

1 Life in the Networked Societies

Our society increasingly relies on interconnected, information networks, which are, more than ever before, shaping the global economic, political, and cultural landscape. In fact, it is argued that we are currently living in an era of networked, information-based societies[1] where 'words, human relationships, data, wealth, and power are manifested by people using computer-mediated communications technology.'[2] The Internet is today an overarching living network that spans the globe and encompasses a milieu of other networks all interacting together and impacting on our lives. Its expansion and transition from a communications medium to a social space where people interact has also given this network of networks the name cyberspace, a term first coined by William Gibson in the 1980s in his *Neuromancer* sci-fi novel.

The Internet, initially a US military project for facilitating the decentralisation of communications in case of a nuclear attack, was introduced to the wider public in the mid-1990s. At the beginning, use was limited to research networks and discussion forums, before being adopted by commercial and governmental actors. Gradually, educational research, communication, and, later, commercial activities started to evolve online,

V. Karagiannopoulos, *Living With Hacktivism*, Palgrave Studies in Cybercrime and Cybersecurity, https://doi.org/10.1007/978-3-319-71758-6_1

taking advantage of the openness and innovation potential of the technologies by which the Internet was created. More particularly, Internet communications were based on technologies and protocols, such as the transmission control protocol/internet protocol (TCP/IP), which broke information into data packets and transmitted them over the network indiscriminately. This preserved the neutrality of the network towards the transmitted information irrespective of its content or originating source and could thus be seen as decentralising and democratising information exchanges further. This core infrastructural element of non-discrimination and openness regarding the various types of information allowed new hardware and software to develop and gave rise to new types of communication and services.

The technological evolution of the Internet began with its popularisation through the World Wide Web technology and the deregulatory decision to entrust important parts of its governance to non-state actors.[3] These initial developments allowed for openness and self-management and reinforced its public uptake. Cyberspace was further transformed into a more interactive, richer social space by a significant twist at around the turn of the century. This was the introduction of a new category of online platforms and software applications (MySpace, Facebook, Twitter), which signified a transition to a second Internet era: the Web 2.0. These new developments empowered users by enabling them to produce their own content in a personalised format, which further decentralised the production and distribution of information and created more dynamic interaction between users. This interaction and potential for collaboration simultaneously empowered civil society and provided it with additional tools for organising and also for influencing the shaping of sociopolitical decisions. The influence of these platforms, both in terms of user interaction and information production, but also in terms of their social and commercial influence can be imagined if one considers the sheer number of users Facebook has attracted to date (2 billion) or the amount of YouTube videos (400+ hours uploaded every minute). Web 2.0 coincided with the gradual popularisation of bandwidth Internet services and mobile smartphones, which greatly increased the speed and proliferation of fast network connections, allowing a quantitative and qualitative increase in the information that could be produced and exchanged.

As we are now entering an era of Web 3.0, where new opportunities for processing large swathes of data are becoming a reality, the importance of information and the knowledge and consequent power this mass information processing can entail is yet to be fully revealed. However, it appears that this new era will signal a more extensive empowerment for those with the power, capacity, and knowledge to store, process, combine, and interpret the 'big data' available. As 'smart' devices have started proliferating in our everyday lives, from connected TVs and fridges to cars and boilers, they enrich the already existing computer networks and the information produced and circulated within them. This expanding 'Internet of Things' is becoming another evolutionary step in the development of networked societies, also creating new ways that data and devices will interact and impact on our everyday lives as well as our socio-political realities.

2 Information: The New Currency of Power

The aforementioned advent of networks, information, and new digital technologies has inevitably also challenged traditional conceptions of linear, top-down power and governance relations, thus offering new challenges to how power is generated and exercised in our globalised world. From the early years of the Internet's proliferation, the cross-jurisdictional nature of these information networks challenged the established hierarchical, law-based models of control. Early thinkers of cyberspace regulation highlighted the weaknesses of legal systems and law enforcement in regulating cyberspace efficiently and legitimately, instead suggesting more decentralised, self-regulatory approaches as more fitting.[4] Even proponents of law as a predominant tool in the service of controlling online behaviours introduce caveats, accepting that whenever laws are challenged by the global and technologically novel nature of the Internet, new actors and tools, such as online intermediaries and new software, could feature in the process of regulating behaviour online.[5] Other theorists, such as Reidenberg and Lessig, argue more explicitly for the need to engage actively with new regulatory actors and tools, mainly through the use of technology as an architectural control mechanism in the networks.[6] These discussions serve to highlight the interplay between law, new norms, and technological developments and demonstrate how power structures are gradually becoming more diversified and decentralised in our expanding social space.

The realisation of the Internet's potential for decentralising power through the empowerment of multiple stakeholders and the gradual popularisation of its use render the Internet politically relevant in modern societies, not just as a communication and commerce tool, but also as a space where political power is generated and shaped and gets dispersed and challenged. As Foucault explains, power is not only decentralised to many people, but also relational and ubiquitous, as it exists within all deliberate, multiple human interactions, instead of just being focused on one agent as a quantum of force to be exercised hierarchically.[7] The Internet by its very nature and structure is an expression of Foucault's realisation, constantly generating and influencing power relations and introducing major challenges to hierarchical operation and control mechanisms.

Within the networked societies, the constitutive element of power also shifts, with information becoming the predominant source and resource of power. Information, despite it being considered central in contemporary societies, has been crucial for economic and sociopolitical development even since the formation of the nation state.[8] However, the Internet and digital technologies have dramatically reinforced and emphasised the role of information in modern societies due to the scale of information being produced and processed. Apart from being the lifeblood of communications networks, information is essential also because it generates knowledge, which inevitably leads to empowerment. As Foucault says, 'it is not possible for power to be exercised without knowledge, it is impossible for knowledge not to engender power.'[9] The hacktivist group Critical Art Ensemble (CAE) also highlights the transition of power and counterpower to a different arena: '[D]isconnected from spatial notions of state and traditional space-related attachments, power has now migrated to the immaterial, information networks, with resistance inevitably following.'[10]

This realisation is also in accord with the Foucauldian view that wherever there is power, there will be a form of counterpower opposing it.[11] Power is, thus, related to information generation and management even more directly than in previous eras, and moderating or liberating information flows and making use of them becomes central for all actors taking part in contemporary sociopolitical struggles.

The importance of information is also reflected in the discussions that focus on the regulatory potential of information technologies, hardware, and software, which Lessig has characterised as 'code,' the building blocks of what constitutes our Internet experience.[12] Technology plays a crucial role for regulation online and strongly interacts with legal restrictions and mandates. In the malleable virtual environment of cyberspace, hardware and software can be very effective in shaping our experience and capabilities based on what the technology enables or prevents us from doing, simultaneously sharing a regulatory and deregulatory potential.[13]

Despite the initial openness and focus on privacy and free information exchange the Internet was built on, as already discussed, these principles have gradually become increasingly challenged, and attempts to now harness the empowering potential of information technologies are becoming increasingly common. This is particularly so due to the medium's extreme popularity and increasing commercialisation, as many corporations, governmental authorities, and even international organisations can see profit-making and/or power-engendering opportunities in influencing information generation, flows, and processing. Governments have become much more active in managing information either through extensive legislation or indirectly through influencing online companies that could exert control over information, such as Internet service providers (ISPs) or content providers and software developers.

However, the Internet's malleable nature simultaneously allows the subverting of control efforts. Technology, as much as it can regulate behaviour, also enables deregulation, and for every technological development that aims to regulate and restrict information production and communication, there are tools developed for bypassing restrictions, which can be easily found online and are massively employed, such as The Onion Router (TOR) network.

The endemic regulatory and counter-regulatory tug of war of the information networks is reflected in Castells' realisation that no power elite can firmly control the setting of norms and goals for the informational networks without these standards being challenged, and no power can eliminate the synergies between various actors that undermine the efforts of others, since they are all engaged in a constant interplay for increasing their own influence.[14] As Terranova aptly argued, '[a]s a political milieu, a network culture looks more like a permanent battlefield than like a neo-socialist utopia. It is the plane over which battles for market shares and for the determination of public opinions are fought.'[15]

From these battles hacktivism developed as a natural expression of counterpower against presumed social injustices in a language more akin to informational networks and adopting norms and values that flow from the nature of the medium and the different groups that engaged with it . As Klang highlights, 'the Internet is used for every conceivable form of communication and it is therefore only natural that it should be used as an infrastructure for protest and civil disobedience.'[16] And hacktivism in a sense personifies at its core a form of civil disobedience (CD) online.

3 The Birth of Hacktivism

The concept of hacktivism can be defined broadly and has been used in so many different contexts that it has come to connote potentially any use of digital technologies for political reasons. This indiscriminate use of the term is also one of the main problems hacktivists face today, as their actions are analogised to purely criminal or even terrorist activities. This is due to the fact that the 'hacktivist mantle' has been adopted by a multitude of individuals and groups attempting to legitimise or glorify their exploits under a political justification. Moreover, the term has been excessively used in sensationalist media reports and by cybersecurity experts and government officials for many incidents of computer network disruption.[17] Vegh[18] and Denning[19] have highlighted the diversity with which hacktivism is portrayed in a spectrum ranging from cyberactivism to cyberterrorism and e-warfare, depending on different viewpoints and interpretations.

However, despite this difficulty in narrowing down hacktivism, the notion of hacktivism adopted in this book relates to activities and tactics that have actual computer access or impairment (or the facilitation of such acts) as their core. For the purpose of this enquiry, then, hacktivism will be considered as 'the use of computer and network access and reconfiguration techniques that transgress or challenge cybercrime laws in order to produce or facilitate symbolic effects that confer a political message or protest a particular policy.'[20]

Hacktivism has its origins in the computer hacker and the activist communities. More particularly, the hacker community, which forms a strong part of the hacktivist community, is intrinsically linked to the resistance-facilitating potential of technology, challenging established operational and behavioural standards. Hacking originally meant 'making use of technology in an original, unorthodox and inventive way'[21] and did not relate solely to illegal acts, as it predominantly does today; or, better yet, the activities perpetrated then, such as software modifications or network penetrations, were not yet explicitly criminalised. Initially, hackers were mostly those who focused on discovering new technological uses and advancing user knowledge and capabilities by sharing information and by cooperating towards innovation, and computer and program reconfiguration techniques were part and parcel of what they were doing in order to develop new technologies as well as have fun within their communities. As Jordan and Taylor highlight, hackers originating from phone phreaks and computer programmers eventually got media attention and developed into a subculture of people who were at ease with new technologies and challenged the norm of fear and insecurity of the information revolution.[22]

By observing the dominant practices and perceptions of, at least, the initial hacker communities, Levy managed to distil certain principles that defined the hacker ethos and also highlight their political potential. The 'hacker ethic'[23] relates to promoting meritocracy, anti-authoritarianism, freedom of information, and optimism for the life-improving potential of technology and the positive effects of computerisation.[24] In societies where information and technology become assets, both from a financial and political/social perspective, it is natural that values such as these would clash with the commercial interests and security-focused policies of surveillance and control. The underground community of hackers was a resisting force to the upcoming dominating influence and control that new technologies would facilitate and a response to the technocratic and control forces of the formulating information societies.[25] Although the gradual spread of digital technologies and the popularisation of the Internet led to an exponential increase of tech-savvy individuals, with many of those using their skills for criminal purposes,[26] even benign hacking gradually became too inconsistent with the general power flows to survive unchallenged.[27]

The second part of hacktivism relates to the evolution of contemporary activist politics. Since information is a source of power and networks of power rely on the integrity of information and unhindered information exchanges, political organisation and the tactics of resistance also change to reflect these developments. The globalisation of politics, in combination with a disappointment in more traditional mainstream political tactics, has led many political collectives to become increasingly devoted to universal political issues (economic crisis, ecology, anti-war) and to the promotion of political diversity and direct participation.[28] The current era is characterised as one of 'meta-politics,' where political activists have shifted their focus from parliamentary democracy and capturing power through party politics.[29] Consequently, activism today has lost much of the concreteness and consistent membership of the past party-based movements. Instead, political contestation takes the form of fluid collectives, 'mobilisations' with ideologically diverse participants, who mostly converge to fight for specific goals, and where solidarity and political sensitisation are not preexisting characteristics, but also aims and products of these mobilising initiatives.[30]

The examples of the Arab Spring protests in Iran, Tunisia, and Egypt or the movements against the economic crisis in the US (Occupy), Greece, and Spain (Indignados) are typical of the new types of political movements with an online and an offline presence highlighting this ideological diversity and tactical looseness. Ideological/party purity has become secondary to a more goal-driven political momentum, which is reinforced by the immediacy social networks afford and the globalisation of political considerations that transcend national political borders—a further consequence of how technologies have managed to collapse traditional notions of time and space. Hacktivism, by its very nature also fits within this new paradigm, where the political message and its underlying rationale become more important than a framing ideology and concrete organisational structure.

This transition to more decentralised and globalised models of political contestation has also impacted on the tactical choices. Activists have abandoned the effort of formal, holistic social reform through the domination of parliamentary processes and focus on circumventing unjust laws and policies and calling on injustice, local and global, by challenging mainstream symbols and meanings (culture jamming) and the disruption of dominant information flows.[31] In addition to being able to uncover the truth by freely accessing the information that is out there and double-checking facts and figures using thoroughly accessible scientific information, activists online and offline introduce additional information by using tactics such as 'signal distortion, graffiti on advertising posters, hijacking of corporate events, all kind of attempts at disrupting the smooth efficiency of the communication machine'[32] in a much similar way as hackers do.

These tactics reflect the difficulty for activists to compete on a level playing field, as regards producing and distributing information over networks compared to incumbent and resource-rich actors, such as states, corporate media, and infrastructure-controlling multinational companies. These new tactics also focus on creating spectacular or controversial effects in order to attract the attention of the mainstream media, in addition to being reported by the activists' own media apparatuses (Indymedia, Facebook groups, Twitter feeds). Web 2.0 has turned users into content creators and broadcasters and has allowed for the viral sharing of information between communities over social networking applications. The broadening of their communication opportunities in addition to their potential for creating spectacular, mediated events allows activists to express their dissent more effectively and widely, sensitise the public, and, eventually, increase the pressure on policymakers for political change.[33]

Hacktivism, as a blend of hacker and activist culture constitutes a manifestation of all these characteristics. Protests are based on media-relating events and in order to attract attention to the protesters' causes and sensitise and engage the public in politics beyond the traditional party processes. Hacktivists aim to bring important information to the fore at the same time that their symbolic protests are drawing attention to it. Their hacker-related background comes to the service of such practices often, as it allows hacktivists to jam cultural and political symbols online and cause noticeable disruptions by intervening on the appearance and functionality of websites and programs. After all, culture jamming and hacking have a lot in common in terms of reconfiguring a cultural artefact or a piece of communication in ways that disrupt or reverse the original purpose and/or message.[34]

4 Conclusion

Before moving on to discuss hacktivist groups in more detail, some conclusions can be drawn from the discussion so far. First, it is a fact that modern society and politics have been radically transformed by the addition of the virtual, online dimension in our everyday lives. The advent of the Internet and digital technologies has created new social, economic, and political spaces and inevitably new ways that power and counter-power are generated and norms and standards are contested. In parallel, politics and social organising have been transformed and new political/activist formations have been shaped and reinvented political goals and values have become the norm.

Within this new situation, the hacktivist movement has also been born and has grown, having its origins deep within these sociopolitical and technological developments, and it seems to be a natural 'child' of this modern era of information politics and the power struggles such politics relate to. This will become much more obvious in the next chapter, which will endeavour to analyse the movement and the relevant groups in more detail.

Notes

1. Various criteria have been used for identifying what is new in the information society, from technological and economic to occupational, spatial, and cultural. Frank Webster (3rd edn, Routledge, London 2006) 8–9.
2. Howard Rheingold, *The Virtual Community: Homesteading on the Electronic Frontier* (The MIT Press, Cambridge (MA) 2000) cited in Suart Biegel, *Beyond Our Control?: Confronting the Limits of Our Legal System in the Age of Cyberspace* (The MIT Press, London 2003) 33.
3. Examples would be the management of the domain name system by the Internet Corporation of Assigned Names and Numbers (ICANN) or the Internet Engineering Task Force (IETF), which was responsible for setting technological standards and protocols for cyberspace.
4. David Johnson and David Post, 'Law and Borders-the Rise of Law in Cyberspace' (1995) 48 Stanford Law Review 1367; David Post, 'Anarchy, State and the Internet' (1995) 3 Journal of Online Law, http://papers.ssrn.com/sol3/papers.cfm?abstract_id=943456.
5. Jack L, Goldsmith, 'Against Cyberanarchy' (1998) 65/4 The University of Chicago Law Review 1199.
6. Lawrence Lessig, *Code v.2.0* (Basic Books, New York 2006); Joel R. Reidenberg, 'Lex Informatica: The Formulation of Information Policy Rules through Technology' (1997) 76 Texas Law Review 533.
7. Mark G.E. Kelly, *The Political Philosophy of Michel Foucault* (Routledge, 2010) 37–38.
8. Webster (n 1) 210–211.
9. Michel Foucault, 'Prison Talk' in Colin Gordon (ed), *Power/Knowledge* (Harvester, Brighton 1980) 52.
10. Critical Art Ensemble, *Electronic Disturbance* (Autonomedia, New York 1993) 111–112.
11. Michel Foucault, *The Will to Knowledge: The History of Sexuality* (Penguin, London 1998).
12. Lawrence Lessig, *Code v.2.0* (Basic Books, New York 2006).
13. Ibid. 24; Tim Wu, 'When Code Isn't Law' (2003) 89 Virginia Law Review 103, 104–106.
14. Manuel Castells, 'Informationalism, Networks, and the Network Society: A Theoretical Blueprint' in Manuel Castells (ed), *The Network*

Society: A Cross Cultural Perspective (Edward Elgar Publishing Ltd, Cheltenham, 2004) 33.

15. Tiziana Terranova, *Network Culture: Politics for the Information Age* (Pluto Press, London 2004) 154.
16. Mathias Klang, 'Disruptive Technology: Effects of Technology Regulation on Democracy' (DPhil Thesis, Goeteborg University 2006) 64.
17. Sandor Vegh, 'Classifying Forms of Online Activism: The Case of Cyberprotests against the World Bank' in Martha McCaughey and Michael D. Ayers (eds), *Cyberactivism: Online Activism in Theory and Practice* (Routledge, London 2003) 83; Alexandra W. Samuel, 'Hacktivism and the Future of Political Participation' (DPhil Thesis, Harvard University 2004) 26–28.
18. Ibid. Vegh.
19. Dorothy E. Denning, 'Activism, Hacktivism, and Cyberterrorism: The Internet as a Tool for Influencing Foreign Policy' in Jon Arquila and David Ronfeldt (eds), *Networks and Netwars: The Future of Terror, Crime, and Militancy* (RAND Corporation 2001).
20. For alternative definitions, see Samuel (n 17) 1–2.
21. Tim Jordan and Paul A. Taylor, *Hacktivism and Cyberwars: Rebels with a Cause?* (Routledge, London 2004) 5–6.
22. Ibid. 10–12.
23. Steven Levy, *Hackers: Heroes of the Computer Revolution* (Bantam Doubleday Dell, New York 1984).
24. The five principles as articulated by Levy are '1) All information should be free, 2) mistrust for authority and promotion of decentralization, 3) judgement should be based on hacking skill and not physical, class or other social criteria, 4) the belief that computers can create art and beauty and 5) that they can change life for the better' (ibid. 40–45).
25. Jordan and Taylor (n 21).
26. For details on the development of the hacker movement and its gradual transition from purely benign programming and 'pranksterism' to more criminal activities, see ibid. 9–12.
27. '[A]s these cultures [openness vs control] came into conflict, real-space law quickly took sides. Law worked ruthlessly to kill a certain kind of online community. The law made the hackers' behavior a "crime," and the government took aggressive steps to combat it. A few prominent and well-publicized cases were used to redefine the hackers' "harmless

behavior" into what the law would call "criminal." The law thus erased any ambiguity about the "good" in hacking.' Lawrence Lessig, *Code and Other Laws of Cyberspace* (Basic Books, New York 1999) 194.
28. Tim Jordan, *Activism!: Direct Action, Hacktivism and the Future of Society* (Reaktion Books, London 2002) 46, 50; Anastasia Kavada, 'The Internet and Decentralized Architectures', in Athina Karatzogianni (ed), *Cyberconflicts and Global Politics* (Routledge, London 2009) 190–191; Jeffrey S. Juris, 'Networked Social Movements: Global Movements for Global Justice' in Manuel Castells (ed), *The Network Society: A Cross-Cultural Perspective* (Edward Elgar Publishing, Cheltenham 2004) 341.
29. Alain Badiou, *Metapolitics* (Jason Barker tr, Verso, London 2005).
30. Robert S. Jansen, 'Populist Mobilization: A New Theoretical Approach to Populism' (2011) 29 Sociological Theory 75, 82–83.
31. Naomi Klein, *No Logo: Taking Aim at the Brand Bullies* (Flamingo, London 2001) 280–283; Terranova (n 15) 17.
32. Terranova (n 15) 17.
33. Juris (n 28) 342; The *Reclaim the Streets* movement in Britain has held many events, where thousands of people would organise a performance with dancers, jugglers, and other artistic events in main street arteries to protest against ecological destruction; Klein (n 31) 312–314.
34. Jordan and Taylor (n 21) 82.

2

The Two Eras of Hacktivism

1 Introduction

Although in reality hacktivism has been realised in the form of a continuum almost since the popularisation of the Internet, I would like to split this discussion of hacktivism into two distinct eras because I feel that there has been a shift in how hacktivism has been realised, perceived, and dealt with after the middle of the 2000s. The first era, therefore, relates to groups that developed and operated mainly in the 1990s and early 2000s. Hacktivists in that first era have been split into groups based on their tactical focus/principles with Jordan and Taylor talking about mass action hacktivism, including groups like the Electronic Disturbance Theater and the Electrohippies, which mostly organised virtual sit-ins, and hacktivists, like Hacktivismo, who focused more on designing activism-facilitating software or, as the authors say, 'the political application of hacking to the infrastructure of cyberspace.'[1] Alexandra Samuel also discusses hacktivists in similar categories (direct action vs digitally correct), adding one more category which seems to be more related to defacements and data compromises, the cracktivists.[2] The discussion will focus on some of these groups that were active during this period.

V. Karagiannopoulos, *Living With Hacktivism*, Palgrave Studies in Cybercrime and Cybersecurity, https://doi.org/10.1007/978-3-319-71758-6_2

The second era of hacktivism, and hacktivist-related literature, is perhaps epitomised in Gabriella Coleman's seminal work[3] and is dominated by the rise of Anonymous. Trying to provide specific categorisations and descriptions during this second era is hard because of the nature of Anonymous and its spin-offs, which essentially encompass all the above categories and typologies. Alongside Anonymous, there have been some individual cases that have attracted much attention and will be important for this analysis. These are the late Aaron Swartz and 'Weev' or Andrew Auernheimer. Both these individuals were involved in activities that had an activist element and employed what the authorities considered hacking/unauthorised access techniques in order to realise their actions, and are thus two major examples of this new era. The attention these cases received from the criminal justice system and the implications of this attention will provide a crucial insight into how hacking-facilitated activism is dealt with currently.

Without wanting to disregard other groups and individuals that might have contributed to hacktivist practice and discussion, this book will focus on the major cases in each era, without implying that this is an exhaustive list. Perhaps two cases that would be expected to feature in this book are those of Chelsea Manning and Edward Snowden and their whistleblower revelations. However, although these cases have been characterised as hacktivism, they are not hacktivism in the sense that this book perceives it, as those were insider revelations from individuals with access to that information and they were not hacks that were perpetrated in order to express a symbolic message. Although I acknowledge the importance of those incidents and the broadness of the term hacktivism, my perception of what hacktivism constitutes is much narrower and focuses more on the use of hacking as an expressive medium.

During this discussion, I will draw from the hacktivists' own writings, webpages, and declarations, but also from a variety of sources in order to sketch the landscape of hacktivism from its birth until today, acknowledging the fact that such an enquiry could be a book on its own. Although this book is about discussing practices and not particular groups per se, becoming familiar with the groups, in terms of background, rhetoric, and tactics will facilitate the understanding of hacktivism. This in turn will also assist in shaping the arguments that will follow regarding the usefulness and risks that such practices can entail.

2 The First Era of Hacktivism and the Birth of Electronic Civil Disobedience

2.1 The Virtual Demonstrators

Hacktivism has existed since the early days of the Internet, even before its extensive popularisation in the early 1990s. The first ever recorded hacktivist act was the circulation of the Worms Against Nuclear Killers (WANK) in 1989, which infected a network shared between NASA and the US Department of Energy. This was the time when there was concern about launching the plutonium-powered Galileo spacecraft and the implications of a potential radioactive accident following Challenger's blow-up. Apart from a number of political messages that the worm was programmed to communicate to those it infected by its alleged Australian creators, its own name and the fact that its manifestation only simulated a file-deleting process are also testament to the aforementioned satirical mentality that characterises hacktivist activity.

Hacktivist action and electronic forms of legally ambiguous, symbolically expressive protests were articulated early on in the writings of the Critical Art Ensemble (CAE), an activist group focusing on general tactical media interventions.[4] CAE's writing focuses on the importance of information generation, control, and distribution in the current networked economies. The main contribution of CAE to the development of hacktivism is an extensive analysis of cyberactivism tactics and philosophy. CAE defines electronic civil disobedience (ECD) as the transition of the tactics of blockage and trespass onto the Internet.[5] It submits that the application of these tactics should always seek to avoid causing damage to websites that are irrelevant to the cause protested or are used for the provision of critical services.[6] However, CAE also accepts that such activities could sometimes provoke unpredictable consequences and collateral damage, as they deem such occurrences inherent in social protests.[7] CAE was one of the initial groups that, as Paglen comments, 'has written the blueprint for Anonymous and Wikileaks-style internet activism while a young Julian Assange probed telecommunications infrastructures, as Mendax, and most of the Anons were still in diapers.'[8]

Multiple tactics have indeed been used by the demonstrator branch of hacktivists, for politically expressive purposes, such as web defacements/redirects, viruses, and virtual sit-ins. Defacements entail gaining unauthorised access to a web page and making modifications that add or modify information on the web page with or without the removal of the original data.[9] Site redirects involve getting unauthorised access into a web server/network and changing its address so that those accessing the site are redirected to an alternative site that is usually critical of the hacked site.[10] Another common tactic is the creation of viruses that were meant to communicate political messages on the computer networks they infected, whilst avoiding any file corruption.

A predominant tactic for hacktivists was and still is virtual sit-ins.[11] Virtual sit-ins simulate the effect of a distributed denial of service (DDOS) attack and aim to block access to a service, network, or website through the coordinated transmission of an overwhelming amount of data at the target server, which consequently slows down or crashes under the excessive traffic. Depending on what ports are enabled on a server, these blockades can be achieved by flooding the server with a large number of emails that are beyond its capability to handle (email bomb), overloading an Internet Relay Chat channel (iRC jamming), or overwhelming the server with small data packets requesting access to information on the website (ping storm).[12]

Virtual sit-ins are in principle based on the deliberate participation of protesters, rather than the deployment of botnets, large networks of computers, which an individual or a small hacker group might control remotely without the owners' knowledge.[13] Public participation is usually facilitated through the use of downloadable software, which users can install on their computers and automate the process of sending multiple information requests or emails to the protested network or site. These pieces of software have developed over the years to allow for more automation and coordination and even enable users to mask their identities in some cases.[14]

The teachings of CAE regarding ECD were put to practice by other groups that focused on symbolic network disturbances. One of the most important groups was the Electronic Disturbance Theater (EDT), which was formed by a small team of four people with artist, activist, and technical backgrounds. As Dominguez, a former member of CAE, and one of EDT's core members, argued, EDT's tactics 'attempted to translate and express the unbearable weight of physical beings into the immaterial informational channels,' without any regard for technical efficiency, as their goal was not 'to bring the enemy down, but be "effective" in side-loading information beyond the local and offering a point of focus for the communities involved.'[15]

EDT did not see their activities as undercover direct action, but instead interpreted them as artistic gestures and performances combined with notions of civil disobedience, which would have to be realised publicly and openly in order to avoid prosecution.[16]

Their online disobedience/performances were mainly virtual sit-ins, through the use of a specialised software tool called Floodnet. Floodnet was freely available for download and essentially automated the process of reloading a web page, thus making virtual sit-ins more efficient and also managing to communicate political messages in an artistic manner, since the information requests were designed to return 404 error pages. The returned error message challenged the lack of respect of human rights in the respective situation, returning an error message saying 'Human Rights not found on this server.' The reconfiguration of the 'not found' 404 message was a common artistic/political gesture in the Internet art communities, demonstrating how culture jamming and hacker understanding can lead to using a mundane technical message in order to express political concerns.[17]

EDT came dynamically to the fore of the hacktivist scene during its support for the Zapatista struggle in Mexico in the late 1990s, and even though the group in its original form has disbanded, some of its original members still participate in similar projects. Dominguez, in particular, still continues to organise many different actions to protest issues ranging from healthcare budget cuts, to US immigration policies, and even police killings in Greece.[18] Despite its controversial tactics and the targeting of high-profile governmental and other websites, such as the Frankfurt

Stock Exchange, EDT was not actively persecuted and Dominguez even acquired a position as a professor of Digital Arts at the University of California in order to teach practices such as ECD, hacktivism, and electronic disturbances. In his own words from a 2011 interview:

> *By 2000, I felt we really needed to stage a new zone for the work to move forward and establish a new series of questions with that knowledge formation–the question of institutional critique, of institutional disturbances. During the middle of the last decade, a need emerged in institutions of higher learning for people to teach students about these practices–most of which came from artists, who had for the most part worked outside of institutional support–that meant that universities had to accept those artists and art groups into the system in order to teach the next generation of researchers and artists–since no degrees existed at that time to get a degree on ECD, networked artivism or hacktivism.*[19]

Through his work at the University of California (UC), Dominguez and others have revived EDT in the form of EDT 2.0. Dominguez even organised a virtual sit-in against the UC Principal's office in relation to budget cuts, invoking the threat of federal prosecution. Investigations were dropped only after an array of online and offline protests led to a private agreement with the University, with Dominguez pledging not to employ such tactics against the UC Office of the President (UCOP) for four years. Inevitably, this news immediately sparked another virtual sit-in against the UCOP.[20] Recently, EDT 2.0 organised a similar protest of e-graffiti, amongst other offline and online methods of protest in solidarity with the Zapatistas, planning to disrupt the Mexican president's website and to write supporting messages for the Zapatistas on the webserver's logs.[21] As Dominguez says, for his collective of banglab/EDT 2.0, the aesthetics and activism are intertwined, but he does not see himself or his group as activists per se, but rather as artists who seek to enhance activist work through their digital art performances.[22]

However, apart from EDT, there were more groups that stirred the waters of online political expression in this early era of hacktivism. Another similarly orientated group which also used mass action tactics was the UK-based group Electrohippies. They are mostly known for having organised a major online disruption in the form of a virtual sit-in during the Seattle World Trade Organization (WTO) meetings in 1999. They promulgated their own protest tool and organised very successful protests against the network servicing these meetings in order to protest capitalist globalisation policies.[23] The Electrohippies focused on achieving community accountability and also published a list of preconditions for using their virtual sit-in tool, ranging from providing information and facilitating the traceability of protesters by the authorities, to providing prior notification to the targets and explanation of the motives and causes for the protest.[24] However, despite the success of their online protests and their principled, organised way of protesting, eventually they abandoned their disruptive tactics, having been intimidated by the intensifying restrictions and punitiveness of the UK cybercrime/cyberterrorist legal regime.[25]

2.2 The Artivists

During the same period, various other web artists (artivists) with political considerations also resorted to cyber activities with illegal and politically expressive effects, such as distributing viruses with a political message or modifying digital artworks exhibited on websites or even creating website parodies, although this latter tactic would probably fall out with the scope of criminal laws. These artists use their technological interventions to protest various political and economic phenomena, from the 'commodification' of artistic expression and the intensification of intellectual property restrictions to the neo-liberal, capitalist policies adopted by governments or the environmental indifference of corporations.[26]

One such group was EpidemiC, which focused primarily, but not exclusively, on viruses, seeking to uncover the artistic and communicative potential in viral code. The underlying software code of the virus they created with 0100101110101101.org, another artivist group, was written as a story trying to highlight the positive aspects of viral code and its undue demonization by the cybersecurity industry. Its code was circulated at a web art festival through various online and offline means, and was even given to antivirus companies as a show of the artists' benign intentions.[27] EpidemiC also created, amongst other projects, a free Windows-based program called 'AntiMafia Action Sharing,' which utilised file-sharing software to help coordinate virtual sit-ins.[28]

0100101110101101.org is another similarly oriented pair of artists and their activities have included in their portfolio of net-related performances many legally ambiguous actions, such as the development of viral software for artistic purposes and modifications of online artworks. For example, in the late 1990s they created fake online gallery websites similar to those offered to limited subscribers/buyers by online galleries and even mutated the works on display in one of those virtual galleries, which resulted in legal action by the owners of those virtual galleries.[29] The purpose was to instigate discussion on intellectual property rights and unveil the pretences of originality and uniqueness in digital works that could be perfectly and easily reproduced digitally.[30] In another potentially illegal intervention, they hacked, as part of their own festival performance, the website of a web art festival, randomly mixing the exhibits with the artists' names.[31] Despite the lack of any legal consequences for the two artists, their performance led to the dismissal of the curator and the banning of the conference, causing the pair to reconsider hack-related performances in the future,[32] without however stopping them from challenging Internet norms and practices through their art.[33]

Although the artists argue that they relate more with the psychological rather than the implicit political elements of their performances,[34] there is an obvious political and also often pranksterist element in their performances. This mentality seems strongly linked with the aforementioned power struggles that are intrinsic in the information networks about the free sharing of information, its commodification, and its control as a means of shaping cultural norms and information, thus demonstrating how such actions can entail political elements, even if the core intention is not political per se.

2.3 The Information Purists

All these groups generate legally ambiguous computer/data modification and impairment effects in order to facilitate the communication of their political messages and performances. However, they also develop software like Floodnet or AntiMafia, which could be considered violations of such laws directly or inchoately, as they can be used to facilitate computer modification and impairment, as will be seen during the analysis of the law. A group that was involved solely in the development of software tools and focused not on the jamming and manipulating of information was Hacktivismo. Hacktivismo, an offshoot of the infamous hacker group, the Cult of the Dead Cow (cDc), aimed to develop encryption and security-enhancing tools for activists in order to enable them to communicate whilst avoiding the threat of authoritarian regimes and censorship efforts.[35] Hacktivismo focused on promoting freedom of information and the privacy of citizens online, two aspects that are core in the current cyberpolitical era, where information acquisition and processing through surveillance and control of communications are crucial in the power conflicts taking place in cyberspace.

Hacktivismo also had strict principles in relation to its chosen tactics, arguing that in democratic regimes the employment of protest methods, such as virtual sit-ins, defacements, and viruses, essentially prevent expression or distort information, thus failing to promote free speech.[36] For these principles and their focus on information liberation, they have been characterised as the 'digitally correct' branch of hacktivism,[37] demonstrating a less directly challenging and more informationally 'purist' hacktivist attitude compared to the other types of hacktivists. However, establishing types of hacktivist groups will become obsolete as will be seen in the new era because Anonymous will prove to be a blend of all the rationales and tactics, thus eliminating these distinctions, which are probably more useful as an analytical tool rather than actual differences anyway.

Even before the formation of Hacktivismo, cDc circulated politically oriented software, such as 'Back Orifice,' which took advantage of security weaknesses in Windows OS allowing for the remote controlling of the compromised computers. The goal of creating and openly publishing such software was to inform users about security flaws in Windows and pressure Microsoft to patch the security holes 'Back Orifice' could exploit.[38] Despite the original benign motivations behind such software, Back Orifice could inevitably be employed to realise the same effect that it was created to prevent, the exploitation of a Windows weakness by hackers. It was exactly this presumption that cDc wanted to take advantage of, in order to induce Microsoft to patch the flaw urgently and avoid risking user security. However, one can easily imagine that such a tool could have legal implications for cDc in jurisdictions where the creation and circulation of hacking tools has been criminalised, such as in the UK, as will be discussed later on.

Apart from the encryption tools they designed such as Six/Four, ScatterChat, and Torpark which appear less controversial,[39] Hacktivismo's final published piece of software work in the late 2000s was 'Goolag Scanner.' This application utilises the Google search engine to uncover website vulnerabilities. Naturally, its dual nature as a security-enhancing application or a tool that enables hackers to find back doors to websites could render it legally ambiguous.[40] Bearing the risk of misuse of their tools in mind, however, Hacktivismo wanted to make sure that their work was not abused for criminal purposes and released them under Hacktivismo's Enhanced-Source Software License Agreement (HESSLA), imposing an obligation of legal, democratic use of the software they release.[41] For one of their encryption projects, Six/Four, they even acquired an export licence from the US Department of Commerce. However, the impossibility of monitoring the use of Hacktivismo's tools, which are freely available, renders the applicability of the licence's terms and the benevolence of their use reliant on the goodwill of the users, without any concrete assurance that these tools will not facilitate criminal actions.

This account of the movements that were active during this era until the mid- to late 2000s is by no means exhaustive and it needs to be highlighted that there are various actions during this period that have been perpetrated by activist groups in general, such as Greenpeace or Kein Mensch ist illegal. The latter group's virtual sit-in against Lufthansa was also considered free expression rather than illegal coercion due to the fact that its organising group had taken all steps to warn the targeted website and do this according to the standards that a legal offline protest would follow.

The particular groups and campaigns mentioned brought hacktivist practices and debates to the fore, both in relation to using technology in political expression and also on the specific philosophies and practices as to how this should happen. If we were to identify some specific characteristics from this era, one could argue that the more obvious ones would be the relative concreteness of these groups in terms of membership, philosophy, and tactics. We can see that we have smaller groups with specific members organising even the public participation-based events, that is virtual sit-ins, and there are general principles as to how these activities should be realised, often in an open and accountable manner, which they promote with the aim to preserve the legal and politically and morally legitimate character of these actions and place them within the context of political expression and civil disobedience. Moreover, there was a much more distinct and relatively obvious core of responsible hacktivists from which the activities originated, even if there were tactical disagreements between the various groups. The following section will demonstrate the transition of hacktivism into the modern era and will primarily discuss Anonymous as well as some important, individual cases.

3 The Second Era of Hacktivism

3.1 The Birth and Politicisation of Anonymous

Anonymous dominates this second era and constitutes an interesting blend of the mentioned groups, further popularising hacktivism, but also challenging the organisational, tactical, and legal limits of it even more.

Anonymous did not start out as a political collective. It originates from 4chan,[42] a compilation of diverse message boards, with topics ranging from Japanese anime and cat videos to sports, music downloads, and pornography. It is considered a space where users converge to discuss their various interests and create Internet culture in the form of trending topics, memes, and even trolling campaigns. The most offensive and challenging content can be found in the particular group /b/, which is where a large part of the trolling roots of Anonymous originate from.

4chan and /b/ are online communities that celebrated various forms of 'geekdom.' The term 'geek' was initially associated with carnival freaks, but has more recently come to denote a label for demonstrating expertise in some field, such as computers and/or other elements of pop culture. These modern, mediated communities are characterised by a fluidity, giving rise to a loose community[43] which further enhances an intrinsic subculture element: resistance to mainstream culture through a semiotic guerrilla warfare.[44] One can easily find in the particular geek and trolling culture of /b/ core elements of carnival, such as satire and masquerade, which Bakhtin links with the countercultural elements of laughter, opposing traditional institutions and reinforcing a culture of order.[45]

The blending of this countercultural spirit at the core of Anonymous and 4chan in conjunction with the sense of community, exchange of ideas, and seeking the 'lulz' through collective interventions eventually led to the more explicit politicisation of the collective. As Coleman argued,

> part of Anonymous has over the last three years moved from disaggregated practices rooted in the culture of trolling[46] to also become a rhizomatic and collective form of action catalysed and moved forward by a series of world events and political interventions.[47]

Despite it being referred to as a particular group, in reality Anonymous is essentially an umbrella identity that can be adopted by anyone, lacking memberships or a clearly delineated and specific coordinating core group. Instead, it encompasses many factions with potentially different ideological and tactical orientations, but often common goals.[48] Coleman identifies the lack of agreed mandates and inevitably the constant flexibility, unpredictability, and lack of institutionalisation as core characteristics of Anonymous, which has, however, certain principles it usually abides by. These are mainly the adoption of a humorous deviant outlook, an anti-celebrity ethic, the use of diverse technological tools and platforms, and the richness of their political intervention techniques.[49]

However, the politicisation of the collective has not been welcomed by everyone associating with it and has created a rift in 4chan. Lulz-oriented members (hatefags) often express their disapproval of the politicised ones (moralfags) and of the transformation of Anonymous from a fun-based collective to an entity with activist sensitivities.[50] On the other side, some more radical members of the politicised factions have also deemed that the activities organised were not adequately confrontational. The diversity of views has also led to the birth of splinter groups, such as the Anonymous Anarchist Action and LulzSec, which distanced themselves from the dictates and practices elaborated by the more moderate factions of Anonymous.[51] Lulzsec, for example, engaged in multiple cyberattacks which led to the apprehension of their members and the handing down of severe penalties by courts.[52] Such fragmentations clearly demonstrate the lack of unanimity in Anonymous, which is crucial in understanding that, despite the controversy surrounding the name of the collective, there cannot be a concrete ideological and tactical set of norms that would be attributed to and followed by all those individuals and factions that operate under the Anonymous umbrella.[53]

The usual rhetoric is also quite diverse and often more confrontational to the first era groups, potentially due to the collective's anti-authoritarian origins and the excitement of its numerous young participants.[54] As Goode aptly suggests, 'the voices articulated through these testimonial texts are simultaneously nihilistic and idealistic, dystopian and utopian, egoistic and collectivist, and dedicated to the negative freedoms of libertarianism yet also concerned with collectivist goals of equality and justice.'[55]

Anonymous is usually meant to function in a direct democratic way, although there are exceptions to that,[56] since decision-making is often based on voting by those participating in the iRC channels.[57] In fact, only a few participants are deemed to be actual hackers, while many participants are computer 'geeks,' as well as other, politically minded individuals and activists.[58] There is no concrete organising core or a spokesperson or leader. The lack of known representatives/organisers is one of the weaknesses of the group, since its representation is done anonymously and from random groups or individuals that might be using the Anonymous identity in order to serve their own purposes, such as de-legitimisation or personal gratification.[59]

There are, however, more concrete subgroups that work towards developing media projects or working on shaping the collective's public relations. These are manned by influential figures within the Anon communication channels, whose opinions carry additional gravity and command a following.[60] In fact, the iRC channels where Anonymous often converge are managed by more experienced members, who have increasing influence on decisions and are also burdened with imparting and employing the channels' constantly evolving self-regulatory norms, such as avoiding the targeting of media outlets or the incitement of violence.[61]

Although the leaderless, memberless collective can be perceived as a disorganised, uncontrollable mob, assessments of Anonymous' operations suggest that the collective can indeed behave with a loose, political conscience and organisation in the form of a 'diffuse crowd.'[62] Anonymous often comes together because of the citizens' need to do something about common socio-political concerns, without a clear understanding of how to realise their goals, yet behaving in a more rational, conscientious manner, where the members have the option to participate or not, without being overwhelmed by a mob mentality.[63] They also say that their goal is not disruption and disturbance per se, but to create symbolic effects and raise awareness with their activities.[64]

Anonymous has also obviously adopted in its majority a policy of anonymity, differentiating it from the more open initial hacktivist groups. Although pseudonymity or anonymity was a norm in the 4chan fora, as a feature of equality and lack of focus on someone's identity, it has also been advocated more recently as a needed precaution against criminal prosecutions and personal attacks.[65] For the same reason of avoiding undue state surveillance, anonymity is even suggested during real-life protests organised under the banner of Anonymous, such as the Million Mask Marches, where many protesters affiliating themselves with the collective wear Guy Fawkes masks as their official 'trademark.'[66]

3.2 Tactics and Operations

Anonymous employs many diverse and often controversial tactics in reflection of the diverse political and tactical perceptions of the people who populate its ranks, ranging from virtual sit-ins and defacements of websites to more controversial acts, such as information hacks and 'doxing' (acquisition and release of private information).[67] Anonymous has also developed its own software for facilitating virtual sit-ins, called Low Orbit Ion Cannon (LOIC). The software can be connected to a general command centre (Hivemind) so that it automatically acknowledges the targets decided upon and engages in the protest when the designated time is reached.[68] LOIC does not include an anonymisation function and cannot be used easily with such software, which means that users can eventually be traced through their IP address, thus retaining a basic way of identification.[69] However, having witnessed the serious legal consequences of the lack of anonymity resulting in prosecutions of virtual sit-in participants regarding their protests against Paypal, members started discussing the need for a more advanced, anonymising LOIC-style tool.[70] Eventually, new tools like Pyloris were also developed, which are more elaborate to use but also have anonymising capabilities.[71]

In a primitive form, parts of the communities that would identify with Anonymous have been active since 2006.[72] What gained them major publicity as a quasi-political movement were their sustained protests against the Church of Scientology, which started in relation to the censoring efforts of the Church regarding a Tom Cruise video talking about his experience as a Church member. Anonymous named this protest campaign Operation Chanology.[73] The protests included online campaigns of hacking Scientology websites and doing virtual sit-ins, and playing telephone and fax pranks. Protests also eventually transitioned offline, with thousands of protesters wearing the Guy Fawkes mask and protesting against the Church of Scientology all around the globe. Members of Anonymous even released information on how to protest legally in the streets, combining an activist mentality with the traditional carnivalesque elements of the collective. After OpChanology, their next major campaign was OpPayback. During that campaign, they organised virtual sit-in protests against the Motion Picture Association of America and Recording Industry Association of America in relation to their denial of service attacks on piracy-facilitating websites. In relation to this operation, members of Anonymous targeted a law firm that was known for acting at the behest of copyright owners sending letters to alleged infringers demanding money and the desistance of further infringement. After a relatively low-intensity virtual sit-in campaign, the security managers of the firm, while restoring the site, made a backup copy of all the emails and passwords available to everyone. This was the final blow for this firm, which was already investigated as a copyright-trolling organisation and was eventually closed down due to its unethical and extortionate practices.[74]

Operation Payback continued as Operation Avenge Assange and made Anonymous the target of media and police attention due to their very successful campaign in support of Wikileaks at the end of 2010, where thousands of users participated in a virtual sit-in campaign against Mastercard, Paypal, and Amazon in protest to the companies' denial to process donations and to offer hosting services to Wikileaks. This denial had come as a response to the release of US diplomatic cables given to Assange by Chelsea (then Bradley) Manning, an army private who was tried and sentenced to 35 years in prison by a military court and was recently released after being pardoned by President Obama.[75]

Even after these actions, which made it generally renowned, Anonymous remained quite active. It hacked into the emails of HB Gary Federal, a security company offering to spy and hinder the operations of Wikileaks through media campaigns, cyberattacks, misinformation, and sabotage in addition to intimidating donors, marring the reputation of supporters and exposing members of Anonymous.[76] It also hacked and exposed information relating to police officers involved in countering protests in San Francisco (OpBART).[77] Anonymous got involved in international politics by helping Tunisian and Egyptian protesters during the Arab Spring, exposed paedophile rings in the dark web, and even declared war on Islamic State of Iraq and Syria (ISIS) for their Paris attacks. It has also targeted international organisations and banks, security organisations and national governments, and even more recently the Ku Klux Klan and Donald Trump. Although some of these efforts have brought praise to the name of Anonymous, its constant threats of war and disruptive campaigns have also reached a saturation point for some others and its actions are not attracting the attention they used to these days.[78] A full account of its actions would be too extensive to provide here, especially since Anonymous has individuals acting under this umbrella name across the globe and many activities have been attributed to Anonymous, without responsibility being taken by the group through their formal channels of communications.[79] This book will focus on some of their most major campaigns, which have also been linked to prosecutions in the USA and the UK.

Apart from any political success, Anonymous' actions have also drawn the attention of the authorities. Two individuals have pled guilty to computer damage charges due to their participating in the Chanology protests, having faced at least one year imprisonment, probation, fines, and restitution penalties.[80] Another 14 members of Anonymous (Paypal 14) have also pled guilty to one misdemeanour and 12 to one felony charge as well. The 12 pleading guilty to both counts will be on probation for a year, after which the felony charge will be dropped, and will also have to pay $5600 each as restitution to Paypal. This was hailed as a final victory after a three-year-long legal struggle, where the group was faced with potential charges for conspiracy and criminal damage to computers that could have reached up to 15 years in prison.[81] Eric J Rosol was also sentenced in 2012 to two years of federal probation and $183,000 in restitution for participating in an Anonymous virtual sit-in against a Koch Industries website for less than one minute.[82] At least four members have also been tried in the UK under similar charges of conspiracy to cause computer impairment regarding the Paypal protests, with the presumed leader of the group, Weatherhead, who did not plead guilty, receiving 18 months in prison on conspiracy charges. He did not participate in the virtual sit-in but was found to be coordinating the communications hub at the time.[83] Many more alleged Anonymous protesters have been arrested and charged or are being investigated in various countries.[84]

3.3 Hacktivism Beyond Anonymous

Beyond Anonymous there have been two incidents that are relevant to this analysis and these are the cases of Aaron Swartz and 'Weev.' Swartz, a wonder kid of the Internet era, with core contributions in the creation of Reddit or the Creative Commons platform, attempted to use his university network access in order to download and make freely available online the whole of the JSTOR database of academic papers in an attempt to free academic knowledge for everyone to access. He was arrested before he managed to realise his goal and was prosecuted under the Computer Fraud and Abuse Act, where he was threatened with punishment as high as 25 years in prison, even though JSTOR did not want to press any charges. His bail reached the amount of $100,000 and his eventual bankruptcy and persecution arguably contributed to his decision to commit suicide. There has been a long discussion regarding the appropriateness and proportionality of the handling of the case in question by prominent scholars and senators, such as Lawrence Lessig and Zoe Lofgren. Aaron's death also gave rise to discussions about managing prosecutorial excess and limiting the overbroad Computer Fraud and Abuse Act, which was the main prosecutorial tool in this case. The impact of the case on the so far fruitless discussions to amend the Computer Fraud and Abuse Act 1986 (CFAA) will be considered in the following chapters, where the CFAA will be discussed in more detail.

Andrew Auernheimer's (Weev) situation is a more particular case. He has been a notorious troll, who along with one of his colleagues, forming a group called Goatse Security, discovered and exposed that AT&T was managing subscriber data without encryption. The data was thus available to whoever knew where to look for them, essentially endangering the security of thousands of its customers without any need to hack into the company's network. Weev's collaborator, Spitler, collected that data and, after advising Spitler on iRC, Weev eventually exposed AT&T's lax data security by providing the data to Gawker, which published the data in redacted form.[85] According to Weev, he had given the chance to AT&T to patch the security flaw before releasing the data.

The main purpose was to shame AT&T for their insecure policies of data retention and motivate them to change their practices and protect their consumers. Weev was also charged and prosecuted under the CFAA and was convicted at first instance under identity fraud and conspiracy to access a computer without authorization charges and was sentenced to 41 months in federal prison and a restitution of $73,000. His co-conspirator, Spitler, pled guilty and received a three-year probation penalty. Weev's case, despite the controversy surrounding many of his acts, attracted the legal support of major legal scholars, such as Orin Kerr, who is a major critic and proponent for change regarding the CFAA.[86] Weev's appeal was accepted on a 'lack of jurisdiction' argument, which left the question as to whether he committed a CFAA offence of unauthorised access unanswered. However, the judges indirectly expressed their concerns regarding the initial conviction considering that there had been no bypassing of technical restrictions and only publicly available information had been accessed.[87] This issue will be discussed in later chapters when the law will be analysed and critiqued in more detail.

Although Weev is a very controversial persona who has been involved or at least linked with various hacking and trolling incidents and has even been characterised as openly racist/Neo-Nazi, it was this particular action against AT&T that led to him being prosecuted. At the moment, Auernheimer lives somewhere in Eastern Europe for fear of further prosecution in the US. Despite the controversy behind most of his activities as a hacker and troll, this book will focus on his particular actions relating to AT&T's lax network security, which actually resulted in him being prosecuted and which are much closer to the hacktivist actions that we will be discussing in general.

4 Conclusion

This chapter has explored some of the main groups and individuals that have played an important role in shaping hacktivism, particularly within the jurisdictions that this book will be focusing on. Undeniably there are more incidents and protesters than those discussed here, which are also active outside the USA or the UK. An exhaustive listing of the groups, rhetoric, and actions is impossible here. However, throughout the analysis more examples will be discussed in order to support or challenge the arguments made. For the moment, if we had to summarise this chapter, I would argue that we have seen a gradual development in the hacktivist movement over the years, which has gone from small activist clusters engaging in technologically facilitated disruption to more loose structures, mainly represented by Anonymous. Compared to other groups that seemed to have a core organising cluster and strategy and even ideological/rhetoric direction, Anonymous feels more like a constantly mutating and evolving living organism that reacts to different socio-political stimuli in a manner that reflects the multiplicity of its origins and the diversity of its aspirations.

It is a constant struggle to try to find concreteness in hacktivists' fluid collectives and diverse goals and tactics but it is also this element that makes the discussion even more fascinating. The only concrete element that we can draw from this discussion is the intrinsic lack of concretisation, which will direct our discussion, but will also divert the analysis from focusing on discussing the usefulness of hacktivist tactics as a reflection of a concrete organisational and ideological background. This liberation of the chosen tactics, not from the particular political cause in each case, but from the overarching ideological and moral confines of a certain group and the realisation of the ad hoc nature of hacktivist tactical choices based on particular rationales and aims, is very important. It is through this process that we are enabled to move away from defining responses to such activities based on the ethos of the perpetrators as a unique legitimising value. The next chapter will thus look more into the nature of hacktivist practice and will try to highlight the positive and negative aspects for democratic societies in the modern information-based era.

Notes

1. Tim Jordan and Paul A. Taylor, *Hacktivism and Cyberwars: Rebels with a Cause?* (Routledge, London 2004) 70.
2. Alexandra W. Samuel, 'Hacktivism and the Future of Political Participation' (DPhil Thesis, Harvard University 2004).
3. Gabriella E. Coleman, *Hacker, Hoaxer, Whistleblower, Spy: The Many Faces of Anonymous* (Verso, London 2014).
4. Tactical media encompasses hacktivism, but generally involves the use of new technologies in artistic projects that, instead of attempting to generate grand revolutionary events, focus on producing micropolitical effects that disrupt, intervene, and educate. Rita Raley, *Tactical Media* (University of Minnesota Press, Minneapolis 2009) 1.
5. Critical Art Ensemble, *Electronic Civil Disobedience and Other Unpopular Ideas* (Autonomedia, 1996) 18.
6. Ibid. 18, 24.

7. Critical Art Ensemble, *Electronic Disturbance* (Autonomedia, New York 1993) 25, 120.
8. Critical Art Ensemble, *Disturbances, 2012*, http://critical-art.net/?page_id=309.
9. Mathias Klang, 'Civil Disobedience Online' (2004) 2 Info, Communications and Ethics in Society 75, 77.
10. Samuel (n 2) 10.
11. Jordan and Taylor (n 1) 74.
12. Sandor Vegh, 'Classifying Forms of Online Activism: The Case of Cyberprotests against the World Bank' in Martha McCaughey and Michael D. Ayers (eds), *Cyberactivism: Online Activism in Theory and Practice* (Routledge, London 2003) 85–86.
13. Jordan and Taylor (n 1) 76–77.
14. Gallagher, Sean, 'High Orbits and Slowlorises: Understanding the Anonymous Attack Tools' (*Ars Technica*, 16 February 2012) http://arstechnica.com/business/news/2012/02/high-orbits-and-slowlorises-understanding-the-anonymous-attack-tools.ars.
15. Bruce Simon, 'Illegal Knowledge: Strategies for New Media Activism: Dialogue with Ricardo Dominguez and Geert Lovink' in Bousquet Marc and Wills Katharine (eds), *The Politics of Information: The Electronic Mediation of Social Change* (Altx Press 2003) 62.
16. Evan R. Goldstein, 'Digitally Incorrect' (*The Chronicle Review*, 3 October 2010) http://chronicle.com/article/Digitally-Incorrect/124649/; Ricardo Dominguez, 'Electronic Disobedience Post-9/11' (2008) 22 Third Text 661, 669–670.
17. Jordan and Taylor (n 1) 87–88.
18. See Dorothy E. Denning, 'Activism, Hacktivism, and Cyberterrorism: The Internet as a Tool for Influencing Foreign Policy' in Jon Arquila and David Ronfeldt (eds), *Networks and Netwars: The Future of Terror, Crime, and Militancy* (RAND Corporation 2001) 266–267; Ricardo Dominguez, 'Electronic Civil Disobedience' (*thing.net*, undated) http://www.thing.net/~rdom/ecd/ecd.html; Ricardo Dominguez, 'Electronic Civil Disobedience in Solidarity with Greek Anarchists' (*thing.net*, 2008) http://post.thing.net/node/2457.
19. 'Interview with Ricardo Dominguez' (*Reclamations Blog*, 24 November 2011) http://www.reclamationsjournal.org/blog/?ha_exhibit=interview-with-ricardo-dominguez.
20. Goldstein (n 16); Ibid.

21. '*Together, we will participate in a conceptual online performance/graffiti and will write the text of "El Dolor y La Rabia" (Marcos' recent communique), all 700 pages of "Don Quixote", and a number of other texts to the error logs of the server that hosts the website of the President of Mexico many times over, depending on how many individuals and groups participate. Through the mass generation of 404-errors, we will collectively establish a performative matrix that imagines books and communiques in mourning and action.*' 'E-Graffiti in Solidarity with the Zapatistas – May.24.2014.' *E-Graffiti in Solidarity with the Zapatistas—24 May 2014*. http://www.thing.net/~rdom/ZapatistasMayo24/.
22. Reclamations (n 19).
23. DJNZ and The Action Tool Development Group of the Electrohippies Collective, 'Client-Side Distributed Denial-of-Service: Valid Campaign Tactic or Terrorist Act?' (2001) 34 Leonardo 269.
24. Ibid. 273.
25. The Electrohippies Collective, 'Cyberlaw UK: Civil Rights and Protest on the Internet' (*iwar.org*, 2000) http://www.iwar.org.uk/hackers/resources/electrohippies-collective/comm-2000-12.pdf.
26. Vegh (n 12) 77; see also Lani Boyd, 'The Yes Men and Activism in the Information Age' (MA Thesis, Louisiana State University and Agricultural and Mechanical College 2005).
27. See Mathias Klang, 'A Critical Look at the Regulation of Computer Viruses' (2003) 11 International Journal of Law and Information Technology 162, 177–178.
28. EpidemiC, 'Antimafia: The Action Sharing' (*EpidemiC*, 2002) http://epidemic.ws/antimafia/action.php?lng=en.
29. 0100101110101101.org, 'Copies' (*0100101110101101.org*, 1999–2000) http://www.0100101110101101.org/home/copies/index.html.
30. Nathan Castle, 'Internet Art and Radicalism in the Digital Culture Industry' (2000) http://www.lulu.com/items/volume_1/89000/89324/2/preview/netart_preview.pdf; 0100101110101101.org, 'Copies' (n 30).
31. 0100101110101101.Org, 'The K Thing: Story of an Infamous Online Performance' (*0100101110101101.org*, 2001) http://0100101110101101.org/the-k-thing/.
32. Ibid.; Tatiana Bazzichelli, *Networking: The Net as Artwork* (*Digital Aesthetics Research Center*, Aarhus University, Aarhus 2008) 200–201.
33. For example, their recent installation/performance called 'Abuse Standards Violations' focuses on the human workforce behind censored

content on the Internet and how this unregulated online censoring impacts on our knowledge, available information, and the shaping of modern culture. Carroll/Fletcher Gallery, 'Eva and Franco Mattes – Abuse Standards Violations' (*Carroll/Fletcher*) http://www.carrollfletcher.com/exhibitions/55/overview/.

34. Thea Ballard, 'Newsmakers: Italian Artist Couple Eva and Franco Mattes' (*Blouinartinfo,* 3 June 2016) http://www.blouinartinfo.com/news/story/1414857/newsmakers-italian-artist-couple-eva-and-franco-mattes.
35. Samuel (n 17) 183.
36. Gar Warner, 'Internet Anarchy: Anonymous Crowds Flex Their Muscles' (*CyberCrime and Doing Time,* 13 December 2010) http://garwarner.blogspot.com/2010/12/internet-anarchy-anonymous-crowds-flex.html.
37. Samuel (n 2).
38. Jordan and Taylor (n 1) 130–131.
39. 'Camera/Shy' is an encryption application that enables the hiding of messages in media images. 'Shatterchat' is an encryption-imbued instant message-relaying system. 'Torpark' is an anonymising web browser that can even be used with a memory stick, hindering the traceability of user identities.
40. Mike Barbwise, 'Google Scanning – Is It Legal?' (*H-Online.com,* 20 February 2008) http://www.h-online.com/security/features/Google-scanning-is-it-legal-746155.html.
41. Samuel, (n 17) 95–96; HESSLA explicitly prohibits the introduction of spy-ware, surveillance technology, or other undesirable code into HESSLA-licensed programmes and any use of the software by any government that has any policy or practice of violating human rights. The licence decentralises enforcement power, empowering plain end users to act as enforcers. Oxblood Ruffin, 'Hacktivism: From Here to There' (*cDc Communications,* 6 March 2004) http://www.cultdeadcow.com/cDc_files/cDc-0384.html.
42. See 4chan website: http://www.4chan.org/.
43. Gallagher (n 14); Andy Bennett, 'Subcultures or Neo-Tribes? Rethinking the Relationship between Youth, Style and Musical Taste' (1999) Sociology, http://journals.sagepub.com/doi/abs/10.1177/S0038038599000371.
44. Dick Hebdige, *Subculture: The Meaning of Style* (Taylor & Francis, 2002).

45. Lachmann, Renate, Raoul Eshelman, and Marc Davis, 'Bakhtin and Carnival: Culture as Counter-Culture' (1988) 11 Cultural Critique 115–152. doi:10.2307/1354246.
46. As it is described in Wikipedia, 'a troll is someone who posts inflammatory, extraneous, or off-topic messages in an online community, such as an online discussion forum, chat room, or blog, with the primary intent of provoking readers into an emotional response or of otherwise disrupting normal on-topic discussion.' Wikipedia, 'Troll (Internet)' http://en.wikipedia.org/wiki/Troll_(Internet).
47. Gabriella E. Coleman, 'Anonymous: From the Lulz to Collective Action' (*The New Everyday*, 6 April 2011) http://mediacommons.futureofthebook.org/tne/pieces/anonymous-lulz-collective-action.
48. Luke Allnutt, 'Old-School Hacker Oxblood Ruffin Discusses Anonymous and the Future of *Hacktivism' (Tangled Web,* 8 June 2011) http://www.rferl.org/content/hacker_oxblood_ruffin_discusses_anonymous_and_the_future_of_hacktivism/24228166.html.
49. Coleman (n 3) 17.
50. Adrian Crenshaw, 'Crude, Inconsistent Threat: Understanding Anonymous' (*Irongeek,* 2011) http://www.irongeek.com/i.php?page=security/understanding-anonymous; Coleman (n 3) 67–68.
51. Harrison Myers, 'Anonymous Anarchist Action Hacktivist Group Founded' (*libcom.org,* 10 March 2011) http://libcom.org/news/anonymous-anarchist-action-hacktivist-group-founded-10032011; Charles Arthur, 'Lulzsec: What They Did, Who They Were and How They Were Caught' (*The Guardian,* 16 May 2013) http://www.guardian.co.uk/technology/2013/may/16/lulzsec-hacking-fbi-jail.
52. See Charles Arthur, 'LulzSec Hackers Jailed for String of Sophisticated Cyber-attacks' (*The Guardian,* 16 May 2013) https://www.theguardian.com/technology/2013/may/16/lulzsec-hackers-jailed-cyber-attacks.
53. Anonymous, 'Anonymous Is Not Unanimous' (*Pastebin,* 17 August 2011) http://pastebin.com/4vprKdXH.
54. Anonymous has named its Wikileaks operation as Operation Payback or Avenge Assange and its punchline is 'we do not forgive, we do not forget.' Similar language can also be seen in iRC chat discussions, when decisions on protests are being realised. See Warner (n 37).
55. Luke Goode, "Anonymous and the Political Ethos of Hacktivism" (2015) 13/1 Popular Communication 74–86, 79.

56. Stephen Mansfield-Devine, 'Anonymous: Serious Threat or Mere Annoyance?' (2011) 1 Network Security 4, 7.
57. Coleman (n 3).
58. Anonymous, 'Fragmented Plurality: An Interview with Gabriella Coleman' (*The Breaking Time*, 14 April 2011) http://thebreakingtime.typepad.com/the_breaking_time/2011/04/an-enormous-plurality-an-interview-with-gabriella-coleman.html.
59. Kevin Rawlinson, 'Inside Anonymous: The "Hacktivists" in Their Own Words' (*Independent*, 2011) https://whyweprotest.net/threads/inside-anonymous-the-hacktivists-in-their-own-words.89494/.
60. Coleman (n 3) 71–73.
61. Coleman (n 3).
62. Warner (n 37).
63. Ibid.
64. Liam Fox, 'From Hacktivists to Spammers: Is Anonymous Failing?' (*News Post*, 12 December 2010) http://newsjunkiepost.com/2010/12/12/from-hacktivists-to-spammers-is-anonymous-failing/.
65. See comments from alleged Anonymous in Scot Terban, 'Anonymous and Their Alleged Propagandist Barrett Brown' (*Infosec Island*, 10 March 2011) https://www.infosecisland.com/blogview/12441-Anonymous-and-Their-Alleged-Propagandist-Barrett-Brown.html.
66. Coleman (n 3).
67. For the various tactics employed, see Crenshaw (n 51).
68. Elinor Mills, 'Wikileaks Fans Should Think before They Botnet' (*CNet News*, 10 December 2010) http://news.cnet.com/8301-27080_3-20025373-245.html.
69. Ryan Singel, 'Dutch Arrest Teen for Pro-Wikileaks Attack on Visa and Mastercard Websites' (*Threat Level*, 9 December 2010) http://www.wired.com/threatlevel/2010/12/wikileaks_anonymous_arrests/#seealsoaff033736dd3e21e1f35daab3a12f8f9.
70. Jon Leyden, 'Anonymous Unsheathes New, Potent Attack Weapon' (*The Register*, 4 August 2011) http://www.theregister.co.uk/2011/08/04/anon_develops_loic_ddos_alternative/.
71. Coleman (n 3) 348; Sean Gallagher, 'High Orbits and Slowlorises: Understanding the Anonymous Attack Tools' (*Ars Technica*, 16 February 2012) http://arstechnica.com/business/news/2012/02/high-orbits-and-slowlorises-understanding-the-anonymous-attack-tools.ars.

72. Their activities started from harassing a virtual hotel for children and white supremacists in order to protest discriminatory behaviour and facilitating the apprehension of an online child predator.
73. Coleman (n 3).
74. 'Copyright Trolls Slammed in UK House of Lords' (*TorrentFreak*, 16 June 2016) https://torrentfreak.com/copyright-trolls-slammed-in-uk-house-of-lords-160616/.
75. Coleman (n 3).
76. Ibid. 207.
77. Aaron Sankin, 'Anonymous' BART Police Attack: Hackers Expose Cops' Personal Information' (*Huffington Post*, 17 August 2011) http://www.huffingtonpost.com/2011/08/17/anonymous-bart-police-attack-personal-information_n_929627.html.
78. B Clark, '"Anonymous" #OpTrump Isn't a "War," It's a Nail in the Coffin of the Encryption Debate' (*The Next Web*, 15 March 2016) http://thenextweb.com/opinion/2016/03/15/anonymous-declares-war-on-donald-trump-again-with-optrump/.
79. For a more extensive list of actions, see https://en.wikipedia.org/wiki/Timeline_of_events_associated_with_Anonymous.
80. Anonymous, 'Teenage Hacker Admits Scientology Cyber-Attack USA v. Guzner – Information' (*Secretdox,* 18 October 2008) http://secretdox.wordpress.com/2008/10/18/usa-v-guzner-plea-agreement-for-defendant-dmitriy-guzner/; See *US v Guzner* (New Jersey, Dist. Court) Case No. 2:09-cr-00087; David Kravets, 'Guilty Plea in "Anonymous" DDoS Scientology Attack' (*ThreatLevel,* 26 January 2010) http://www.wired.com/threatlevel/2010/01/guilty-plea-in-scientology-ddos-attack/.
81. Howard Mintz, '"Anonymous" Defendants Appear in San Jose Federal Court in Paypal Cyberattack Case' (*Mercury News,* 1 September 2011) http://sip-trunking.tmcnet.com/news/2011/09/01/5747845.htm.
82. John Ribeiro, 'Wisconsin Man Sentenced for Participating in Anonymous DDOS' (*PCWorld*, 2 December 2013) http://www.pcworld.com/article/2068600/wisconsin-man-sentenced-for-participating-in-anonymous-ddos.html.
83. *R v Weatherhead, Rhodes, Gibson, and Burchall* (Unreported) Southwark Crown Court, 24 January 2013; Josh Halliday, 'Anonymous Hackers Jailed for Cyber Attacks' (*The Guardian,* 24 January 2017) http://www.guardian.co.uk/technology/2013/jan/24/anonymous-hackers-jailed-cyber-attacks; Coleman (n 3) 140.

84. Mary Watkins, Tim Bradshaw, and Joseph Menn, 'Global Police Moves against "Hacktivists"' (*The Financial Times,* 27 January 2011) http://www.ft.com/cms/s/0/db6f5ab0-2a34-11e0-b906-00144feab49a.html#axzz1YaNDtzCj; Giles Tremlett and Agencies in Istanbul, 'Turkish Arrests Intensify Global War between Hacker Activists and Police' (*The Guardian*, 13 June 2011) http://www.guardian.co.uk/technology/2011/jun/13/turkish-arrests-global-war-hackers-police; John Leyden, 'Spanish Police Cuff Three Anonymous Hack Suspects' (*The Register,* 10 June 2011) http://www.theregister.co.uk/2011/06/10/spain_anonymous_arrests/.
85. David Kravets, 'Appeals Court Reverses Hacker/Troll "weev" Conviction and Sentence [Updated]' (*Ars Technica*, 11 April 2014) https://arstechnica.com/tech-policy/2014/04/appeals-court-reverses-hackertroll-weev-conviction-and-sentence/.
86. Orin Kerr, 'United States v. Auernheimer, and Why I Am Representing Auernheimer Pro Bono on Appeal Before the Third Circuit' (*The Volokh Conspiracy*, 21 March 2013) http://volokh.com/2013/03/21/united-states-v-auernheimer-and-why-i-am-representing-auernheimer-pro-bono-on-appeal-before-the-third-circuit/.
87. Kravets (n 86).

3

Looking into the Positive and Negative Aspects of Hacktivism

1 Introduction

Having seen the various hacktivist groups and movements and their rationales and tactics, this chapter is meant to discuss the importance of such actions for democratic politics, but also the risks that these political actions entail for users and networks. This analysis will be done through the lens of free speech and civil disobedience (CD), which will enable us to better focus and analyse in depth all the potential concerns that might be generated from symbolically expressive illegal acts. By reframing the free expression/CD debate on a cyberspace level we will be able to better conceptualise the ways in which hacktivism could be beneficial for democratic politics and the reasons and conditions that it could prove harmful.

Trying to assess new forms of online protest, based on free expression and CD criteria shaped during a pre-Internet era, when most of free speech, and especially CD theory, was developed, could end up generating seemingly difficult analogies. Although this analysis will attempt to demonstrate that perceptions and assessments of political legitimacy, harmfulness, or risk could and should be perceived based on well-established principles that operate within the existing framework of

V. Karagiannopoulos, *Living With Hacktivism*, Palgrave Studies in Cybercrime and Cybersecurity, https://doi.org/10.1007/978-3-319-71758-6_3

Western democracies, the new social, economic, and political conditions introduced or exacerbated by the advent of digital technologies should not be disregarded. On the contrary, it is a consistent theme of this book that a re-contextualisation of moral and practical arguments is required for providing a realistic and practical, instead of an abstract, theoretical analysis. This process will acknowledge that with societies' gradual progress, perceptions cannot remain unchanged, since that would render them obsolete or stifle social progress. Since hacktivism is considered political speech, which usually falls within the scope of human rights protected by state intervention, it would be interesting to see whether and to what extent such analogising is feasible and reasonable.

2 The Links Between Hacktivism and Freedom of Expression

The symbolic political acts, such as those employed by hacktivists and more traditional, offline CD protesters, are usually some form of conduct that acquires its expressive quality according to the context it takes place in, thus taking on a certain meaning without being explicitly put into words. For example, a sit-in at a University Dean's office by students for reasons relating to unequal university policies is, thus, upgraded from a mere illegal act of trespass to a message about the students' disapproval of the protested policies. Although expression through symbolic conduct that can also entail law-breaking is often more implicit than pure verbal expression of dissent, symbolic protests are usually part of a wider campaign for a political cause, where the role of such acts is to intensify the direct expression of dissent through communicative acts. It is also often a fact that the illegality of expressive conduct relates to an act of disruption (such as trespass, breach of peace, or computer impairment for hacktivists) in order to attract additional attention.

That element of disruption and the usual illegality of symbolic speech acts are, however, crucial differentiating factors between fully protected speech and conduct-facilitated expression, despite views which argue that 'actions which are clearly symbolic and only incidentally illegal ought to be protected for what they are.'[1] In the US, where free speech jurisprudence is far more extensive and detailed, the right to free speech and the consequent protection are afforded to pure speech, which has been considered distinct from expression through symbolic acts.[2] The common law origin of a right to protest is that people could do whatever they wanted, so long as their actions did not break the law.[3] Therefore, under common law, illegal acts of expression would not be considered protectable legal speech. Even pure speech in the form of verbal (slander) or written expression (libel) can be exempt from free speech protection and, thus, punishable.[4] Moreover, even when exercising freedom of expression in the forms of speech, assembly, or petition, one is not allowed to commit a breach of peace,[5] while restrictions can be imposed in relation to the time, space, and manner of the expression of dissent.[6] After all, free expression is not absolute and can be restricted by conflicting serious interests, such as the protection of private property or public safety.[7] Even in the US, where the First Amendment is considered fundamental, case law has prioritised property rights and has accepted time, manner, and place restrictions, if these restrictions do not relate to the content of the speech, are narrowly tailored, serve a governmental goal, and allow for speech alternatives.[8] Hacktivism, being an outright violation of cybercrime laws, also impacts on public and private property, and thus, under the above-mentioned rationale, would not qualify as protected expression.

To further reinforce this conclusion, case law in both the US and the UK has given priority to private property rights, when conflicting with free expression rights, even for pure speech-related events on spaces that are not designated for public speaking, despite these places simulating public fora, such as shopping malls.[9]

A similar rationale seems to be followed in cyberspace cases regarding pure speech and private property.[10] The existence of legitimate alternatives online, such as websites, social networking sites, and blogs, allows for speech to be expressed via the same medium, and therefore hacktivists would not be justified in arguing a lack of chances to express their protest online. Moreover, the tendency to give priority to private property rather than speech online has been further reinforced by designating even government-owned websites[11] and public-access computers as non-public spaces.[12]

A question arising from these cases is whether the intrinsic lack of adjacent, or any, public spaces, such as roads, pavements, or town squares, in cyberspace could have an impact on the decision to allow speech on private websites. Perhaps one could argue that, much like the exceptional *Logan Valley* (see note 9) case, the lack of any interstitial spaces online in conjunction with the potential relevance of the protest to the website accessed could justify the act of unauthorised access by hacktivists. As Lemley argues, the economic rationale, which relates to protecting private property, in addition to the absence of physical proximity online should be seriously considered by courts when creating analogies from offline private property to online spaces.[13]

However, the disruptive effect of the designated function of the website that hacktivist tactics usually entail would probably negate any claim to legality. This is further reinforced by *Tanner* (see note 9), which argued that protectable speech should have no disruptive effect on the proper function of the protested space, on the space itself, and on its visitors.[14] It appears then that it would be unrealistic to argue that hacktivist tactics such as defacements and virtual sit-ins could be considered free expression and, consequently, render its perpetrators fully protected from criminal liability. This is even more so since courts in the US have considered even the provision of advice and suggestion to commit virtual sit-ins as unprotected speech,[15] while numerous arrests and criminal convictions of cyberprotesters in the US and the UK clearly show the general presumption is to consider hacktivism criminal, rather than an exercise of free speech.

The sole exception can perhaps be found in Germany, where the Frankfurt appellate court, trying a case of virtual sit-ins against Lufthansa's website for its assistance to state deportation policies, found that a lack of any substantial coercion of the online protesting impairment would allow it to be equated to protected speech.[16] The court of appeal acquitted the organiser of the protest, Thomas Vogel, after the court of first instance had found him guilty and had imposed a monetary fine, with the appellate verdict spreading optimism for the future legality of virtual sit-ins.[17] However, prosecution was based on charges of coercion rather than cybercrime laws and the trials took place before the explicit EU-wide criminalisation of denial of service attacks—two elements that weaken the impact of this precedent.[18] Nevertheless, this case demonstrates an official acknowledgement of the expressive quality inherent in hacktivism.

Irrespective of whether hacktivism could be considered free speech, though, this acknowledgement at least reinforces the need to assess hacktivism as a new form of CD, which has historically compromised politically expressive action with illegality. The history and theory of CD has shown that it has an intrinsic value to democratic regimes in terms of promoting justice and effecting political change and progress, yet its inherent law-breaking also generates concerns that seem to be similar to those of hacktivism regarding security, coercion, and impact on the rule of law. Considering how hacktivist actions are often characterised as electronic civil disobedience (ECD), it would be useful to discuss this link in more depth in order to expand our understanding of what the benefits, but also the negative elements, could be from ECD.

3 The Links Between CD and Hacktivism

3.1 Definitions and Initial Clarifications

CD has been a core element of contemporary democratic politics that has been employed by protesters in relation to multiple causes, with cases like Gandhi's salt protests or Rosa Parks' violation of segregation rules in the American South being historic examples of how symbolic law-breaking contributed to political change and the downfall of authoritarian and racist practices and to the achievement of more equality and justice in society. The presumed political justifiability of these activities flowing from their sociopolitical benefits has induced theorists to suggest that CD should be attributed a 'legitimate yet informal place' in democratic states.[19] This acceptance of moral political law-breaking as a legitimate political activity rather than plain criminal activity consequently also supports calls for leniency or even tolerance and milder sanction to no punishment or resort to alternative sanctions for disobedients.[20]

Many theorists have attempted to define this elusive and multifaceted practice and identify the elements that render law-breaking morally and politically justifiable and useful in contemporary democracies. Rawls describes CD as 'a public, nonviolent, conscientious yet political act, contrary to law usually done with the aim of bringing about a change in the law or policies of the government.'[21] For Habermas, it is a 'non-violent, symbolic, and illegal form of protest, undertaken with the intention of appealing to the formal institutions of the state on the one hand and the sense of justice of the wider political community on the other.'[22] Power is even more inclusive: 'it is a deliberate, public, articulated infraction of regime rules, aimed at changing a regime's law or policy, non-injurious to the physical person, considerate of the rights of others, and pursued within the state's jurisdiction to expand and apply the democratic ethos.'[23]

Considering these points, the definition of hacktivism as 'the use of computer and network access and reconfiguration techniques that transgress or challenge cybercrime laws in order to produce or facilitate symbolic effects that confer a political message or protest a particular policy' is indicative of, at least, an initial conceptual connection between CD and hacktivism.

The primary element of CD is the voluntary violation of a valid criminal law provision. It can involve directly violating a law considered unjust, in order to induce a reconsideration of this law or achieve a constitutional review of it (direct CD). CD can also be indirect, which relates to staging a protest through breaking other valid laws, usually property-related, or in the case of hacktivists, cybercrime laws (which are also essentially property-protecting), as a means to communicate a political message, attract attention to an injustice, sensitise the public, and induce policy changes (indirect CD).[24] Usually the focus of hacktivist practices is on criticising other political decisions and social injustices. Therefore, their protests are mainly indirect, using the legal violations as a means for creating a political message in online spaces that are relevant to their various causes.[25] In fact, the violation of cybercrime laws could be an inevitable requirement for realising their expressive protests.

Regarding unauthorised data acquisition and exposure (doxing), the symbolic element can be secondary in them, or in some cases absent, but can still exist in cases where the data exposed are meant to highlight security flaws in corporate systems that leave users exposed to potential criminal exploitation of their information. Here the case of 'Weev' will be of particular interest as a controversial example of data acquisition that could be considered authorised and thus not illegal per se and which was done as a means of sensitising the public regarding problematic corporate practices and putting pressure on those responsible for remedying the situation. Undeniably, though, there have been instances where data exposures would be harder to analogise to symbolic, indirect CD, both practically and in terms of moral justifiability, since these acts often constitute a more radical form of direct action[26] or vigilantism. This ambiguity highlights the fact that even practices that would be considered identical in terms of the actual effect, such as doxing, could be viewed differently based on the context they are realised in.

Having discussed the initial elements, it will now be useful to discuss the concept of CD in more detail and also extract the criteria that have been considered crucial in preserving the positive elements of it, whilst mitigating the harmful effects such practices can have. We will then try to link hacktivist practices to those elements in order to see how contemporary conditions reconfigure our conceptions of what is politically legitimate and useful or unjustifiably harmful political practice. One should bear in mind that this is not a discussion that will render absolute results of either good or bad practice. The aim is to distil some core elements that help us define good and problematic practices and to see how hacktivist practices fit within the framework constituted by those elements.

3.2 The Value of CD and the Analogy of Hacktivism

A first question would be when we should consider law-breaking as legitimate. Habermas and Calhoun, approaching it from a social contract perspective, introduce the free and rational personal assessment of laws as a criterion for the legitimacy of a social contract-based society and a prerequisite for obedience in addition to coercion, found in more traditional contract theories.[27] For Habermas, illegitimate law that undermines the need for obedience is either one that violates basic rights of citizens or one that is created without proper democratic deliberation.[28] The first element is straightforward, focusing on natural rights of citizens. The second criterion refers to cases where less influential minorities, politically and/or financially, are excluded from democratic deliberation processes or where powerful economic and political minorities promote decisions without engaging in public dialogue or manipulate decision-making with their influence.[29] Apart from the need to protect citizens' basic rights, Habermas acknowledges the potential obsolescence or corruption of democratic institutions by strong influences and he considers the democratic social contract an open process, where its norms have to be consistently challenged and revised.[30] The challenging is realised through the generation of crises within the public sphere that reinvigorate the polity and ameliorate the inevitable communication and power deficits in contemporary democracies.[31] Essentially, Habermas and Calhoun submit that CD functions as a means for the polity to maintain its legitimacy by attempting to reinstate the moral balance implicit in the basic contractual arrangements that have been corrupted and by further developing these contractual terms, like an informal, crisis-inducing correctional device.[32]

Based on this, indirect CD as an illegal, yet symbolic, act of protest is considered justified as a means to reinstate the moral bases of deficient democratic regimes. The correctional function relates to the protests appealing to the core foundations of legitimacy of the constitutional democratic order, democratic deliberative decision-making, and the protection of established citizen rights.[33] Essentially, it is believed that CD can reinstate marginalised citizens as participants in legislative processes, from the formal procedures of which they might feel excluded, such as deliberation procedures, to facilitating the more direct exposure and confrontation of corruptive influences and deficiencies that could nullify the democratic social contract.[34] Consequently, CD is usually 'suspended between legitimacy and legality' and even though the state has a right to bring its perpetrators to justice, if it considers it necessary, it should do so with the consideration that such protesters are also guardians of the state's legitimacy.[35] In order to maintain the moral legitimacy of CD, Habermas articulates certain moral criteria that CD protesters will have to consider.

These are the need for protesters to act publicly, non-violently, and accept their punishment for their law-breaking, but also the need to demonstrate respect for the legal order and justify their protest based on constitutional principles.[36]

In relation to these criteria, Rawls offers some additional clarity. He discusses the concept of moral justifiability of CD in his theory of justice, which he builds on notions of fairness between co-citizens. Justice, for Rawls, is interrelated with fairness and equality. Fairness, for Rawls, entails that duties and obligations derive from ethical principles, defined as principles people would have chosen if their social status and interests were 'unknown' to them—his famous 'veil of ignorance.'[37] Second, Rawls also submits that societies are just when they maintain conditions of equal opportunity between citizens within social institutions and that social and economic inequalities (i.e. of wealth, authority) are considered just only if they result in compensating benefits for everyone, particularly the underprivileged.[38]

For Rawls, the prima facie duty to obey the law and promote just institutions gives way only when disobedience is realised for the political reason of addressing the sense of justice in the community and for cases where there is substantial and clear injustice.[39] Rawls designates as substantial injustices any serious infringements of the principles of equal liberty or fair equality of opportunity.[40] However, he also recognises that in contemporary pluralistic societies, absolute descriptions of justice would be void, as there is an abundance of liberal conceptions which might share similar structural characteristics of society, yet interpret and balance them differently.[41] This acknowledgement of diverse perceptions of justice, along with his acceptance of reasons for justifying disobedience if it is opposing serious injustices, renders the justifiability of disobedience open to interpretation, thus, broadening its scope.

Rawls explicitly accepts the justifiability of CD and also discusses indirect CD. He acknowledges that, sometimes, it is less harmful and practically feasible to break a minor law, such as trespass, in order to protest a major law that might be practically difficult to break, such as more abstract foreign policy decisions, or might have very grave consequences if directly violated for the purposes of protesting it, such as homicide.[42] Moreover, he acknowledges that protests might also relate to inaction of the government to take measures to prevent an ongoing injustice where there is no law to be protested, but the object of the protest might be the creation of a law in order to deal with the injustice in question.[43] Rawls also argues that CD should not be confined to cases of constitutional challenge, since, if a law is considered unjust, the protesters will disobey it even if it is eventually considered constitutional.[44] As he argues, 'CD expresses disobedience to law within the limits of fidelity to law, although it is at the outer edge thereof.'[45]

Rawls further discusses criteria he considers constitutive of CD as a morally justifiable practice identifying some ways that the negative aspects of law-breaking could be mitigated or justified. First, he believes that CD should be based on shared political principles of justice and not personal morality, religious beliefs, or self-interest.[46] Rawls further focuses on the non-violent character of CD and argues that protesters should avoid harming other citizens or seriously impacting on their civil liberties, although he concedes that sometimes after legitimate, non-violent attempts have failed, force might be an acceptable option.[47] Another criterion influencing justifiability is whether CD is employed after an effort has been made to facilitate change through legitimate means.[48] Rawls also argues for coordination of CD between minorities with valid claims to exercise it in order for it not to become so pervasive as to severely weaken the rule of law, which he believes can be achieved through competent leadership.[49] Furthermore, he links the moral justifiability of CD to its potential punishment, arguing that the civil and moral nature of the act and its justifiability on the basis of political constitutional principles should lead the courts to either reduce the penalties or even suspend any punishment.[50] Even though he considers these elements constitutive of CD as a moral practice, he accepts at the same time that they can be relative criteria in relation to the specific context of the protest.

Looking at CD from a more utilitarian perspective, Mill enriches the theory of utility by introducing certain rights that formulate a more complete concept of justice based on rules and principles that usually produce utilitarian results. Mill specifies those rights as personal liberty, property, or any other thing which belongs to a person by law, moral rights, just deserts, the protection of expectations raised by promised obligations, and impartiality in the appointment of rights, which is also related to equal treatment.[51] Utilitarianism, as Mill explains, is not a theory that disregards justice for the maximisation of public good, but one that acknowledges the diversity of interpretations of justice and the inevitability of conflicts between those different interpretations in culturally diverse societies and finds utilitarianism as the best resolution to conflicting justice claims.[52] He argues, however, that although the rights and expectations constituting justice are of paramount social utility, sometimes, one might be allowed to break laws that support some of the less important ethical duties, which should be followed in principle, in order to serve a higher moral duty.[53]

Based on Mill's rationale, the utility of indirect CD is also based on the rationale of a balance of conflicting disutilitarian actions. CD is employed, even though prima facie considered immoral as law-breaking of a normally utilitarian, legitimate law. In essence, justification is, therefore, based on the balancing of evils between the immorality inherent in the breaking of a valid law as a protest act and the important moral aim of trying to change a seriously disutilitarian law or policy. Utilitarianism also identifies higher utility in CD when it relies, not just on appeal to the majority's sense of justice, but also on the need to protest against potential harms that derive from misguided, yet formally legitimate, political decisions, where the potential effect might be of great social disutility.[54] Although this lack of reliance on justice principles has been deemed potentially problematic for the justification of disobedience,[55] Greenawalt asserts that protesting against foreseeably harmful policies could be morally justifiable, because one should not expect citizens to 'disregard their fears about harms that do not derive from injustice.'[56] After all, it appears that, contemporarily, many offline CD and hacktivist protests are also realised for reasons relating to lack of social consideration in political decision-making, despite it having gone through normal validation processes.[57]

By going through this theorisation on CD, it was my aim to show that, despite the general acceptance of a prima facie obligation of citizens to obey the law, disobedience has been considered morally acceptable and politically useful as a practice by various influential theorists, when done for reasons that are based on strong moral grounds. It was important to have this discussion in order to demonstrate that even though law-breaking is not taken lightly by those discussing justice and law-breaking, there are still strong political arguments within diverse democratic regimes that identify great value in acts of law-breaking, when done with political, justice-based motivations.

Theorists, such as Habermas, Rawls, Mill, and Greenawalt, seem to accept that disobedience could be justifiable and useful, if based on strong moral reasons, even if breaking legitimate laws. From the discussion we can distil certain elements that are meant to highlight and preserve the positive elements of CD and also ameliorate any negative consequences. It is through this process that a discussion regarding the positive and negative elements of hacktivism will become clearer. Some of the criteria that will be discussed include non-violence, protesting openly and for a moral political purpose, the need to trust in the legal system and use of CD only after legitimate measures of amelioration have been attempted, the coordination of protesters to minimise disobedience and disruption, the realisation of the protest within the normative framework of contemporary societies, and acceptance of the general validity of the legal order and of the punishment society would hand down. Utilitarians also highlight the importance of proportionality for the justifiability of CD, arguing essentially for a balancing of harms between the consequences of the disobedient act and the consequences of the injustice protested against.

However, the main conclusion is that, even for the criteria which have been identified, the particular context of a protest plays a crucial role in assessing the extent they could be followed. Contextuality is, thus, the most crucial overarching element that informs most discussions of the moral justifiability of CD and any relevant analysis should not consider the aforementioned criteria as absolute edicts, but more as indicative elements that try to morally and practically compromise a diverse political practice with the moral requirements of an even more culturally and politically diverse society.

The use of the term justifiability, instead of justification, declares exactly the graduated nature of the notion, but also highlights that there is a graduated level of political legitimacy and usefulness, as well as risk and harm, in many acts of political law-breaking. This relativity encompassed in the term justifiability will become more obvious in the following sections, where the criteria identified will be discussed and linked to hacktivism, thus revealing its positive and negative dimensions and the challenging balance between those more clearly.

4 The Positive and Negative Aspects of Hacktivism Through Its Link to CD

4.1 Conscientious, Yet Political

As CD is a response to a perceived injustice, a basic criterion for demonstrating its political legitimacy and utility is the conscientious belief of the protesters that there is a serious injustice or a legitimate political cause justifying their protesting. The question arises as to whether a general public consensus is required in relation to the actual existence of an injustice or whether personal beliefs would suffice. The motivation for the illegal act has to involve a moral reason that deserves more respect than the legal violation the protest involves.[58] However, in contemporary societies, sanctifying personal conscience unqualifiedly has been considered dangerous, as it could lead to justifying activities that relate to every personal whim and render CD dangerous for the social order if exercised superficially.[59]

Rawls tries to avoid this potential generalisation of justifying disobedience by highlighting that CD activities should be based on established political principles of justice and not just personal morality, religious beliefs, or self-interest.[60] That is why he describes CD as 'conscientious, yet political.' According to Rawls, for a person to act with autonomy and responsibility, they would have to find and assess how the political principles that inform the interpretation of the constitution relate to their particular context of disobedience and decide their course of action in accordance to how they think these principles should be interpreted.[61] Only after this process can the decision to disobey, even if the interpretation is wrong, be deemed conscientious and, thus, moral, rather than just selfish.[62] After all, Rawls accepts that there cannot be a single correct interpretation of constitutional principles, even if coming from the legislature or the courts and, therefore, citizens are responsible for their interpretation of the principles of justice and their conduct according to these.[63] This primary criterion is also often related to hacktivist actions, since in most protests there is indeed a reference to the violation of certain important rights, principles, or policies, from privacy and free speech online to the violation of international conventions regarding environmental concerns or the financial and social impact of austerity policies.

The broader interpretation Rawls gives to conscientious protesting also relates to another important concern, namely, whether CD as an informal, law-breaking, policy-changing tool contradicts formal, majority-based decisions within a democratic regime. Arguably, considering CD by minorities as morally legitimate and politically beneficial in a democracy could compromise decisions taken by democratically elected legislatures and lead to the majority acceding to the coercive minorities' demands.[64] This is a very serious challenge for CD, which is usually portrayed as beneficial for democracies and raises a more general question of whether CD is in conflict with democracy if protests originate from minorities and/or aim to change the policies of the officially elected government. As discussed earlier, a crucial criterion of justification is the existence of a level of respect for the current legal order, which constitutes an overarching moral expectation that relates to many elements. Therefore, it is crucial to assess whether CD acts and, by extension then ECD acts, undermine majoritarian democracies by morally justifying actions that would oppose the decisions of the government.

In order to assess whether CD and ECD violate the democratic ethos by challenging majoritarian decisions based on minority interpretations of morality and justice, one should first assess the importance of majority rule for democratic regimes. Is majority rule the absolute and unchallengeable principle of democratic states? This cannot be said with certainty. Despite its intrinsic importance for democratic decision-making, majority rule does not absolutely overrule all other concerns of a democratic society. This is because ensuring inclusive processes of deliberating decisions by the public and the protection of minorities' interests are also crucial democratic elements that balance majority rule.[65]

Therefore, majority rule cannot be considered flawless and protests that challenge injustices that the majority (or its representatives) might have facilitated against minorities should not be characterised as undemocratic, since their purpose could often be to act correctively against majorities' excesses or corrupt decisions of the majority's representatives.[66] In an era where governmental decision-making can be strongly influenced by financial interests, with the more obvious example of open lobbying and financing of candidates in the US elections, even the decisions of a democratic government can be challenged in relation to whether they are influenced and express the interests of the underlying financial interest rather than citizen well-being. This becomes even more relevant when protests turn towards private organisations that yield policy-influencing power or strongly impact on citizen rights, such as large financial institutions or Internet corporations. Challenging their views is not an anomaly for CD and ECD, but a consequence of the diversification of the role of such companies and their sociopolitical impact on matters of public interest.

Moreover, since CD and hacktivism often involve attempts to inform the public and sensitise more people into facilitating political change, this implies that the protesters have an ultimate belief in the majority's rule. It would thus be an oxymoron to criticise CD protesters as disregardful of the majority, either in the form of government representatives or the political body, since protesters often aspire to communicate to both these political bodies the need for change though their protests. One could even counterargue that CD protests reinforce the rule of the majority by ultimately recognising its authority to correct the mistakes of its representatives.

One should also bear in mind that certain views that are expressed by CD/ECD protesters might be shared by a far wider range of citizens than those obviously making a stand through their active protesting. This realisation makes the degree of public acceptance or at least the tolerating acknowledgement of a certain protested view by the general public very hard to gauge, especially for protests relating to international issues. Consequently, it is more important for moral assessment to focus on whether the hacktivist efforts have a moral background informing their efforts as appeals to the majority and/or its representatives in response to potential deficiencies of the democratic governance. Obviously there are cases where the desired effect is not to appeal to the public or its government, and in those cases, the legitimisation of the protest is of course impacted upon, as it is disconnected from what Habermas expects CD to be, a correctional tool for the polity.

Related to this tis whether the moral motivation for the conscientious act can be proven by the number of people joining the protest. Particularly in relation to the choice of tactics for online protests, small group/individually realised protests have been characterised as selfish, undemocratic actions of technical and political arrogance.[67] Especially in cases where the activities are perpetrated by single hacktivists or small groups, such as redirects/defacements or the promulgation of a political virus or even doxing, the above-mentioned consideration becomes even more important. For proponents of virtual sit-ins, their distributed nature decentralises the blameworthiness—something which presumably emphasises their democratic legitimisation of these protests,[68] without this meaning that virtual sit-ins have not been criticised as selfish and undemocratic.[69]

However, this argument will not always be valid, since less disruptive tactics, even if perpetrated by fewer people, such as a web defacement, could be more appealing to the public than a mass online sit-in causing serious service disruption.[70] Gandhi even considered individual or small group CD far safer and less prone to corruption than massive acts, without considering it less morally legitimate, as long as disobedience was consistent with the same moral cause as mass actions.[71] This is particularly relevant for virtual sit-ins and the trend that has seen networks of involuntarily engaged computers (botnets) being employed in order to enhance the disruptive effect of virtual sit-ins. As online mass action could be corrupted in such a way, one could argue that solitary or small group acts could indeed prove equally, if not more, morally legitimate. Even in these cases of botnet-enhanced virtual sit-ins, one could adopt Raz's argument that the disobedient should only be responsible for the morality of his or her own acts.[72] Therefore, the fact that someone from the protesting crowd might be acting immorally by joining the virtual sit-in and using a botnet to enhance its effects should not undermine the justifiability of the principled protestors' actions.[73] This could be assessed differently if those joining the protest are aware of such an occurrence and still do not attempt to prevent it.

Consequently, one could argue that there is a tenuous link between the assessment of the moral conscientious character of disobedience and the actual choice of tactics or numbers of participants. The choice of tactics might even be related to the particular context, and thus, the number of engaged protesters can be a matter of practicality and efficiency, since many tactics off- and online require or allow only for smaller groups.[74] After all, both offline CD and hacktivist acts cannot practically engage every person who might be supportive, while the legal ambiguity of such actions can also be discouraging for the masses for fear of punishment. If collective conscience behind the protest has expressly opposed certain tactics or political aims, considering them excessive or inconsistent with the purposes and the goals set, the activities of an individual could be considered personal and detached from shared perceptions of injustice, and, thus, selfish and less justifiable as democratically/socially useful.[75] We could, for example, argue that a defacement from a small group of far-right activists in order to promote the violation of the human rights of immigrants not only impacts on the network through the illegality of the protest, but has a negative impact on established social values that democratic institutions in multicultural environments are there to protect, such as equality, diversity, and tolerance.

4.2 Non-violence and Virtual Harms

The requirement to avoid violence in discussions about the justifiability/political utility of CD relates to preserving the proportionality of harms between the protesting law-breaking and the injustice the protest relates to. Physical injury to citizens would usually adversely impact on the justifiability of protests because physical harm will often be disapproved as a means of protest and can also undermine the expressive character of the protest. A demand for non-violence is also considered important for preventing political law-breaking from deteriorating into serious social disorder, where harm to individuals and property destruction—both characteristic of violent behaviour—could lead to similar acts of retaliation and generalised vigilantism. The fear that the justification of disobedience, especially when violent, could lead to generalised lawlessness and social disorder has been a common concern,[76] yet it has never been historically proven and has been considered an exaggeration by supporters and critics.[77] The requirement for non-violence thus reflects the need for the protest to avoid challenges on the state's monopoly of the use of coercive physical force, but also, mainly, the need to act in ways that would minimise any chances for serious harm or damage to citizens or property that would detract from the public approval of the political message behind the protest.[78]

In reality, the contextual, multifaceted nature of CD often involves minor violence or coercion, the absolute condemnation and exclusion of which would be an unrealistic and disempowering demand of protesters.[79] After all, CD has also been considered as a means for correction of antisocial and unjust political decisions and even as a less harmful outlet of social disaffection, instead of more radical opposition, due to its symbolic, non-violent nature.[80] Similarly, hacktivism, with its relatively low-intensity disruptions, could also partially operate as a release valve for social tensions, indicating the sources of public disaffection before public reactions become so radical as to deteriorate into more violent outbursts. Considering our discussion will transition online, defining violence is a necessary first step before embarking on any further analysis.

The threshold between violence and non-violence is hard to define and the term 'violence' has often become distorted, since virtually any unwelcome activity might be considered violent if it causes inconvenience or offence.[81] DeForrest proposes defining it by using accepted legal definitions in order to prevent vagueness and exclude forms the law has not strictly prohibited.[82] According to the United States Code, Title 18, Part I, Chapter I, S. 16, 'crime of violence' means

(a) an offense that has as an element of the use, attempted use, or threatened use of physical force against the person or property of another, or
(b) Any other offense that is a felony and that, by its nature, involves a substantial risk that physical force against the person or property of another may be used in the course of committing the offense.[83]

In the UK, Public Order Act 1986,[84] Section 8, defines violence as:

> [A]ny violent conduct, so that
>
> (a) except in the context of affray, it includes violent conduct towards property as well as violent conduct towards persons, and
> (b) it is not restricted to conduct causing or intended to cause injury or damage but includes any other violent conduct (for example, throwing at or towards a person a missile of a kind capable of causing injury which does not hit or falls short).

Despite the relatively unhelpful tautological nature of the latter definition, the focus on physical damage or injury or the threat of it is obvious, since, even if the desired damage and injury does not come about, the behaviour will still be considered violent based on someone's intention to achieve such a result.

Beyond legal definitions, Greenawalt defines violence as 'acts of force against persons that cause death, substantial physical pain, or impairment of physical faculties or that restrain physical liberty for a significant period of time, and acts of force against property that destroy or gravely impair its physical integrity.'[85] Although perceptions of the degree of force or the nature of the acts that constitute violence might be different according to different contexts, Greenawalt's definition relates to CD more particularly and focuses on the consequences that suggestions of non-violence when engaging in CD were meant to prevent. However, what is apparent is that all definitions relate to an extensive degree of physical force and the respective severe effects, supporting the presumption that the traditional notion precludes the possibility of non-physical violence.[86]

Defining violence in strictly physical terms would in most cases resolve the need to discuss non-violence in the context of hacktivist actions, the effects of which mostly take place online, presumably without any actual physical damage to people or property. Hardware is almost never physically damaged and software is often restorable as it was before the attack. On the Internet, citizens only deal with abstract, electronically structured representations of physical entities, therefore eliminating the chance for direct physical violence.[87] Yar moves one step further from physicality when discussing violence online and includes as cyberviolent behaviours only those that relate to 'psychological harm or inciting physical harm against others,' such as cyberbullying or suggestions inducing offline violence.[88] Owen also links cyberviolence to similar activities such as trolling and bullying[89]; physical violence online is not considered in other ways.

In relation to hacktivism one could argue that doxing by Anonymous, for example, regarding the addresses and names of police officers could be linked to Yar's latter category of violence, but in general the expressive hacking acts, such as viruses, defacements, or sit-ins, would rarely communicate a message inciting violence in the physical sense discussed in this context.

Regarding force and damage to property, US case law supports the view that the transmission of unwanted messages, such as spam[90] (which could be similar virtual sit-ins involving the transmission of multiple information requests) could be considered physical damage to a computer system.[91] Similarly in the UK, under s.1 of the Criminal Damage Act 1971, as interpreted in *R v Whitely*,[92] damage need not be physical in itself, but should have an impact on the value and usefulness of something physical, interpreting the concept of damage widely so as to include permanent and temporary physical harm or even just impairment of the value or usefulness of the property in question. In our case, the physical objects would potentially be the computer hardware in the form of computer storage devices and servers, the functionality of which would be modified in a way that impacts on their quality.[93] The extent to which the damage caused by data impairing/modifying acts, which might have temporarily impacted on the functionality of a computer or network, could also be considered violence, however, this is not very clear, unless we consider every impact on the quality and availability of computer equipment as violence.

Focusing on when damage could be considered violence supports a more teleological interpretation of the necessity for non-violence which links with the preservation of a proportionate harmfulness during protests and the demonstration of respect to the rights of others by avoiding overtly forceful, coercive behaviours. In his definition of CD, Power seems to argue for activities which are non-injurious to the person, something which would relate to the physical aspect of violence, but he also mentions that protests must be realised in ways respectful to the rights of others.[94] We could argue that this element of 'respect to the rights of others' could lead us to highlight a potential dimension of violence that could apply to cyberspace activities as acts that hinder the exercise of rights of others. Since physical violence seems to be quite obscure to conceptualise, especially with hacktivist actions that are not destructive or might have short-lived disruptive effects, the requirement of non-violence in cyberspace could, thus, be translated as a need to moderate the cyber-protests' imposition on the rights of others, so as not to be disproportionately coercive.

As argued,[95] expectations of complete non-violence can be unrealistic and, thus, CD can also entail an element of coercion and still be justifiable as politically legitimate and useful if it retains its initial persuasive character and attempts to induce change primarily through voluntary reconsideration of policies and not as a response to unavoidable coercion.[96] For example, a virtual sit-in could be employed in order to attract attention to a cause and initiate a discussion for change, but if it is realised in ways that totally hinder the functionality of a web page for long periods in order to force the desired change as a precondition for stopping the protest, the level of coercion would be much higher and the act less justifiable. Conversely, low coerciveness can serve publicity goals and even facilitate persuasion between protesters and protested, since it reduces conflict while still being acceptable.[97] This is because the rights that protesters violate, such as property or access to information, are not absolute, and thus minor infringements could be more acceptable when promoting higher moral goals.[98]

Morreal acknowledges that justifiable low coercion relating to non-absolute rights could eventually reach a degree that would be similar to what could be considered morally reprehensible violence by assessing the duration and intensity of the effects of the act.[99] The question should be, thus, whether this nuisance reaches high and disproportionate levels so as to be felt more as an unavoidable force. Acts that impinge on rights can be considered violent when they disproportionately hinder the exercise of rights, such as physical health, pursuit of happiness, and enjoyment of property.[100] In the cases of online CD, the rights that can be compromised are the enjoyment of property and potentially the right to free expression and access to information.

As McGuire clarifies, for genuine harm to manifest on a cyberspace level, it will have to relate to a practical or functional loss of a valued right or asset that citizens generally take for granted in their online environment and to reduce its capacity to an almost absolute degree.[101] For example, he argues that, if the right of access to the Internet becomes extremely pervasive and a social necessity, even temporary loss of the capacity for remote interaction could be instituted as harm.[102] At least for now, however, permanent connectivity has not attained such importance for individuals. However, it is a question as to whether we could say the same for a company, the business of which primarily takes place online and thus requires constant connectivity and accessibility for its financial survival.

Therefore, assessing the impact of the intensity and the duration and, thus, the coercive nature of the protest brings us back to assessing the potential damage and loss caused by the impairing act, since even short-lived protests can potentially cause financial loss, which is perhaps the primary counterargument against ECD protests. Consequently, the choice of targets becomes especially relevant to assessments of potential coercion, since impairing the functions of certain websites offering critical services to the public could prove damaging, not only to the direct target of the protest, but also to the wider public. Moreover, the targeting of private actors, such as financial organisations or commercial websites, could produce large amounts of assessed losses, even when minor disruptions are involved. PayPal, for example, claimed $5.5 million in damages from Anonymous' virtual sit-in during Operation Payback/Avenge Assange. Consequently, the notion of risk of harm to property as a potential aspect of violent behaviour becomes more pertinent in those cases where private actors are prevented from making use of their resources due to a virtual sit-in slowing down or causing a server to crash or a defacement requiring the restoring of a web page.

The realisation that the existence and degree of violence in CD are context-dependent, relative, and not easily measurable[103] is also consistent with the analogy created earlier, perceiving violence in the online context as the coercive infringement of property rights. This conceptualisation of violence could function as a viable alternative regarding notions of non-physical violence, when discussing the harmfulness of hacktivism. However, considering an act as violent for CD, at least, involves the question of the degree of infringement of rights of property or physical integrity, which would have to be generally high in order to constitute coercive activity.[104] Low-intensity acts, such as short-lived virtual sit-ins or easily 'healable' viruses might be law-breaking and rights-impinging, but their effects would not be adequately severe or persistent to be considered harmful/violent. Even in those cases where we would characterise these acts as violent, it can be argued that, when violence has no chance of leading to the injury of a person or the risk of it, it is a priori much less morally reprehensible.[105] Of course, the financial impact of such attacks on the web pages and networks targeted should not be taken lightly. Hacktivists themselves have deliberated and have often been selective when choosing their targets in order to minimise the harmfulness of their actions and the impact of their protest, acknowledging damage minimisation as a crucial element in establishing the political usefulness and legitimacy of their actions. However, this is not always the case, since many actions are done spontaneously, especially in relation to Anonymous' decisions. The issue of damages and financial harm is a core criticism for hacktivism and thus needs to be taken seriously in order for these protests to be considered proportionate and politically legitimate.

4.3 Efficiency and the Conflict of Speech

Another element that relates to retaining the proportionality between harms and benefits deriving from the act of protest as well as promoting democratic institutions is the need of the act of dissent to be realised in a way that is publicly visible and allows those experiencing it to link it to the cause it relates to. In other words, there needs to exist an obvious, communicated causal nexus between the protest and the cause. Particularly for online CD, due to technological issues, such as the lack of public fora online, efficiency also encompasses a dilemma between the free expression of protesters and that of the targeted actors. Before proceeding to discuss efficiency more particularly, one should, therefore, discuss one crucial precondition for the efficiency of online protests, which is the conflict of speech rights between protesters and their targets. This issue also relates to severe criticisms even from within the 'hacktivist' movement, finding information impairment and modifications to be inconsistent with the core principles of free exchange and preservation of information.[106]

An argument against the disruptive practices of ECD is that in contemporary democracies, with all the new possibilities for expression, especially online, from online radio to blogs or social networks, political opinions and dissent could be expressed without employing tactics that impinge on the speech opportunities of those protested against. Websites include content that forms an expressive message on behalf of those running them, be they private or state actors. Hacktivist tactics that impair the functionality of and impede access to these websites consequently infringe on the exercise of the expressive rights of those represented behind targeted websites. Especially for private commercial entities, the courts have recognised a right to free expression, both in the US and in the European Union.[107]

The response to these criticisms focuses on the inevitability of expressive tools that enable users to compensate for the reduced opportunities for expressing dissent online, compared to established organisations and authorities with extensive and multifaceted media access.[108] The idea of 'publicness' is complexified in the cyberspace context as there are many opportunities for one to express oneself through a personal website, blog, or social media like Facebook. However, such expression will normally be restricted to a small circle of friends and peers and will not have the popularity and visibility of more mainstream websites.[109]

Moreover, the nature of the content will be managed by the content providers, which usually have the right to take down content that has been reported or is deemed offensive. A typical example here is the denial of Amazon to offer hosting services to WikiLeaks when the diplomatic cables provided by Chelsea Manning were released in 2010. Although there was no legal action pending at the time against WikiLeaks, Amazon decided to stop offering its services to the whistle-blower website. The same happened with a Facebook page of Anonymous, where users were sharing information regarding an operation targeting terrorist websites. Facebook initially gave no explanation for the takedown apart from it being against its terms of service, but reversed its unjustified decision after a number of Anonymous members protested against it.[110] Even online Internet service providers often employ personal policies in relation to the speech they allow on their social spaces, while Internet search engines such as Google promote more popular search results, thus impacting on the audience reach of minority views.[111] Consequently, minority political views can be marginalised due to their inability to employ similarly popular information channels for reaching an equally significant audience.

Therefore, in assessing the extent to which hacktivist actions disrupt the speech rights of their targets in a manner that harms the democratic ideal of free speech and free exchange of information, one ought to also focus on the argument regarding the multiplicity of alternative expressive channels that the protesters' targets have available, compared to the channels that protesters and minorities might have to reach a similar audience. Governments or big corporations, which are usually the main targets of hacktivist protests, often dominate time, space, and information distribution on the popular mainstream communication channels of the Web, which can potentially facilitate their influence on democratic and norm-building processes and, thus, disproportionately impact on the sociopolitical discourse, steering public perceptions towards their desired directions.[112] Obviously, hacktivists can target websites, such as those of ISIS, which potentially complicates the argument discussed earlier about the imbalance of communication channels, but then the rationale behind the disruption relates to speech that would not be protected because it is hateful and incites violence.

Essentially then, efficient communication of the political message on a space that is relevant to the cause of the protest and frequented by the general public essentially requires that it is expressed on third-party websites without authorisation. Hacktivist tactics intervene on the proper functioning and speech of an existing speaker. Yet they also broaden the scope and diversity of expression and social debate by offering the opportunity to speak on the same popular space with those parties hacktivists protest against and, consequently, they gain access to similar numbers and types of audiences.[113] We therefore need to evaluate each particular context in relation to the speech opportunities of each side of the conflict and the overall level of impact of hacktivist protests on the sum of speech opportunities of the protested parties. Where in the offline world the crucial element had been the struggle for unhindered speech, in the interconnected island space of the Internet, free expression struggles focus more on audience capture and equating speech opportunities, rather than the capacity of a person to say what they want. It is not what you are saying, but who and how many will hear it that is important in the current era of information overload.

Returning to the main issue of the efficiency of the message, there seems to be another concern that detracts from the value of hacktivist protests. This relates to the implicit symbolic nature of indirect CD tactics, which might obscure the clarity of the protest message and, consequently, the protest's relation to the injustice protested. The absence of an obvious effect and, thus, a causal link between protest and goal can render the law-breaking protest less effective in terms of it being registered as an appeal to a just cause and, consequently, in terms of its contribution to remedying the injustice, which would be the anticipated positive, utilitarian effect. When the causal link between protest and goal is obscured or too vague, moral assessments based on a balancing of benefits and harms may result in the protest being considered excessively harmful compared to its actual contribution to remedying the injustice.[114]

In relation to the issues of clarity and actual impact, defacements or redirects are quite straightforward in terms of having a visible effect and communicating a message for as long as they remain protested on the website. However, virtual sit-ins sometimes prove inefficient, breaking the law without any actual speech effect being registered. This can happen if the disruption is absorbed with no practically visible impact on the targeted site through the employment of defensive measures or the renting of additional bandwidth. It can also happen when the number of participants is not so high as to attract public or media attention. Even if some form of temporary disruption is generated it could be perceived as a technical problem. Obviously, when the effect is negligible, there could be no actual legal concerns. But what happens when there is a disruptive effect, but it is not clearly registered?

Despite the general efforts to publicise protests in advance, so that the actual nature of a potential disruption is acknowledged by the public for what it is irrespective of the actual effect on the website, especially for virtual sit-ins, the potential low popularity of alternative media that promote hacktivist events could result in the actual message of the protest reaching only small audiences.[115] The same could apply to viruses countered by antivirus software. The example of virtual sit-ins best highlights the vicious circle between efficiency and harmfulness, since hacktivists will often have to find ways to balance between generating an adequate level of disruption to be noticeable, yet also not be as disruptive so as to be considered disproportionately coercive. For example, even though prior announcement of a protest might reduce its disruptiveness and potential harmfulness, as it would give the target site time to prepare a defence, notification would also compromise the actual message of the protest realised through the disruption if it were countered by the targeted site.[116]

However, hacktivist efficiency goes beyond the disruptive effect and the communication of the message can be facilitated even if the disruption is weak. After all, the usual aim of CD and hacktivism is to publicise injustices and sensitise the actors engaged. These online protests are only part of wider sociopolitical, multi-action struggles that function in a mutually reinforcing way and form a continuum, with multiple efforts aiming to achieve the same goal.[117] Despite the danger of not being noticed by the public, in cases where multiple users are engaged in the protest, these efforts can still be politically mobilising and engaging, as they can often be supported by hundreds or thousands of people.[118] As Denning admits even from the early days of ECD activity in the early 2000s, the protesters' causes can be communicated not just through the crashing of the website, but also due to the mass engagement of citizens, even without any major network interruption.[119] Protest groups such as the EDT have actually implemented a code in their virtual sit-in tools that returns an error screen with a political message included or registers a political message on the access logs for those operating the site to view, thus making their political message more obvious, in addition to the campaign to publicise it beforehand. Moreover, other hacktivist tactics, such as defacements, might be mirrored by many users in social networking sites and, thus, achieve greater publicity and communicate the message more effectively, even if the defacement is speedily amended. After all, the actual impact of a hacktion, both short- and long-term, cannot be foretold or gauged easily, as it also relies on external elements, complex, large-scale events, and slow political processes.

Therefore, the interplay of efficiency with the problems of speech and proportionate disruption could lead one to conclude that justifiability would have to be linked with the intended effectiveness and causality between targets and protested cause and not the existence of an immediate effect and political change. Protesters should therefore make choices that would render the protest as relevant as possible to the cause in terms of targets, tactics, and communicated messages. The actual disruptive outcome, which can rely on pure luck or even unanticipated countermeasures from the protested side, should not greatly impact on assessments of morality, unless it reflects an intentional effort of the protesters to cause disruption without any causal relation to an injustice or any underlying message.

4.4 CD as a Last Resort

Another element of legitimacy and utility for CD protests, which links to the respect protesters demonstrate towards the democratic rule of law, is the expectation that CD should be used only as a last resort after the exhaustion of all legal alternatives.[120] Illegal protest action is deemed unnecessary, since the democratic system allows citizens to express their dissent to various decisions, laws, and policies. This expectation also expresses the essence of proportionality, where the choice of means should be the least damaging possible, and thus more preferably legal, to achieve the desired result.[121] This particular requirement would thus imply that, if all the other equally efficient legal remedies are not exhausted, recourse to law-breaking would be disproportionately harmful per se and therefore immoral in a democratic regime, where there are usually legal political means available for seeking redress. This demand is nowadays reinforced, not only by the fact that, in contemporary democracies, free political expression is considered strongly established, but also by the aforementioned expressive opportunities afforded by digital technologies, which allow citizens to create and distribute their own content. Arguably, then, the various different legal means of expression and political participation are considered adequate for facilitating political dissent and change, consequently rendering all illegal acts of protest unnecessary and, thus, less justifiable.[122]

However, the above-mentioned assumption fails to realistically acknowledge the potential deficiencies in formal law-making and accountability processes, such as capture of political processes by lobbying interests or the increasingly governing role of private actors, especially in cyberspace, that do not have to abide by constitutional standards of review.[123] Furthermore, such a requirement seems to disregard cases where legal means of protest could have more serious social effects than illegal ones.[124] The relative nature of such a requirement is more evident when acknowledging the common fact that judicial and legislative mechanisms are overburdened in most countries and initiating proceedings can be very slow and costly.[125] Citizens might arguably even resort to CD due to unsuccessful and arduous efforts to gain access to formal legal remedies.[126] Where the injustice is current and ongoing, and has persisting consequences for a social group, these inefficiencies are further emphasised.

Although moral theories on disobedience would converge on the fact that when obviously accessible and possibly effective legal alternatives exist, political law-breaking should not be resorted to lightly, the requirement to exhaust all possible legal remedies could constitute an insurmountable moral demand on acts of CD and hacktivism.[127] Especially in an era when politics have transcended national sovereignties and are formulated by international groups[128] and financial organisations,[129] this requirement becomes untenable in its absolute form. Therefore, the strictness with which one should assess the morality of CD in relation to the existence of alternative, less harmful means of amelioration ought to relate to the particular context and the accessibility or potential success of legal means. Both Rawls and Greenawalt, for example, acknowledge that in cases of urgency or when the legal options appear potentially fruitless, the moral requirement to first exhaust legal ways of amelioration could be bypassed.[130]

Adding to that, it needs to be mentioned that CD can often be a way of inducing those capable and/or responsible for supporting legal or judicial action to actively do so. Regarding ECD, it also expresses, at least partly, the popular frustration for a gradual increase in inaccessibility or inefficaciousness of formal means of amelioration in contemporary democracies. Hacktivist projects bring together people globally in protests against social matters for which the legal remedial means are often beyond their jurisdictional or financial reach, despite the global implications of the political acts or policies protested. For example, the act of Visa and PayPal to arbitrarily freeze donations towards WikiLeaks, which fuelled the Operation Payback/Avenge Assange protests by Anonymous, was considered an act with political dimensions that had a serious censoring impact regarding online speech on an international level.[131] Naturally, few will have the resources to challenge such a decision in court, despite its global implications on speech and political debate. Even if that happens, the slow court proceedings would probably mean that by the time a final decision is reached, WikiLeaks would be financially exhausted and defunct.[132] Considering that the protests and the subsequent publicity eventually reversed the decision of PayPal to block donations to WikiLeaks,[133] one could see how protesting after all legal remedies have been exhausted could have made an efficient protest meaningless.[134] Moreover, hacktivism, with its usually provocative, eye-catching nature can often act as a precursor to the employment of legal measures of amelioration by generating public discussion and bringing the issue to the fore of even global mainstream media.

The need for careful consideration on behalf of protesters before the employment of illegal means of protest is a valid concern, in order to avoid the full substitution of legitimate democratic procedures by unprincipled and generalised vigilantism in the form of disproportionately coercive protests. However, moral assessments of CD should take into account the actual contemporary political conditions in relation to the possibility of access and success of prior legal means. Such an evaluation process would entail assessing whether legal recourse was possible, accessible, and potentially efficient; whether such measures have been sought prior to employing illegal ones; and even whether CD could function as a way to activate these legal processes.[135]

On the other hand, of course we should be wary not to condone every form of vigilantist and damaging protest if it mainly expresses a disconnected or exaggerated response on behalf of the perpetrators. For example, the constant declarations of war by Anonymous do not really serve to demonstrate a coherent and consistent connection of hacktivist efforts to worthwhile goals, even if they are consistent with big issues like terrorist attacks by ISIS or President Trump's controversial political decisions. What needs to be carefully thought out and avoided is the realisation of protests with a frequency and manner that would potentially exhaust the tolerance of even those who are positively predisposed to such efforts.

4.5 Taking Responsibility Versus Anonymity

Another important element affecting the justifiability of CD and relating to the protesters' demonstration of respect for the legal order they operate in is the acceptance of punishment by the protesters. This requirement is considered indicative of the protesters' altruistic intentions and their respect for their political regime and their co-citizen rights, which are compromised by their law-breaking.[136] Moreover, the openness of identity that an expectation to accept punishment presupposes is also a justificatory factor, because it ensures the public nature of the protest and distinguishes protests from covert criminal acts, essentially confirming the moral intentions of the protesters.[137] This element is also linked with criticisms towards hacktivists and mainly Anonymous for not openly revealing their identities and thus acting in the shadows like criminal hackers.

Nevertheless, the interpretation and true implications of such a moral requirement have been strongly contested. As Arendt argues, society cannot expect that the disobedient will simply accept any punishment, since that would require that the disobedient does not defend their case, consequently nullifying their basic defendant rights.[138] Moreover, although Gandhi and Raz have argued that accepting punishment is linked with the state's acknowledgement of the moral motives of the protesters and with the imposition of lenient penalties, they find it unlikely that the authorities will ever accept any potential legitimacy of the protesters' cause.[139] This is further exacerbated in the case of hacktivism, where protesters have faced very high penalties for their actions, way higher than what serious offline offences could involve. The punishment for CD offline for vandalism or trespassing usually consists of misdemeanour charges, which are substantially different in seriousness from the felonious charges faced by hacktivists.[140] As Coleman argues, for example, Eric J. Rosol was given a two-year probation and $183,000 fine by US courts for joining a virtual sit-in of Anonymous against the Koch Brothers industries website for 1 minute, while more serious crimes like arson would involve a much lower fine.[141] For online protesters who are knowledgeable of the very high penalties, their willingness to openly protest might be curbed by the feeling of the illegitimacy of the threatened penalty compared to the seriousness of their actions.

Considering the above, this criterion should not be interpreted narrowly to mean that protesters should seek and accept whatever punishment is handed down. Acceptance of punishment relates more closely to the protesters expressing their dissent publicly and being identifiable and traceable in order to be tried, if the maintenance of public order renders this necessary. These aims, however, could be equally served through a moral expectation that the disobedient should not try to actively avoid the risk of arrest and prosecution[142]—an interpretation which resolves the problems that an unqualified acceptance of any punishment creates. The acceptance of, at least, the prospect of arrest and punishment by protesters could function as a guarantee that alleviates public frustration caused by the protesters' law-breaking and also tests the protesters' conviction in the legitimacy of their cause.[143] Adopting the acceptance of the risk of prosecution rather than of punishment as a moral criterion also avoids the judicial unreasonableness of expecting the protesters not to pose any legal defence in court or at least stand their ground during plea bargaining.

Acceptance of the prospect, rather than the punishment per se, will allow the protester to defend their case properly and publicise the justness of their cause and allow them to remain politically active.[144] Therefore, acceptance should not be read as acceptance of the specific punishment handed down by courts, but instead acceptance of the prospect of being faced with sanctions for their activity and also their need to defend their actions and justness of cause in court. This course would, consequently, avoid the delegitimisation of just causes and the elimination of the politically sensitised part of society, which could result from an unquestioning acceptance of any punishment.[145] The state would, instead, have to convince the court that it has good reasons to punish these protesters who have beliefs so strong as to risk punishment for them.

This reading of accepting the risk of prosecution would be consistent with how cyberspace protests are realised and the specific difficulties of identifiability online, where prima facie anonymity and distance create difficulties in locating, apprehending, and punishing deviants. From the Internet's inception, anonymity has been the standard norm and has generated and facilitated criminal behaviours, but also the more acceptable values of privacy, freedom of expression, and creativity, and is therefore deemed worthy of preservation.[146] Hacktivists have adopted varying degrees of identifiability, from full openness to full covertness, which are related to their degree of acceptance of accountability and influence their moral legitimacy,[147] yet undeniably also reflect their concerns regarding the increasing instances where protesters have been prosecuted under very serious charges.

Many of the first-era groups were open about their identities as artists/performers and activists or used traceable pseudonyms.[148] Members of the Electrohippies argued that total exposure of identity, instead of their adopted pseudonymity, could endanger their livelihoods due to potential social and workplace prejudice towards their activities, without substantially facilitating their traceability by the authorities.[149] Moreover, Ricardo Dominguez is a typical example of a person who has even been employed openly by a university for his hacktivist background and he has never tried to mask his involvement and in fact his organising of such events, along with his fellow EDT group mates, even risking an FBI prosecution in his attempt to practise what he was employed to teach. Hacktivismo has also been quite open about the identity of at least their spokesperson, Oxblood Ruffin.

The diversity of practices reflects the diversity of different perspectives and the concerns for the risks of openly engaging in such activities in relation to the potential penalties. After all, even for those who have tried to remain anonymous in the Anonymous IRC channels, the FBI has managed to infiltrate these channels and has even allegedly used informants like Monsegur, a leading persona for Anonymous, as agents provocateurs.[150] Constantly evolving technologies of control in cyberspace have ultimately rendered full anonymity difficult to achieve, especially for everyday users who lack the willingness or knowledge to employ 'anonymisation' techniques.[151] As Lessig argues, the trend towards extreme identity-authentication technologies on the Internet is unstoppable, especially since Internet infrastructure has the potential to facilitate the development of such techniques.[152]

Again, as with every element discussed so far, we can see a variety of approaches and responses/reactions to how the authorities have responded to such openness, but we also need to perceive anonymity through the lens of cyberspace norms, where pseudonymity or anonymity is far more established normatively, especially in the spaces that Anonymous originates from. We also need to bear in mind that difficulties in potentially apprehending protesters can be based not just on anonymity efforts by hacktivists, but also on resource availability, jurisdictional challenges, or the discretion and prospect of successful apprehension/prosecution on behalf of law-enforcement agencies. Several Anonymous protesters have been prosecuted anyway, as they did not mask their identities when participating in virtual sit-ins.

These interpretations of openness in conjunction with the acceptance of punishment through identifiability highlight a difficult balancing process between the potential need to sanction protesters for their law-breaking, if required, with the need of protesters to demonstrate a basic respect for the legal system, but also retain some sense of privacy in relation to their expressive actions and deal with prosecutorial excesses. However, this discussion might take a different turn once we see that, apart from exceptional cases, those persecuted and/or prosecuted are the protesters who did not try to mask their identities, thus being easy targets, which would seem to be rewarding rather than delegitimising those who do try to act in a more undercover manner.

5 Conclusion

This chapter has evaluated the potential positive aspects of hacktivism against the criticisms using a discussion on free speech and mainly CD as a platform. It first discussed the links between free expression and hacktivism and the reasons why symbolic hacktions cannot be considered identical to protected free speech due to their law-breaking aspect, despite the strong links of these activities to free expression. Subsequently, the analysis focused on CD as a political practice and the positive and negative consequences that such practices could have. We discussed how arguments that have related to similar offline activities could be translated into the online environment and the impact this translation has on understanding and assessing hacktivist actions.

What this discussion demonstrated was that hacktivist practices have both positive and negative potential as a form of contestational political expression that relates to the violation of existing laws within modern, globalised, and information-based democracies. An overarching conclusion to be drawn is that hacktivist actions are neither a priori dangerously criminal nor totally justifiable political practice and, in many cases, deciding on their political usefulness or harmfulness will be a challenging assessment process based on the particular context. However, the aim of this chapter was to demonstrate that hacktivism entails positive and negative aspects that need to be holistically and also contextually considered when making a decision as to how such actions should be perceived and dealt with.

The following chapters will review whether the current norms and laws that relate to hacktivism as a combination of political protest and hacking allow for balanced contextual assessments that take into account both the negative and positive aspects of such activities. This process will allow us to assess whether the current responses reflect this duality inherent in hacktivism and thus also whether the responses produced could be considered to be promoting just and efficacious responses towards hacktivism.

Notes

1. Robert Hall, 'Legal Toleration of Civil Disobedience' (1971) 81 Ethics 128, 132; Mead equates peaceful speech with symbolic expressive acts, even if incidentally or inevitably obstructive/disruptive with a requirement that protests do not entail disproportionate disruption that could seriously impair the functionality of the protesters' targets. He considers such activities to be legitimate civic responses that should be considered lawful, unless there is contradicting evidence. David Mead, *The New Law of Peaceful Protest: Rights and Regulation in the Human Rights Act Era* (Hart Publishing, Oxford 2010) 11–12.
2. Barbara J. Katz, 'Civil Disobedience and the First Amendment' (1985) 32 UCLA Law Review 904, 906–907.
3. Mead (n 1) 26; Noah Hampson, 'Hacktivism: A New Breed of Protest in a Networked World' (2012) 35 Boston College International & Comparative Law Review 511, 526–527.
4. Susan Tiefenbrun, 'Civil Disobedience and the US Constitution' (2003) 32 Southwestern University Law Review 677, 697. Criminal libel was only abolished for England, Wales, and Northern Ireland in 2010 with the Coroners and Justice Act of 2009, Ch 3, section 73.
5. J.L. Legrande, 'Nonviolent Civil Disobedience and Police Enforcement Policy' (1967) 58 The Journal of Criminal Law, Criminology, and Police Science 393, 395–396.
6. Hampson (n 3) 527; Mead (n 1) 100.
7. Council of Europe, 'The European Convention on Human Rights' (Rome, 1950) art 10.2: 'The exercise of these freedoms, since it carries with it duties and responsibilities, may be subject to such formalities, conditions, restrictions, or penalties as are prescribed by law and are necessary in a democratic society, in the interests of national security, territorial integrity, or public safety, for the prevention of disorder or crime, for the protection of health or morals, for the protection of the reputation or rights of others, for preventing the disclosure of information received in confidence, or for maintaining the authority and impartiality of the judiciary.'
8. *Ward v Rock Against Racism* 491 U.S. 781 (1989).
9. The picketing against a company operating within a shopping mall was considered protected speech. The two crucial elements justifying this decision were, first, that the protest was strictly related to the space

where it was taking place and, second, there were no public space alternatives close by due to the nature of the area where the shopping mall was located. *Food Employees v. Logan Valley Plaza, Inc* 391 U.S. 308 (1968) (*Logan Valley*). However, this case has been superseded by.*Lloyd v Tanner*. In this case, the denial to leave the mall's premises at the request of the owner, when leafleting against the war in Vietnam, was considered a violation of the mall owners' right of private property. The court concluded that the cause of the protest was unrelated to the place of protest (the mall), as there were also adequate alternative places for expression that were publicly accessible, such as pavements, adjacent to the shopping mall. *Lloyd* Corp. *v Tanner*, 407 U.S. 551 (1972) (*Tanner*). See also *Hudgens v NLRB* 424 U.S. 507, 96 S. Ct. 1029, 47 L. Ed. 2d 196, 1976 U.S.

A similar conclusion was reached by the European Court of Human Rights in *Appleby v UK*. In *Appleby*, the rights of property of the mall-owning company Postel were considered superior to the right of free expression (art.10 ECHR) and assembly (art.11 ECHR) of three protesters who were petitioning inside one of its malls. (2003) 37 EHRR 38 (*Appleby*). Similarly, in the UK, an example would be the case of *City of London v Samede & Ors* [2012] EWHC 34 QB (*Samede*). Here, protesters were prevented from protesting within the privately owned Canary Wharf area, even though the cause of their protest, the economic crisis allegedly exacerbated by the policies of the banks hosted in Canary Wharf, was very relevant to the space the protesters had chosen.

10. For example, the court in *CyberPromotions, Inc. v America Online, Inc.* 948 F. Supp. 436 (E.D. Pa. 1996) (*CyberPromotions*) found that, if non-Internet alternatives exist that would allow expression to reach the desired public, then private actors, such as America Online (AOL), could not be forced to accept speech on their private online network web pages in order for speech to reach its subscribers. The court argued that AOL's service did not have the character of a public forum and, thus, was under no obligation to allow speech as a private space. See Dawn C. Nunziato, 'The Death of the Public Forum in Cyberspace,' (2005) 20 Berkeley Technology Law Journal 1115, 1136.
11. In *Sutliffe v. Epping Sch. Dist.*, 584 F.3d 314, 333–34 (1st Cir. 2009) the court found that a town's website could not be considered a public forum. See also *Hogan v. Twp. of Haddon*, 278 F. App'x 98, 102 (3d Cir. 2008) and *Vargas v. City of Salinas*, 205 P. 3d 207, 215 n.8 (Cal. 2009)

regarding whether websites of government organisations could be considered public forums. A more extensive analysis can be found in Xiang Li, 'Hacktivism and the First Amendment: Drawing the Line between Cyber Protests and Crime' (2013) 27 Harvard Journal of Law & Technology 301.

12. *US v. American Library Association*, 539 U.S. 194 (2003) (*Library Association*) the US Supreme court argued that public library Internet access did not constitute a public forum and, therefore, filtering restrictions on patrons' access to information were considered constitutional.
13. Mark A. Lemley, 'Place and Cyberspace' (2003) 91 California Law Review 521, 536–537. http://scholarship.law.berkeley.edu/californialawreview/vol91/iss2/5.
14. The court respected the private property right and the desire of the owners of the mall to prevent protests that could cause disruption or annoy any of the patrons.
15. *US v Fullmer* 584 F.3d 132 (3d Cir. 2009) (*Fullmer*).
16. See the Lufthansa virtual sit-in case: *OberlandesGericht Frankfurt am Main v Thomas Vogel* (No. 1 Ss 319/05) case available in German: http://www.libertad.de/service/downloads/pdf/olg220506.pdf.

    See also commentary in English in European Digital Rights, 'Frankfurt Appellate Court says Online Demonstration Is Not Coercion' (*European Digital Rights,* 07 June 2006) https://edri.org/edrigramnumber4-11demonstration/.
17. Ricardo Dominguez, 'Electronic Disobedience Post-9/11' (2008) 22 Third Text 661.
18. Federico Biancuzzi, 'Achtung! New German Laws on Cybercrime' (*Security Focus,* 10 July 2007) http://www.securityfocus.com/columnists/448.
19. Mark E. DeForrest, 'Civil Disobedience: Its Nature and Role in the American Legal Landscape' (1998) 33 Gonzaga Law Review 653, 654.
20. John Rawls, *The Theory of Justice* (Harvard University Press, Cambridge 1999) 339; Juergen Habermas and Martha Calhoun, 'Right and Violence: A German Trauma' (1985) 1 Cultural Critique 125, 137; Robert Hall, 'Legal Toleration of Civil Disobedience' (1971) 81 Ethics 128, 132–133.
21. John Rawls, *The Theory of Justice* (Harvard University Press, Cambridge 1999) 320.
22. Juergen Habermas, 'Civil Disobedience: Litmus Test for the Democratic Constitutional State' (1985) 30 Berkeley Journal of Sociology 95, 99.

23. Paul F. Power, 'Civil Disobedience as Functional Opposition' (1972) 34 The Journal of Politics 37, 40.
24. Hugo A. Bedau, 'Civil Disobedience in Focus: Introduction' in Hugo A. Bedau (ed), *Civil Disobedience in Focus* (Routledge, London 2002) 50.
25. An exception could be the creation of a virus that attempts to express concerns about the undue demonisation of viral software in contemporary cybercrime regimes. 0100101110101101.org, 'Contagious Paranoia: 0100101110101101.org Spreads a New Computer Virus' (0100101110101101.org, 2011) http://0100101110101101.org/biennale-py/.
26. CAE characterises direct action as policy subversion tactics, including information thefts and more destructive interventions that have a more coercive and less expressive character than ECD. Critical Art Ensemble, *Digital Resistance* (Autonomedia, New York 2001) 14.
27. Habermas and Calhoun (n 20) 134–135.
28. William Smith, 'Civil Disobedience and Social Power: Reflections on Habermas' (2008) 7 Contemporary Political Theory 72, 79–80.
29. Ibid. 81–82; See, for example, how the Supreme Court connected the elimination of limitations to spending money and effort in promoting or defeating political adversaries with free speech, surrendering election decisions even more to the influence of rich corporate elites. Adam Cohen, 'Case Study: The Supreme Court and Corporate Free Speech' *(Time,* 07 July 2010). http://www.time.com/time/nation/article/0,8599,2001844,00.html.
30. Juergen Habermas, *Between Facts and Norms: Contributions to a Discourse Theory of Law and Democracy* (William Rehg tr, Polity, Cambridge 1996) 384.
31. Ibid. 382; Smith (n 28) 78.
32. Habermas and Calhoun (n 27) 137.
33. Smith (n 28) 79–80.
34. Ibid. 78.
35. Habermas and Calhoun (n 20) 137.
36. Ibid.
37. John Rawls, *The Theory of Justice* (n 20) 301; John Rawls, 'Justice as Fairness: Political Not Metaphysical' (1985) 14 Philosophy and Public Affairs 223, 236–237.
38. Rawls, *The Theory of Justice* (n 20) 13.
39. Rawls, *The Theory of Justice* (n 20) 326–327.

40. Ibid.
41. John Rawls, *The Law of the Peoples; with the Idea of Public Reason Revisited* (Harvard University Press, London 2000) 14–15; Rawls, *The Theory of Justice* (n 20) 342.
42. Rawls, *The Theory of Justice* (n 20) 320.
43. Alan M. Schwarz, 'Civil Disobedience' (1970) 16 McGill Law Journal 542, 564.
44. Rawls, *The Theory of Justice* (n 20) 320–321.
45. Ibid. 322.
46. Ibid. 321.
47. Ibid. 322.
48. Ibid. 327–328.
49. Ibid. 328–329.
50. Ibid. 339.
51. John Stuart Mill, *Utilitarianism* (Original Edition 1879, The Floating Press, 2009) 78–83, 90.
52. Ibid. 99–104.
53. As Mill says, '[j]ustice is a name for certain moral requirements, which, regarded collectively, stand higher in the scale of social utility, and are therefore of more paramount obligation, than any others; though particular cases may occur in which some other social duty is so important, as to overrule any one of the general maxims of justice' (ibid. 113).
54. As Greenawalt says, '[i]f [...] what has happened is only a very bad policy decision and disobedience is likely to produce a careful reappraisal and possible reversal, the disobedience might well be warranted. The intensity of opposition demonstrated by self-sacrificing disobedience can serve to promote re-examination of crucial factual data as well as claims of justice.' Greenawalt, *Conflicts of Law and Morality* (Oxford University Press, New York 1989) 234–235.
55. Daniel Markovits, 'Democratic Disobedience' (2005) 114 The Yale Law Journal 1897, 1900–1901.
56. Greenawalt, *Conflicts of Law and Morality* (n 54) 234.
57. Markovits (n 55) 1901.
58. Bedau, 'Civil Disobedience in Focus: Introduction' (n 24) 9.
59. Power (n 23) 42.
60. Rawls, *The Theory of Justice* (n 20) 320–321.
61. Ibid. 341.
62. Ibid.

63. Ibid. 342.
64. Steven R. Schlesinger, 'Civil Disobedience: The Problem of Selective Obedience to Law' (1976) 3 Hastings Constitutional Law Quarterly 947, 953; Rawls, *The Theory of Justice* (n 19) 312; Smith (n 28); Menachem M. Kellner, 'Democracy and Civil Disobedience' (1975) 37 The Journal of Politics 899, 900.
65. Rawls, *The Theory of Justice* (n 20) 313; Kellner (n 64) 901; The European Court of Human Rights in *Gorzelik v Poland* (2005) 40 EHRR has argued that democracy identifies with the protection of minorities and the avoidance of abuses of the majority's dominant position; Mead (n 1) 32.
66. Alexander M. Bickel, 'Civil Disobedience and the Duty to Obey' (1973) 8 Gonzaga Law Review 199, 210; Habermas and Calhoun (n 20) 137.
67. Kenneth E. Himma, 'Hacking as Politically Motivated Digital Civil Disobedience: Is Hacktivism Morally Justified?' (2005) 17 http://papers.ssrn.com/sol3/papers.cfm?abstract_id=799545#.
68. Alexandra Samuel, *Hacktivism and the Future of Political Participation* (Harvard University, 2004) http://alexandrasamuel.com/dissertation/pdfs/index.html, 12.
69. See Gabriella Coleman, *Hacker, Hoaxer, Whistleblower, Spy: The Many Faces of Anonymous* (Verso Books, 2014) 107–109.
70. Small-scale actions like web defacements often cause less disruption and inconvenience than mass actions, like virtual sit-ins. See Meiring De Villiers, 'Distributed Denial of Service: Law, Technology & Policy' (2007) Paper 7, University of New South Wales Faculty of Law Research Series, 1, 25–26.
71. Vinit Haksar, 'The Right to Civil Disobedience' (2003) 41 Osgoode Hall Law Journal 415. For example, small groups could be more politically and tactically considerate than more expansive collectives, such as with Anonymous, where motivations and beliefs of participants could vary.
72. Joseph Raz, *The Authority of Law: Essays on Law and Morality* (Oxford University Press, Oxford 1979) 269.
73. Ibid.
74. Web defacements and redirects are examples of individual or small group efforts, while a sit-in at a small office could not accommodate all the protesters that a march for a similar cause would.

75. For example, Anonymous might criticise attacking certain websites as irrelevant to a cause and yet some members might still proceed with a protest, despite the general condemnation of the choice.
76. Raz (n 72) 237; Kent Greenawalt, 'A Contextual Approach to Disobedience' (1970) 70 Columbia Law Review 48, 56–57.
77. Martin C. Loesch, 'Motive Testimony and a Civil Disobedience Justification' (1990) 5 Notre Dame Journal of Law, Ethics & Public Policy 1069, 1112–1113; Alan M. Schwarz, 'Civil Disobedience' (1970) 16 McGill Law Journal 542, 553–554; Hannah Arendt, *Crises of the Republic* (4th edn, Harvest Books, San Diego 1972) 69–70, 74; Rawls, *The Theory of Justice* (n 21) 342.
78. Rawls, *The Theory of Justice* (n 21) 321–322.
79. Raz (n 72) 267; Schwarz (n 77) 565–566; Anthony D. Woozley, 'Civil Disobedience and Punishment' (1976) 86 Ethics 323, 325; Greenawalt, *Conflicts of Law and Morality* (n 54) 245.
80. Rawls, *The Theory of Justice* (n 21) 336; Craig P. Colby, 'Civil Disobedience: A Case for Separate Treatment' (1968) 14 Wayne Law Review 1165, 1167–1168. Arendt recognises that many changes in the US legal system have happened because of the pressure CD has exerted on reformative political mechanisms and legislatures: Arendt (n 77) 80–82; Moreover, the government is forced by confronting such incidents to also witness the social disaffection for its practices, realise its shortcomings, and try to minimise points of friction with citizens. Power (n 23) 47.
81. Mark E. DeForrest, 'Civil Disobedience: Its Nature and Role in the American Legal Landscape' (1998) 33 Gonzaga Law Review 653, 657–658.
82. Ibid.
83. U.S.C., Title 18, Part I, Chapter I, Section 16.
84. (c.8).
85. Greenawalt (n 54) 245.
86. Himma (n 67) 2–3; Calabrese seems to agree, characterising as forms of violence only extreme hacking acts that irreparably destroy server files. Andrew Calabrese, 'Virtual Nonviolence? Civil Disobedience and Political Violence in the Information Age' (2004) 6 info www.emeraldinsight.com/1463-6697.htm, 332.
87. Michael McGuire, *Hypercrime: The New Geometry of Harm* (Routledge Cavendish, Oxford 2007) 80.

88. Majid Yar, *Cybercrime and Society* (Sage Publications, London 2006) 10–11.
89. Tim Owen, 'Cyber-Violence: Towards a Predictive Model, Drawing upon Genetics, Psychology and Neuroscience' (1 September 2016) 9 International Journal of Criminology and Sociological Theory 1, 1–11.
90. See *America Online, Inc. v IMS et al.* 24 F.Supp. 2d 548 (E.D.Va. 1998); As it was argued, 'AOL's loss of good-will when customers complained about the slow and balky operation of their service was an element of actionable damages, above and beyond physical damage to the system itself.' Richard A. Epstein, 'Cybertrespass' (2003) 70 The University of Chicago Law Review, Centennial Tribute Essays 73, 81.
91. De Villiers (n 70) 41.
92. (1991) 93 Cr App R 25.
93. For discussion, see Andrew Murray, *Information Technology Law: The Law and Society* (1 edn Oxford University Press, USA, Oxford; New York 2010) 340–341.
94. Power (n 23).
95. See (n 79).
96. Mathias Klang, 'Civil Disobedience Online' (2004) 2 Info, Communications and Ethics in Society 75, 76–77; John Morreal, 'The Justifiability of Violent Civil Disobedience' in Hugo Bedau (ed), *Civil Disobedience in Focus* (Routledge, London 1976) 130–143, 135–138.
97. Morreal (n 96); Vinit Haksar, 'Civil Disobedience and Non-Cooperation' in Hugo Bedau (ed), *Civil Disobedience in Focus* (Routledge, London 2002) 144–158, 146–147.
98. Morreal (n 96); Haksar (n 97) 146–147.
99. Morreal (n 96). For the need of some degree of coercion in CD, see Kimberley Brownlee, 'The Communicative Aspects of Civil Disobedience and Lawful Punishment' (2006) 1 Criminal Law and Philosophy Journal 179, 181.
100. Morreal (n 96).
101. McGuire (n 87) 124.
102. Ibid.
103. Bedau, 'Civil Disobedience in Focus: Introduction' (n 24) 8; Schlesinger (n 64) 956; Raz (n 72) 267.
104. Quint (n 16) 125.
105. Greenawalt, 'A Contextual Approach to Disobedience' (n 76) 61–64; Jonathan Simon, *Governing through Crime* (Oxford University Press, Oxford 2007) 154.

106. Luke Allnutt, 'Old-School Hacker Oxblood Ruffin Discusses Anonymous and the Future of *Hacktivism*' (*Tangled Web,* 8 June 2011) http://www.rferl.org/content/hacker_oxblood_ruffin_discusses_anonymous_and_the_future_of_hacktivism/24228166.html; Tim Jordan and Paul A. Taylor, *Hacktivism and Cyberwars: Rebels with a Cause?* (Routledge, London 2004) 90–91.
107. Bruce Johnson and Ho Youm, 'Commercial Speech and Free Expression: The United States and Europe Compared' (2008) 2 Journal of International Media & Entertainment Law 159; see also *Citizens United v Federal Election Commission*, 558 U.S 310 (2010).
108. Klang (n 96) 82–83.
109. Lijun Tang and Peidong Yang, 'Symbolic Power and the Internet: The Power of a Horse' (2011) 33 Media Culture Society 675, 676.
110. D Zeidy, 'Facebook Just REVERSED Ban Against Anonymous Group That Has Been Targeting ISIS' (*MintPress News*, 18 March 2015) http://www.mintpressnews.com/facebook-just-reversed-ban-against-anonymous-group-that-has-been-targeting-isis/203449/.
111. Stephanie Winston, '"Don't Be Evil": Uncovering the Implications of Google Search' (2011) 7 Dalhousie Journal of Interdisciplinary Management 1; Nunziato (n 10).
112. Manuel Castells, *Communication Power* (Oxford University Press, Oxford 2009) 298; Scott Burris, Michael Kempa, and Clifford Shearing, 'Changes in Governance: A Cross-Disciplinary Review of Current Scholarship' (2008) 41 Akron Law Review 1, 28.
113. Samuel (n 68) 210–212.
114. Carl Cohen, 'Civil Disobedience and the Law' (1966) 21 Rutgers Law Review 1, 4–5; Hugo A. Bedau, 'Civil Disobedience and Personal Responsibility for Injustice' (1970) 54 The Monist 517.
115. Jordan and Taylor (n 106) 79–80; 2600 Magazine, 'Press Release – 2600 Magazine Condemns Denial of Service Attacks' (*2600 Magazine,* 10 December 2010) https://dear2600.wordpress.com/2010/12/10/press-release-2600-magazine-condemns-denial-of-service-attacks/.
116. An example of this is the protest against Lufthansa, where the company had been notified in advance and had taken precautionary measures in order to absorb the increased traffic with less disruption. See (n 16).
117. Pamela E. Oliver, 'Bringing the Crowd Back In: The Non-organizational Elements of Social Movements' (1989) 11 Research in Social Movements, Conflict and Change 4, 7–8; Jordan and Taylor (n 106) 152–153; Bruce

Simon, 'Illegal Knowledge: Strategies for New Media Activism: Dialogue with Ricardo Dominguez and Geert Lovink' in Bousquet Marc and Wills Katharine (eds), *The Politics of Information: The Electronic Mediation of Social Change* (Altx Press 2003) 55–65, 58–59; see, for example, use of hacktivism in struggles against the Iranian regime and the global support these protests generated. Jon Leyden, 'Iranian Hacktivists Hand-Crank DDoS Attack' (*The Register,* 22 June 2009) http://www.theregister.co.uk/2009/06/22/iranian_hactivism/.

118. Ricardo Dominguez, 'Electronic Civil Disobedience' (*thing.net,* undated) http://www.thing.net/~rdom/ecd/ecd.html.
119. Dorothy E. Denning, 'Activism, Hacktivism, and Cyberterrorism: The Internet as a Tool for Influencing Foreign Policy' in Jon Arquila and David Ronfeldt (eds), *Networks and Netwars: The Future of Terror, Crime, and Militancy* (RAND Corporation, 2001) 266–267.
120. Rawls, *The Theory of Justice* (n 21) 327–328; Merton Tice, 'Civil Disobedience: A Study of Law and Its Relation to Society' (1968) 13 South Dakota Law Review 356, 361; Lasse Thomassen, 'Within the Limits of Deliberative Reason Alone: Habermas, Civil Disobedience and Constitutional Democracy' (2007) 6 European Journal of Political Theory 200, 203.
121. Greenawalt, 'A Contextual Approach to Disobedience' (n 76) 61.
122. Himma (n 58) 4–5; US courts have supported that there can be a presumption that petition and elections could always bring change legally, rendering the potential exhaustion of legal means impossible. See John A. Cohan, 'Civil Disobedience and the Necessity Defense' (2007) 6 Pierce Law Review 111, 141–142.
123. Castells documents the power imbalances in modern information society democracies. Castells, *Communication Power* (n 112); Black also discusses the deficiencies of state regulatory processes and agencies, suggesting the need for regulation to move beyond the core democratic state: Julia Black, 'Critical Reflections on Regulation' (2002) 27 Australian Journal of Legal Philosophy 1; Schwarz (n 77) 558–559.
124. Raz (n 72) 269; A strike of ambulance drivers would most probably generate more social distress than a virtual sit-in on the website of the Ministry of Health.
125. Kellner (n 64) 904.
126. Ibid. 903–904; Arendt (n 77) An example is when strongly supported petitions are ignored without due consideration.

127. Cohan (n 122) 141–143. For example, in *US v Schoon,* 22 Ill.971 F.2d 193 (9th Cir. 1991) (*Schoon*), the Court argues that even the possibility for Congress to change its mind on an issue was sufficient to satisfy a reasonable assessment on the existence of legal alternatives.
128. Examples are the European Commission or the United Nations Security Council.
129. World Trade Organization in Africa, International Monetary Fund in Greece, Argentina, Romania.
130. Greenawalt (n 54) 229; Rawls, *The Theory of Justice* (n 21) 327–328.
131. See Yochai Benkler, 'Free Irresponsible, Press: Wikileaks and the Battle over the Soul of the Networked Fourth Estate' 46 Harvard Civil Rights-Civil Liberties Law Review, 311, 331–332.
132. WikiLeaks argued that after the donations froze, they witnessed a revenue drop of 95%: Alex Fitzpatrick, 'Wikileaks Wins Battle against Visa, Mastercard' (*Mashable,* 12 July 2012) http://mashable.com/2012/07/12/wikileaks-wins-battle-against-visa-mastercard/.
133. Charles Arthur 'Inside "Anonymous": Tales from within the Group Taking Aim at Amazon and Mastercard' (*The Guardian Technology Blog,* 13 December 2010) http://www.guardian.co.uk/technology/blog/2010/dec/13/hacking-wikileaks.
134. Fitzpatrick (n 132), The legal battle between Wikileaks and Visa for restoring their service to Wikileaks was decided more than a year after the processing of donations was suspended.
135. Cohan (n 122) 142–143; Eric Engle, 'The Rights' Orchestra: Proportionality, Balancing, and Viking' (2011) New England Journal of International Law and Comparative Law http://papers.ssrn.com/sol3/papers.cfm?abstract_id=1704503; although the US approach is called means–ends rational review, the elements examined are similar.
136. Herbert J. Storing, 'The Case against Civil Disobedience' in Hugo A. Bedau (ed), *Civil Disobedience in Focus* (Routledge, London 2002) 86; Stephen R. Alton, 'In the Wake of Thoreau: Four Modern Legal Philosophers and the Theory of Non-Violent Civil Disobedience' (1993) 24 Loyola University Law Journal 39, 63–64.
137. Greenawalt, *Conflicts of Law and Morality* (n 54) 238–240.
138. Arendt (n 77) 54–55.
139. Haksar, 'The Right to Civil Disobedience' (n 71) 421–422.
140. Coleman (n 69) 140.
141. Ibid. 140.
142. Woozley (n 79) 330.

143. Greenawalt, 'A Contextual Approach to Disobedience' (n 76) 69–71.
144. Colby (n 80) 1173–1174. However, in direct disobedience, one might object to punishment, since he considers the law disobeyed should not exist in the first place.
145. Ibid.
146. Joseph M. Kizza, *Ethical and Social Issues in the Information Age* (Springer-Verlag, New York 2010) 83; Katja F. Aas, *Globalization & Crime* (Sage Publications, London 2007) 156; Lawrence Lessig, *Code v.2.0* (Basic Books, New York 2006) 18–20, 190–192; 'disassociation and lack of physical proximity encourages people to participate in illegal activities in the Internet, such as hacking, denial of service[...]. They do not feel that in reality they are doing any serious harm'; Gregor Allan, 'Responding to Cybercrime: A Delicate Blend of the Orthodox and the Alternative' (2005) 149 New Zealand Law Review 175–176.
147. These can range from total anonymity to open declaration of identification: Samuel (n 68) 214–215.
148. Ibid. See the transparency policies of EDT and pseudonymity of Electrohippies in Jill Lane and Ricardo Dominguez, 'Digital Zapatistas' (2003) 47 TDR 129; DJNZ and The Action Tool Development Group of the Electrohippies Collective, 'Client-Side Distributed Denial-of-Service: Valid Campaign Tactic or Terrorist Act?' (2001) 34 Leonardo 269, 274; Even Anonymous, who generally advocates anonymising techniques, often employs software that allows IP-tracing and cannot be used through anonymising websites, eventually resulting in detection and prosecution of protesters. Stephen Mansfield-Devine, 'Anonymous: Serious Threat or Mere Annoyance?' (2011) 1 Network Security 4, 6; Evgeny Morozov and Will Oremus, "In Defense of DDoS" (*Slate*, 13 December 2010) http://www.slate.com/articles/technology/technology/2010/12/in_defense_of_ddos.html. 'Unlike fingerprints, IP logs cannot specifically designate the person that was using that IP address. Law-enforcement will have to use real-world evidence to eventually find the last user of the terminal of interest.' Allan (n 145) 151–152.
149. Klang (n 96) 81.
150. Coleman (n 69) 390–391.
151. Lessig (n 145) 203; Constance Zhang, 'Regulation of the Internet-New Laws and New Paradigms' (2006) 17 Journal of Law, Information & Science 53, 67–68. Morozov has also emphasised how social media and

the Internet in general can also facilitate the tracking down and deterrence protests and how new technologies of surveillance have struck a serious blow to the early-year presumptions that the Internet was a place of deliberate, impenetrable anonymity: Evgeny Morozov, *The Net Delusion: The Dark Side of Internet Freedom* (Public Affairs, New York 2011). See the counterargument in Trevor Thompson, 'Terrorizing the Technological Neighborhood Watch: The Alienation and Deterrence of the White Hats under the CFAA' (2008) 36 Florida State University Law Review 537, 547–548.

152. Lessig (n 145) 45–46.

4

Contemporary Norms and Law and Hacktivism

1 Introduction

The previous chapters reviewed the nature of hacktivism and its role as a modern manifestation of counter-power in cyberspace and established that hacktivism is an alternative online political practice that entails positive elements for democratic polity, but also involves risks and is prone to corruption. Hacktivism has been linked to civil disobedience (CD), which has also been a controversial practice throughout history in relation to how it should be considered and dealt with. DeForrest, for example, is of the view that CD should be attributed a 'legitimate yet informal place' in the polity.[1] Habermas submits that the democratic state should first acknowledge the conflict between political legitimacy and illegality inherent in CD and prosecute, if necessary, but must simultaneously recognise, the civil disobedient as a guardian of its own legitimacy.[2] Raz also argues that the courts should take weighty moral reasons for law-breaking under consideration, even if these justifications are not formally included in the law, in the form of justification defences.[3] Similarly, Hampson argues that 'forms of hacktivism that are primarily expressive, that do not involve obtaining or exploiting illegal access to computers or networks for commercial advantage or financial gain, and that cause little or no

V. Karagiannopoulos, *Living With Hacktivism*, Palgrave Studies in Cybercrime and Cybersecurity, https://doi.org/10.1007/978-3-319-71758-6_4

permanent damage, should receive at least some protection as a legitimate form of protest.'[4]

However, discussions and practices surrounding how hacktivism is perceived and dealt with are far less straightforward, and despite the links between hacktivism and CD, calls for leniency and tolerance could not be considered self-evident, since they are not commonly accepted. Theorists, for example, have supported full criminal punishment for CD and hacktivists, analogising these activities to plain criminality, if not terrorism.[5] In fact, as we will see here, the reality today regarding hacktivist actions actually seems to be far closer to the views of the critics, rather than those acknowledging the value of CD for modern democracies, which has significant consequences, not only for hacktivists themselves, but also for the nature and exercise of political contestation online, as well as for overall cybersecurity.

The purpose of this chapter will thus be to discuss the dominant norms relating to cybercrime and cybersecurity and their relation to hacktivism and how it is dealt with. Subsequently, we will assess applicable legislation and its impact on hacktivist practices.

2 The Normative Framework and Its Impact on Hacktivism

2.1 Focusing on 'Command and Control'

At the beginning of this book, we discussed how the Internet developed and elaborated on the various power structures and conflicts that take place online and shape how regulation is shaped by multiple nodes in an ever-expanding network of networks. A shift towards more decentralised models of regulation inevitably reflects the networked, decentralised nature of cyberspace, which inevitably challenges the already contested state-based forms of regulation.[6] However, irrespective of expectations of decentralisation, there seems to be a persistent trend to deal with cybercrime and consequently also hacktivist incidents through a more traditional, criminal law-based 'command and control' approach.

This approach relates to the use of state legal rules backed by criminal sanctions.[7] Currently, this translates into the state promulgating orders and imposing penalties and trying to increase its grasp on information production and regulation of technology and those developing and manipulating it.

Despite the challenges for a state-based type of regulatory approach,[8] especially for cyberspace, as Palfrey argues, after the initial deregulation period in the 1990s, governments have gradually taken more regulatory initiatives and are not only regulating state-to-individual interactions, but are also trying to control private entities and induce or coerce them to do the government's biding.[9] As will become obvious from the following analysis, at least some of the suggested deficiencies of a top-down, law-focused approach are evident in the cybercrime law regime and are often even exacerbated when dealing with hacktivism in particular. This is due to the legal and moral ambiguities inherent in the practice of hacktivism, which aims to challenge the limits of law and contest the applicability of cybercrime legislation to cross-jurisdictional activities. Let us then proceed to discuss these issues in more detail, beginning from the normative framework behind the current regime.

2.2 Fear of Risk and Security Discourses

The regulation of behaviours and the shaping of laws are influenced by the pervasive sociopolitical norms and symbolisms, and thus, the treatment of hacktivism will initially be related to the directions posed by dominant norms and regulatory policies. Cyberspace and hacktivist practice per se have developed at a time when welfarism has been abandoned and governance philosophies focus instead on managing risks and increasing order.[10] Fear of crime has become a main driving force for establishing policies that attempt to reduce risk-related activities, legitimising the gradual shift of democratic regimes towards public safety and national security.[11] As Sunstein argues, regulation is currently dominated by the 'precautionary principle,' which dictates that regulators should try to protect society from hypothetical harms, even if the causal links between these harms and public safety are unclear and their realisation only probable.[12] Policies of zero tolerance towards risk have also overwhelmed and substituted fiscal efficiency tactics that entailed increased rationalisation processes.[13] This lack of rationalisation processes facilitates more emotive and, consequently, less well-considered and more reactionary approaches.

Zedner summarises the elements of the general theory of security in criminal justice: first, there is a temporal shift towards pre-emption and reduction of criminal opportunity; second, risk is the framework for security, with security policies mainly designed to locate and manage diverse risks; third, the focus of crime does not centre on wrongdoing, but aims to pre-empt and minimise loss.[14] Security becomes a commodity in the balance between the cost of measures that promote it and the potential losses from risk-related activities, and consequently, the provision of security becomes a profit-making process.[15] This prominence of security as a measure for political and financial success is reflected on all levels, from politicians' declarations and legislative initiatives to business sector policies and the judiciary's punitive trends.

The policymaking focus on security is further reinforced by the multiple terrorist attacks and relative rhetoric that have naturally proliferated, especially after 9/11, and even more so after the recent terrorist attacks in Europe, from Belgium to France and the UK. The persistence and unpredictable nature of terrorist attacks and their high death toll have forced governments to increase their levels of security emergency and have further fuelled public fears. Inevitably, the panic of terrorist trauma facilitates the rushed, non-deliberated imposition of harsher, more punitive emergency policies and laws.[16] Terrorist fears also strengthen the role of the state as a dominant actor that is capable and burdened with managing risk control.[17] The 2015 UK Conservative Party manifesto, for example, contained promises of dealing with non-violent extremism as well as violent extremism, essentially expressing a desire to create provisions that would impose banning orders on groups that are deemed dangerous, yet do not fall within the proscription criteria.

Moreover, since information is fast becoming a core resource of society, the protection of informational and network integrity is often analogised to protecting public safety or national security.[18] Indicative of this is the declaration of cyberattacks as a Tier 1 threat for the UK, alongside terrorism in the 2010 National Security Strategy. All these shift the state towards a more controlling and punitive approach in order to demonstrate its capacity to deal with controversial political groups that are labelled as security threats.[19] Simon emphasises the danger for dissidents, arguing that the major terrorist attacks, such as that of 9/11, have often been perceived by the authorities as a licence to persecute future non-violent demonstrations and to prosecute ideologically radical groups, irrespective of terrorist motivations or actions.[20] As one can imagine, hacktivists, as dissident groups that combine political controversy along with information and network compromises, could very well be at the centre of attention.

The Internet is unavoidably influenced by such normative tendencies and also fuels them.[21] It feeds fears of crime and concerns for risk due to its unpredictable technological nature, which entails an inherent risk for technology to malfunction or be misused[22] and can often challenge the average citizen's capacity to understand the various phenomena of cyberdeviancy within it. This tendency is also further reinforced by the medium's inherent potential for anonymity that generates uncertainty and can hinder crime prevention. The difficulty to understand, measure, and predict the potential risk also magnifies the salience of cybercrime, eventually inducing the public to support more preventive and punitive measures that presumably maximise security.[23] Research regarding the rhetoric of US presidents in relation to cybercrime reinforces this, as it has found that presidents often use symbolic rhetoric that corresponds and is meant to address the public's technopanic and fear, whilst cybercrime is often included in presidential talks that relate to even more serious issues, such as national security or terrorism.[24] With cybersecurity becoming a global agenda issue, hacktivism has also come to the fore, especially after the explosion of activity documented in recent years.[25]

Moreover, cyberterrorist/national security considerations are intensified by the mass use of the medium by terrorist and extremist groups, combined with the migration of infrastructural services to cyberspace, which makes the connection between terrorist attacks and accessibility to critical resources more plausible.[26] The controversial political nature and the cyberspatial interventions of hacktivism are inevitably linked to those fears and regulatory trends.[27] As Meikle also argues, even though acts like virtual sit-ins are exercises of symbolic power, they are portrayed as primarily coercive, which delegitimises such practices.[28] Samuel also agreed that the events of 9/11 placed information security and cyberterrorism at centre stage and generally reduced tolerance towards politicised cybersecurity threats.[29] Hacktivists have also documented an increasing tendency of governments and e-commerce lobbyists to portray electronic civil disobedience (ECD) as terrorist activity.[30] For example, the National Security Agency director, along with other federal officials, has expressed his concern that Anonymous could soon have the ability to bring about a limited power outage through cyberattacks.[31]

2.3 The Deviant 'Other' and Hacktivists

Normative systems that are based on the existence of risks and the need to eliminate them naturally require a risk-provoking agent to be the deviant 'Other,' against which the community will have to rally.[32] Garland characterises this process as the criminology of 'essentialised difference,' which trades in archetypes and symbolisms, rather than careful research and analysis of findings.[33] Perceptions of criminality in the current era, where fear of crime has become a dominant policymaking rationale,[34] increasingly detach deviance from social causes and attribute it to the personal characteristics of a dangerous 'Other' that incorporates the dominant social fears.[35] Even though security is considered to be a general public good that all citizens should enjoy, the balancing of security against human rights often exaggerates the interests of the majority, which results in generally adversely infringing the rights of weaker and marginalised minorities.[36] Even when tolerance is advocated for some minority opinions, this is a politically charged tolerance that presumes the approval of the minority's demands from the ruling majority, thus preventing any excessive challenges to the establishment.[37]

The cybercriminal archetype is the masterful and evasive hacker.[38] It presumes a highly skilled, malevolent 'super-user,' functioning as the target and justification for the broadening of the scope and intensification of strictness of cybercrime legislation.[39] Risk and counterterrorist discourses have gradually also politicised this initial archetype, instituting the cyberterrorist and, to an extent, the hacktivist, due to its presumed association with political disruption, as a contemporary super-threat.[40] The unpredictable hacker collective dominates cybercriminal discussions, with authorities even from the early years relabelling hackers and online activists as 'information terrorists,' thus inevitably also increasing popular condemnation for hacktivists, while legitimising stricter online controls and crackdowns against them.[41]

The negative labelling of ECD is also intensified by the nature of hacktivist groups. Due to the pseudonymous or anonymous character of these collectives and their lack of any specific political constituency and much offline contact with the wider public, most citizens are largely ignorant of the ideology, motives, goals, and tactics of these groups.[42] This opaqueness facilitates the corruption of the hacktivist image and promotes homogenised perceptions of cybercriminality that blur any moral and tactical distinction between profit-seeking cybercriminals and hacktivists.[43]

2.4 The Influence of the Media, Experts, and Security Firms

The structuring of online norms largely relies on power networks that manage information production and distribution. Consequently, mainstream media, despite the alternative channels of communication online, still dominate norm-setting. Mainstream media often tend to generate, repeat, and magnify the normative messages of risk and fear in order to satisfy viewers, corporate sponsors, and their stockholders by attracting audience attention through sensationalist accounts that hopefully guarantee their viability.[44] As Klein highlights, there is rich literature regarding how the media tend to portray anti-government protests in a less serious and more trivialised manner, and focus more on the spectacle rather than the message.[45] Research has also shown that the media have an 'agenda-setting' and 'priming' effect on the public in relation to crime, thus intensifying fear and support for punitive policies.[46] Spectacular media representations also tend to overstate the role and power of technology in order to satisfy the socially pervasive technophobia.[47] Inevitably, this can also impact negatively on the public's view of hacktivist practices, especially since research has shown that it is very common that hacktivist actions by Anonymous, for example, are mostly portrayed by the media in a negative light, with a focus on the victims rather than the protesters' motivations.[48]

Moreover, incidents of criminality are intensely magnified by the hyper-connectivity and the ease of transferability and reproduction of news of crime through digital media (videos, photos), and thus eventually aggravate the tendency to exaggerate risk possibilities.[49] The Internet provides access to diverse sources of information through blogs, social networking sites, or alternative news sites that filter and tone down sensationalised and dramatised reporting and public discussion.[50] However, the majority of citizens would usually visit the traditional major media, which generally reproduce the TV-based news that the same corporate group broadcasts.[51] Although cross-posting of information in social media has allowed for the proliferation of more views, simultaneously, the capacity the Internet offers for personalised filtering and customisation of user experience partly neutralises this effect, with people focusing and interacting more with sources that align with their views.[52] Because the public demands quick and efficient public policies to deal with the social problems at hand, the proliferation of crime reporting online intensifies the public sense of abstract danger, infusing web forums with 'moral panics'[53] and discursive 'cascades' that support stricter security measures.[54] Hacktivism, which has recently become a prominent cybercrime concern, will inevitably also feature in these popular discussions, which would render its negative perspectives more salient.

Information about risk is also presumed to be structured on expert assessments that influence public perceptions.[55] Beck has argued that our social focus on risk is not because of an intensification of risk, but because our perception of risk has changed through the bombardment of the public with scientific material that magnifies risk.[56] The privatisation of security alongside the intense commercialisation of the Internet has generated an increasing interest for private corporations to support and promote security-focused discourses and regulations.[57] This focus on security serves to protect the companies' goods and investments more intensely and also enables security companies and experts to promote their own products and services.[58] Moreover, corporate lobbying facilitates the generation and circulation of many security assessments and expert claims that often emphasise and exaggerate the potential criminal risks in cyberspace,[59] thus reinforcing their own position and necessity.

However, there have been doubts whether expert and security company assessments reflect the true extent of the risks.[60] This is because the decentralised and obscure environment in which cybercrime thrives undermines the reliable collection of data, since victimisation reports do not flow through a single official portal and, in fact, official sources for assessing cybercrime risks are very few.[61] It was not until last year, for example, that cybercrime started featuring in the National Crime Survey for England and Wales. This serves to show our slow progress in mapping the full scope of an ever-expanding phenomenon such as cybercrime.

Researchers have also challenged the methodological structures behind cybersecurity research and have highlighted potential conflicts of interest.[62] Leyden, for example, has deconstructed spyware infection reports by a cybersecurity firm, demonstrating how the survey was methodologically structured in a way that greatly increased the reported number of computer compromises.[63] Consequently, the difficulty to validate expert claims that shape public opinion and governmental policies often leads to excessive reliance on traditionally inflated statistics about cybercrime.[64] Within such a climate, multiple security compromises that are put under the broad label of hacktivism can end up portraying these activities as part of dystopian cybersecurity predictions by security firms and experts.[65]

Moreover, the labelling that ensues from these cybersecurity reports marginalises the targeted citizens and could even induce a part of them to play into the deviant role prescribed for them.[66] The labelling of hacktivists feeds a vicious circle, where concerns for hacktivist dangerousness are sometimes further reinforced by the protesters' tactical choices and their radical and retaliatory rhetoric. Anonymous, for example, demonstrates inconsistent, diverse behaviours, with moral, but also often war-declaring, rhetoric and tactical choices,[67] which can result in portraying hacktivists as potentially dangerous or immature.[68] Due to the lack of hierarchy and the anonymity that characterises Anonymous, users acting under the banner of Anonymous can produce videos and suggest protest targets that would be inconsistent with other parts of the collective. Various radical declarations, such as an intention to shut down the Internet, have been attributed to Anonymous, for example, only to see members of the collective dispute such claims through the online channels of communications later on.[69]

In sum, we can see that the general norms that dominate cybercrime-related policymaking and public discourse more generally are predominantly oriented towards increasing the fear of crime and risk and support harsher controls in the name of security. Overall, the often exaggerated information that proliferates in relation to the risks and dangers of cybercrime and hacktivism specifically is bound to have an impact on how cybercrime policy is shaped and enforced, since public views influence policies and vice versa.[70] The marginalisation of hacktivism and its labelling as a social threat would also flow from the prioritisation of security-enhancing policies at the expense of civil liberties and human rights of users. Furthermore, the prioritisation of security and the populist tendencies in law-making, trying to satisfy media-enhanced moral panics, would often mean that the positive aspects of hacktivist actions, such as their focus on protecting human rights, would be given much less attention than the potential risks hacktivists protests pose for online security. The impact of all these will become even more obvious with the following description of the issues arising from cybercrime legislation.

3 Cybercrime Laws and Their Application on Hacktivism

3.1 The Making of Cybercrime Laws

Considering the norms and policymaking trends just discussed, one can see how cybercrime legislation would be a reflection of these norms and prominent regulatory tools in the processes of security norm-setting, risk minimisation, and information/network control. Indeed, cybercrime legislation has been a peculiar area of law that was first created as a response to public fears generated by a hacker-related movie, War Games, even before the advent of the Internet.[71] Cybercrime laws have been expanding and becoming more inclusive ever since, based on the consistent political support for intensification of controls of activity online and also on a general indifference of policymakers to the practical effects of such a growing intensification of restrictions and penalties.[72]

On a less critical note, Decker argues that, consistent with the policy-making focus on risk minimisation and prioritisation of security, the main reason for promulgating cybercrime laws has been the prevention of the increasing damages and losses that cybercrime causes.[73] Moreover, the increasing dependence of critical infrastructures, such as the electricity power grid or even banking systems, on networked computing, in conjunction with the rising concerns for cyberterrorism, has further intensified the concerns for building a robust and all-encompassing cybercriminal law structure.

How then does a cybercrime regime generated under the aforementioned conditions function when having to deal with hacktivist incidents and be employed as the main tool for resolving such cases? The following section will discuss some main legislative examples in the US[74] and the UK that are applicable and have been applied to hacktivist incidents and will also analyse whether and to what extent the changes in law, but also the systemic problems of the cybercrime regime, can have an increasingly adverse impact when used as a tool to regulate hacktivism.

3.2 The Applicable Unauthorised Access Offences

The US cybercrime regime has become increasingly stricter over the years, with higher penalties, lower standards for felonious liability, broader criminalisation of recklessness and negligence, and mainly an increased focus on damage and loss, and more broad-reaching provisions. On a federal level, the main applicable act for hacktivist actions that has also been employed in prosecutions of hacktivists is the Computer Fraud and Abuse Act of 1986 (CFAA).[75] Since 1984, when it was fist passed, it has been amended many times, often in response to the ever-growing challenges and the sociopolitical influences that have gradually led to a more inclusive and harsher approach to cybercrime.[76]

There are various provisions in the updated CFAA that are applicable to hacktivist actions, such as Sections 1030(a)(2)(B) and (C) criminalising whoever intentionally accesses a computer and obtains information from any department or agency of the US or accesses a 'protected computer' without authorisation or exceeds authorised access, and thereby obtains information.[77] These sections would apply to hacktivists causing web page modifications (defacements and redirects) that inevitably require unauthorised access to gain control of the underlying code of the web page layout (root access) in order to modify it or modify the Universal Resource Locator (URL) of a certain page, so as to link to another website instead.[78] Data acquisition from 'protected computers' or governmental computers are also prosecutable under these provisions, but even obtaining the passwords and any other information related to the unauthorised access would probably fit within the scope of the provision.

Obtaining information from a protected computer after unauthorised access was secured, which could be interpreted as just viewing the information,[79] is a misdemeanour, punishable by up to one year imprisonment and/or a fine.[80] If the accessed information is further used for personal gain or other criminal purposes or the information has a value of at least $5000, this act could be considered a felony, punishable by up to five years imprisonment and/or a fine.[81] For recidivists, the penalty could go up to ten years in prison in addition to a fine.[82]

Similar to Section 1030(a)(2), Section 1030(a)(3) is also applicable to defacements/redirects, data acquisition, and political viruses, but differs on the nature of the targeted computer network. It criminalises the intentional, unauthorised access (even without obtaining any information) to 'any **non-public** computer of a department or agency of the United States or the accessing of such a computer of that department or agency that is exclusively for the use of the Government of the United States or, in the case of a computer not exclusively for such use, is used by or for the Government of the United States and such conduct affects that use by or for the Government of the United States' (emphasis added). This offence is usually punishable by fine and/or a maximum penalty of one year imprisonment, unless the perpetrator of the crime has a purpose of commercial advantage or private financial gain or to further any criminal or tortious act in violation of the Constitution or laws of the US or of any state or the value of the information obtained exceeds $5,000, in which case the penalty is five years.[83] Considering how this unauthorised access could also violate state laws relating to unauthorised access, it is easy to understand how the range could easily be increased for plain unauthorised access. Kerr has highlighted the consequences of such double counting in his analysis of the Andrew (Weev) Auernheimer case.[84]

Similar offences in the UK can be found in Sections 1 and 2 of the Computer Misuse Act 1990 (CMA).[85] Section 1 criminalises unauthorised access, which only demands that the computer is manipulated intentionally to perform any action in order to secure unauthorised access. The offence is now punishable by up to two years imprisonment on indictment, making it extraditable and also enabling prosecution for aiding, abetting, counselling, and procuring the principal offence.[86] Additionally, Section 2 of the CMA criminalises unauthorised access if it is realised with the intent to commit or facilitate the commission of a further serious offence.[87] Section 2 is a more serious offence, covering unauthorised access with a further intent to cause harm, such as stealing information to commit fraud.[88] The maximum penalty on indictment is five years imprisonment and a fine.[89] It is questionable, however, whether such an offence would ever be employed against hacktivist actions, especially since more focus is given to Section 3, which we will discuss in more detail in the following section. Furthermore, the purpose of this offence is to punish unauthorised access more seriously when this is done with an ulterior criminal motive and not just as the plain unauthorised access. For hacktivists, the only motive would be to cause computer impairment and modification as a form of expressing dissent and therefore computer damage/impairment offences would be more relevant.

3.3 The Dominating Provision of Computer Damage/Impairment

Despite the applicability and expansive reach of unauthorised access provisions to specific hacktivist tactics, the most appropriate and all-inclusive section of the CFAA for prosecuting hacktivists is Section 1030(a)(5)(A), which deals with knowingly causing a transmission of a program, information, code, or command, which results in intentionally causing damage without authorisation to a 'protected computer.' Moreover, two additional offences are included which deal with intentional unauthorised access to a protected computer that results in reckless damage (Section 1030(a)(5)(B)) or damage and loss (Section 1030(a)(5)(C)).

Damage is limited to economic damage and this is defined in Section 1030(e)(8) as 'any impairment to the integrity or availability of data, a program, a system, or information.' The concept of loss is far more abstract and is defined as 'any reasonable cost to any victim, including the cost of responding to an offense, conducting a damage assessment, and restoring the data, program, system, or information to its condition prior to the offense, and any revenue lost, cost incurred, or other consequential damages incurred because of interruption of service.'[90] Most hacktivist tactics which manipulate, impair, suppress access and availability of information, or compromise the integrity of websites and even servers would generally fall within the scope of the aforementioned provisions.[91]

The CFAA felony triggers were amended to include low damage/loss requirements that can be satisfied even by minor criminal acts, such as the expressive hacks (defacements, redirects, virtual sit-ins) often perpetrated by hacktivists. The relevant harms that trigger felonious liability—also requiring the causing of some amount of damage—are as follows:

> (I) Loss to one or more persons during any one-year period (and, for purposes of an investigation, prosecution, or other proceeding brought by the United States only; loss resulting from a related course of conduct affecting one or more other protected computers) aggregating at least $5,000 in value[92]; (V) damage affecting a computer used by or for an entity of the United States Government in furtherance of the administration of justice, national defense, or national security[93]; (VI) or damage affecting 10 or more protected computers during any 1-year period.[94]

The more directly and generally applicable are triggers (I) and (VI). Starting with trigger (I), after 2001, the need to prove intent to cause $5000 of loss was eliminated and prosecutors are only required to prove intent to cause damage.[95] Moreover, despite the already broad definition of loss,[96] the types of loss included are not deemed exclusive and assessments can include additional types of financial setbacks, which are unlisted.[97] The easily satisfied expectation that simply relates to causing only some amount of damage, in addition to the multiple elements that can be calculated as damage and loss, could result in simple web defacements or very temporarily disruptive virtual sit-ins easily exceeding the $5000 felony-triggering limit, especially for commercial websites.

The potential excesses in relation to calculations of damage and loss are evident when one assesses the various cases that relate with Anonymous. For example, PayPal conceded in relation to OpPayback/Avenge Assange in late 2010 that there was no actual damage and disruption of services was restricted,[98] yet still protesters were prosecuted for losses of up to $5.5 million.[99] Even the eBay boss (PayPal's parent company) Pierre Omidyar has highlighted the excessive damage/loss assessment process employed, arguing that damage estimates should only include staff pay and overtime for dealing with any issues and not costs of systems upgrades. Furthermore, he argues that every protester should be responsible for his individual contribution to the damage and not to the whole amount.[100] The penalties of Weev and Eric J. Rosol, which are premised on broad calculations of damage and loss, are indicative of the potential exaggerated responses that damage and loss assessments could lead to. The former was prosecuted on the basis of $73,000, which were the costs for AT&T to send out letters through the post to its clients regarding the data compromise resulting from Weev's actions even though it had already informed them via email. The latter was penalised not on the basis of the actual loss for the Koch Brothers, which amounted to less than $5000, but on the amount of $183,000, which was the cost of the consultancy hired beforehand in order to get advice on how to mitigate the protest effects. Coleman has also highlighted that in the case of PayPal harms, the company officials claimed the attack had much more severe effects and harms in courts than what they did in other fora.[101]

The other two felony triggers are more straightforward. First, virtual sit-ins and viruses could easily satisfy the 'damage to ten or more computers' requirement, especially since no specification on the amount of damage exists again. Consequently, even if one commits $1 of damage on every computer out of ten, that action would be a felony. Moreover, ECD protests against computers that are used in the furtherance of administration of justice or national security could also be a very realistic possibility for triggering felonious liability for hacktivist actions, since this broad term could definitely include websites that protesters target, such as those of the Departments of Justice or other military or police websites.[102] Fafinski et al. have also commented on the focus on harm and loss and the broadness and abstract nature of those terms. In their own words:

> Loss is a particularly common component of cybercrime harm: how should such fiscal harm be assessed and recorded in cash terms? The discussion ultimately appeared to result in a simple agreement: it would be incredibly difficult to achieve, coding it correctly would be near impossible and the figures would likely be meaningless. Although quantifying harm in economic terms is useful in attracting policymaking attention, correctly coding and assessing particular losses would either require an extensive framework or substantial effort when acquiring data.[103]

Finally, the CFAA contains a civil suit provision that can also be brought against those criminally charged for restitution, making the ultimate impact from a successful prosecution even higher.[104] For the CFAA, current penalties can reach up to 10 years imprisonment for first-time offenders, whereas penalties could rise up to 20 years in addition to fines.[105] Since many ECD protesters could be involved in more than one protest as part of a general political campaign or organisation, the high recidivist penalties could eventually become applicable if convicted hacktivists participate in future protests. Moreover, consecutive prosecutions become even more probable when one considers that, under normal circumstances, hacktivists protesting openly could be identified and prosecuted more easily than anonymous, skilled cybercriminals, although the latter are the primary purpose cybercrime legislation was designed to be so broad and punitive.[106] The strict calculating philosophy that permeates cybercrime legislation thus renders the traditional route of applying the cybercrime legal regime to acts that are not meant to cause damage and loss as their primary goal problematic, since hacktivists would easily be charged with felonies and the ensuing high penalties from those charges.

A relatively similar inclusive and increasingly punitive rationale is followed in the UK. The analogous UK provision is Section 3 of the CMA, providing that whoever knowingly performs any unauthorised act in relation to a computer with the intention to impair the operation of any computer, prevent or hinder access to any program or data held in any computer, impair the operation of programs or reliability of data or enable such actions[107] could incur penalties of imprisonment of up to ten years and/or fine on indictment, while up to a year and/or fine on a summary conviction (6 months in Scotland).[108] Section 3(3) also broadens the scope of the offence by criminalising the recklessness of the offender regarding the realisation of these impairing/damaging effects.

The Serious Crime Act 2015 recently introduced through Section 41 a new addition to the CMA (Section 3ZA) meant to deal with more serious unauthorised acts that cause, or create a risk of, serious damage. The act is meant to explicitly criminalise acts that could have an impact on national security and critical infrastructures of a state, such as transportation, water, and electricity supply or healthcare. In relation to hacktivism, the act involves the causing of significant risk of serious damage to human welfare, which is further defined to include disruption of a system of communication. In fact, according to Section 4, it is immaterial whether the unauthorised act causes that damage directly. Mens rea also extends to recklessness in relation to whether such damage is caused.

It has to be highlighted that this is a hard section to navigate as it is extensive and quite broad-reaching. Liability could potentially range from someone intentionally attacking a healthcare network system with the purpose of wreaking havoc at a hospital and causing loss of life to cases where someone organises a virtual sit-in protest that targets a network of computers, which ends up impacting on the functionality of a wider communications system, with the perpetrator only being reckless towards this. As the government's guidance mentions, the new section is meant to deal with cases where there is significant risk for the unauthorised act to cause social disruption amongst other more serious consequences, such as loss of life or threat to national security.[109] Commentators have actually expressed concern regarding the broadness of definitions of applicable acts in the Act, but also its expanded jurisdictional reach which could be used 'in targeting other, arguably less serious cyber acts, still falling within the scope of the Act.'[110]

Although the US example is far more extreme in its focus on damage and loss, there are some aspects of the relevant UK laws that indicate a similar turn towards stricter, loss-based assessments of punishment. In the UK, the 2006 amendments to the CMA 1990 UK provisions followed the US example, doubling the penalties for computer crimes[111] and extending the scope of liability, criminalising reckless in addition to intentional impairment caused by an unauthorised act.[112] The recent Serious Crime Act 2015 and the new 3ZA offence penalties have also increased to up to 14 years for cases where cyberattacks cause, or create a significant risk of, severe economic or environmental damage or social disruption, or even life in cases where lives are lost or serious illness or injury ensues.[113]

The recent addition of recklessness further extends liability despite guidance, explicitly arguing for the criminalisation of only intentional interference.[114] As MacEwan argues, the extension of liability to reckless impairment could increase vagueness and lead to questionable prosecutions, especially since the addition of recklessness had also not been suggested by the Convention or the Framework Decision and was inserted at a stage where it did not allow for public scrutiny.[115] This extension could broaden the scope of liability and punishment significantly since it would be very difficult to assess whether protesters without much technical expertise could foresee the level of disruption of their protests. It is an important question, for example, whether they would be aware of the risk of potentially enhanced harmfulness through the addition of hackers' botnets, which could contribute thousands of compromised computers to the protest and consequently increase its impact.[116] Naturally, the changes that expand culpability, such as the criminalisation of reckless damage, even in the form of short-lived, minor disruptions, essentially enable the criminalisation and punishment of even minor offences.

Furthermore, liability in the UK can be incurred irrespective of the duration of the impairment or the extent of damage caused, even though the 2005 EU Framework Decision (Art.3)[117] suggested that minor system interferences should not be criminalised.[118] However, this has not been explicitly included in the amendments of the CMA. Moreover, both the Council of Europe Cybercrime Convention[119] (Arts 4–5) and the Framework Decision (Art.3) suggest that intentional and serious hindering or interruption of the functionality of computer systems or data should be criminalised, potentially excluding less serious compromises from criminal liability.

However, the term 'serious' does not feature in the CMA regarding the criminalising of illegal interference. The Framework Decision was also superseded by the Directive 2013/40/EC on attacks against information systems, which explicitly retained the guiding suggestion that minor cases should not be criminalised by member states. Moreover, in particular for system interference, the Directive also called for the criminalisation of cases that are serious. However, these suggestions have been neglected by the UK legislature, which just added Section 3ZA, as discussed earlier. In general, the increasingly broadening cybercrime legislation in conjunction with its highly punitive character reduce any opportunity for generating responses towards hacktivists that would reflect a balanced assessment between the potential positive and negative aspects of such activities.

Under such conditions, hacktivists would be less incentivised to organise their actions with a mindset of avoiding damage or following other moral safeguards, since the level of damage required for liability is very low and there seem to be very few mitigating circumstances that could impact on the current system of attributing liability and respective penalties. The presumed lack of tolerance and the application of punitively orientated provisions and penalties can thus often lead to more numerous and radicalised protests, as a form of backlash.[120] This is because punitive responses can be considered disproportionate and illegitimate by the protesters and also those supporting their views and causes.[121] Although research has supported that state repression can often tame protests rather than intensify them, it is crucial to remember that cyberspace creates more positive conditions for easy participation from a distance (mainly jurisdictionally) as well as more opportunities for anonymity, and therefore could impact on the deterrent efficaciousness of repression and also allow for a wider population to offer support internationally.[122] Moreover, if the punishment is felt to be unfair in relation to the protesters' actions and the legitimacy of their cause, it could also lead to bystander backlash, with the general public getting involved in further protesting against the excessively punitive response itself or in generally supporting the hacktivists' cause.[123]

3.4 The Further Criminalisation of Inchoate Offences and Jurisdictional Expansion

The chance for potential felonious liability in the US is even higher, since the scope of inchoate offences, such as attempt, incitement, and conspiracy charges and their punishment, has increased accordingly, being punishable as consummated offences.[124] Especially conspiracy was only added in 2008 with the Identity Theft Enforcement and Restitution Act 2008.[125] Similarly in the UK, all cybercrime offences (even plain unauthorised access) can now be prosecuted for aiding or procuring the principal offence, incurring penalties at the level of a consummate offence, even for just divulging information on computer weaknesses and even orally offering advice on how to participate in a virtual sit-in.[126] Weatherhead, for example, was sentenced to 18 months in prison for the PayPal attacks even though he was not considered to have actively attacked, but was responsible for the communications hub that coordinated the attacks. Furthermore, hacktivists have been charged with conspiracy to impair a computer network based on Section (1)(1) the Criminal Law Act 1977,[127] while Section (1A) of the same act could also be used to criminalise conspiracies outside England and Wales, as amended by the Coroners and Justice Act of 2009.[128]

The increasing criminalisation of inchoate offences generates even more complicated scenarios for hacktivists since even failed or weak virtual sit-in attempts could be prosecuted and have, indeed, been prosecuted as conspiracy offences, thus increasing the potential penalties.[129] Naturally, if certain hacktions are considered terrorism-related, hacktivists who even incite such protests could also be prosecuted for several inchoate offences like public provocation or recruitment.[130]

Further, in relation to aiding, the production and distribution of hacking tools is not included in the CFAA apart from enabling fraud in Section (a)(6), which only discusses trafficking in passwords and information enabling unauthorised access with the purpose of committing fraud. The production and trafficking of unauthorised access devices[131] is also considered an aggravating factor for cybercrime offences in the US Sentencing Guidelines.[132] The applicability of Section (a)(6) to hacktivist software, however, is unclear since prosecutors need to also prove a purpose to defraud, which is not relevant to our case due to the different aims of the protesters.

On the contrary, the UK has explicitly criminalised the production and distribution of articles that facilitate unauthorised access and impairment. Section 3A of the CMA 1990 criminalises the making, supplying, or obtaining of articles for use in offences under Sections 1, 3, or 3ZA of the CMA.[133] It provides that a person is guilty of an offence if they make, adapt, supply, or offer to supply any article (including any program or data held in electronic form) intending it to be used or believing it is likely to be used to commit or assist in the commission of offences under Sections 1, 3, or 3ZA of the CMA 1990. It even criminalises obtaining such an article with a view to its being supplied for the reasons specified, with penalties reaching two years' imprisonment.

This provision requires that the perpetrator has a double intent, both to supply the article and to intend it, or believe it is likely, to be used for computer misuse offences. The proving of the second part of intent and the vagueness of the term 'likely,' the interpretation of which has been left to the discretion of the courts, have caused great controversy amongst politicians, cybersecurity firms, software vendors, and network operators.[134] The main reason is that the criminalisation of the ownership or sale and use of such tools without providing any clear legitimate use defence, as the Cybercrime Convention had advised,[135] could potentially incriminate many legitimate users, creators, and sellers of such software for network security purposes.[136] This provision could further criminalise hacktivists that generate and openly distribute relevant software tools and political viruses with a view to facilitate political activism. Again, such a theory has not been tested, since prosecutors tend to use the more serious computer damage/impairment provisions for prosecuting hacktivists, but it is a real possibility, demonstrating the all-encompassing nature of cybercrime legislation.

3.5 The Complexities of Establishing Lack of Authorisation

The issue of lacking and exceeding authorisation is one of the most contested in relation to cybercrime laws. The CFAA is the most characteristic case regarding lack of clarity on the issue of authorisation, which can seriously impact on the core issue of the actual illegality of certain hacktivist actions. To begin with, the courts in the US have disagreed on when an act might be authorised or not, with *US v Czubinski*[137] establishing an 'intended use' test. This case related to whether an employee had exceeded his or her authorization to access information because he or she has used the work password without permission in order to access confidential Internal Revenue Service data out of curiosity without making any further use of that data. The appellate court confirmed that Czubinski had exceeded his authorisation to access the work computers, based on the fact that he had used his authorisation out of personal curiosity and not for his official duties.

The intended use test was further clarified by civil courts in *EF Cultural Travel BV v Explorica Inc,*[138] where it was decided that employing software, which automates data collection (Scraper) when accessing a publicly accessible website for which manual access and collection is authorised, would be exceeding the use for which authorisation was given. This decision was based on the fact that the design and use of the automated search software violated a confidentiality/non-competition agreement signed between the plaintiff and the CEO of the defendant. Although the appellate court focused more on the violation of the confidentiality agreement for establishing the exceeding of authorisation, it also seemed to accept the district court's view that the appellants had exceeded authorised access, since the use of the automated software for competitive reasons went beyond the reasonable expectations of use that would be authorised by the website owner and its users.[139]

The concept of reasonable expectations was challenged, however, by the appellate court in a related case *EF Cultural Travel BV et al. v Zefer Corporation (Zefer),*[140] finding that the vague, implicit concept of reasonable expectations could not form the basis of establishing whether access using a Scraper was unauthorised and that this should be explicit in the terms of service. This case lands the first blow to the concept of 'intended use' as it requires that there exists clarity and explicit mention of such terms between the interacting parties.[141]

The concept of exceeding authorised access was reconfigured though in the case of *US v Nosal I.*[142] This case related to former employees accessing the network of their previous employer after they had formed a competitive business venture, using the credentials of an existing employee.

Although the court in *Nosal I* after an *en banc* hearing acquitted the defendants on the basis that exceeding authorisation required the bypassing of technical restrictions, the case has been discussed again more recently in *Nosal II*,[143] where the 9th circuit reversed its previous decisions and found Nosal and his accomplices guilty on the basis that they had been explicitly excluded from accessing the database of their former employer. This case focused on the lack of authorisation ensuing from using someone else's password—a colleague still working at Nosal's previous employer, Korn/Ferry. Apart from the general controversy surrounding the CFAA that these reversals indicate, what is important for our discussion is also the existence or lack of authorisation in relation to a website's terms and conditions which could impact on virtual sit-ins and also on activities such as data exposure in the sense of what Aaron Swartz and Weev did. Let us try to unpack the Nosal cases and get a clearer idea of the important issues involved.

Nosal I had discussed the concept of unauthorised access more generally arguing that employer–employee and company–consumer relationships, both based on private agreements, are usually regulated by tort and contract law and that the *Czubinski/Explorica* 'intended use' test or even the *Zefer* request for explicit guidance in the terms of use regarding allowed access would result in these relationships being manipulated by private parties in order to police them through criminal law. More particularly, the *Nosal I* court expressed its concern that attaching felonious liability for the CFAA on the violation of vague and unknown or arbitrarily changeable Terms of Service could criminalise millions of plain users bypassing private contracts or terms and conditions of websites. As the court further argued, despite governmental assurances that prosecutors would not resort to prosecuting superficial cases of exceeding authorisation, the current interpretation of exceeding authorisation (*Czubinski/Explorica*) cannot be allowed as it would force citizens to greatly rely on the discretion of the prosecutors for avoiding excessive prosecutions. The court further dared Congress to explicitly dictate if it wanted such cases included, since the rule of lenity requires that penal laws are interpreted strictly. It considered that exceeding unauthorised access could only be established if there was bypassing of technical restrictions, which was an important shift from relying on the vague intentions of the website/

network owners' will, implicit or explicit, to depending on the existence of an actual technical hurdle that prevented access.

Nosal II reversed the decision, indicating that there was not a need for technical restrictions to be bypassed and finding that the use of log in credentials of an existing employee could not be considered authorised access, when the network owner had explicitly banned these former employees from using the network. A dissenting Judge Reinhardt still highlighted the difficulties this decision presented for cases where there was no explicit ban for a particular user, such as when the terms of service of a website just prohibited commonplace practices, such as Facebook password sharing. The constant shifting in the case of Nosal is indicative of the ambiguity of the particular concept of lacking or exceeding authorisation and further highlights the complexity of the CFAA.

The *Nosal I* rationale regarding whether terms of service violations by users could incur CFAA liability gained momentum both in other courts[144] and also regarding suggestions to amend the CFAA.[145] Discussions on amending the CFAA and a new bill were proposed after the death of Aaron Swartz, highlighting the potential for excessive prosecutorial discretion and suggesting a move towards the more restrictive *Nosal I* approach[146]; however, this did not materialise initially. More recently, there have been attempts to revive the bill, but nothing major has taken place.[147] In fact, in a recent case involving Facebook[148] that was decided shortly after *Nosal II,* the court put some limitations on authorisation relating to terms of service. In this case, the court found that if someone is given someone else's password to access a service that prohibits this password-sharing in the terms of service, the access would be authorised and would then become unauthorised only if the website owner expressly forbade this again.[149] This development has seemingly established a compromise between the views expressed in *Nosal* regarding more everyday use incidents, but it is not clear whether it might have confused things even more. How does all this then relate to hacktivist actions?

In the case of most intrusive protests, such as defacements, redirects, and viruses, there would not be much to discuss as these acts would obviously be unauthorised, perpetrated by individuals accessing presumably secured networks, and therefore lacking authorisation per se and bypassing access controls. This would satisfy even the relaxed *Nosal I* standard for unauthorised access. However, for activities such as virtual sit-ins or the acquisition of data in the case, where that data might be publicly available, as in the case of Weev, the proving of authorisation or the lack of it would be far more ambiguous.

To begin with data acquisition, which is more straightforward, Weev's case was decided on the basis of 'intended use' and he was initially convicted on grounds that his accessing the AT&T data that were freely available online was unauthorised.[150] However, as Kerr highlights, these email addresses were freely published on the Web under particular publicly accessible URLs, and according to *Pulte Homes, Inc. v Laborers' International Union Of North America*,[151] everyone is authorised to visit an 'unprotected website' that is 'open to the public.'[152] Consequently, access would not be unauthorised unless AT&T had implemented technical restrictions, such as encryption, as is usual practice in order to prevent access to the customer data 'Weev' acquired. Even if AT&T explicitly stated in its terms of service that such data should not be accessed and collected, access could be considered to be exceeding authorisation under a *Zefer* rationale, but would still fail to justify the *Facebook* standard of repeating the prohibition to Auernheimer or the even higher standard proposed by *Nosal I* which entails the bypassing of technical restrictions.

The cases of virtual sit-ins are slightly more complex. The Senate has explicitly articulated its view that the two latter sections of the computer damage offence, Sections a.5(B) and (C), should only relate to those fully lacking authorisation and not to insiders or users accessing publicly accessible websites, as for the latter, authorisation to access is presumed due to the publicness of the site accessed.[153] This would mean that the only section applicable to virtual sit-ins would be Section a.5(A) whereby there needs to be an intent to cause unauthorised damage through knowingly transmitting information to a protected computer. However, it is not clear whether the data sent to the website should also be considered unauthorised access or exceeding authorised access, since publicly available websites are considered free to access and thus everyone is considered authorised to send information requests to them. Therefore, even if damage is caused by the sending of data, it could prove challenging to establish users' intention that the data were meant to cause unauthorised damage if the sending of data is authorised in the first place.

However, the confusion does not stop here. As discussed earlier, Sections a.5(B) and (C) are meant to apply only to those fully lacking authorisation to access the protected computers. Yet, some participants of virtual sit-ins have been offered guilty plea agreements on charges based on those two sections of reckless damage or negligent damage and loss.[154] These cases relating to virtual sit-ins yet linking those to provisions that require solely unauthorised access could mean three different things.

First, they could be demonstrative of prosecutorial disregard of the Senate's intentions regarding the exclusion of reckless or negligent computer damage charges for users with some degree of authorisation, as would be those accessing a publicly accessible website. Second, such prosecutorial plea offers could be interpreted as denying the existence of a prima facie authorisation of users to send information requests to a publicly accessible website, thus considering their access unauthorised. This could mean that prosecutors have applied the contested *Czubinski* 'intended use' test discussed earlier. The third one is that these plea agreements on an inapplicable provision of the CFAA were offered as they usually incur lower sentences than the main Section a.5(A) and therefore would be more likely to be accepted, but would also help prosecutors avoid having to go to court to prove the intention of virtual sit-in protesters to cause damage.

It is obvious that this lack of clarity in the interpretation of a very complex, but very important provision in the CFAA by prosecutors and courts increases the risks of hacktivists accepting punishment for charges that would not even be applicable in their cases or would be hard to establish, if these were pursued in court. The lack of clear instruction also enables prosecutors to charge protesters with an array of sections, with the hope that at least one would prove convincing to the courts, which have expressed a wide range of views when interpreting concepts such as lack of authorisation. Hacktivists could thus be at the mercy of the court to pick from the various interpretations that coexist as precedent regarding unauthorised access as well as the range of activities that could be considered within the scope of each section. The lack of legal clarity here is combined with two issues to be discussed in the next chapter relating to the wide prosecutorial discretion and also the courts' lack of familiarisation with cybercrime and its intricacies, which would result in risk-averse hacktivists submitting to any plea deal offered.

The case in the UK is different in the sense that for the computer impairment section, there is no distinction between insiders and outsiders to the network accessed in terms of defining what type of lack of authorisation will exist between total lack (unauthorised access) or partial lack (exceeding authorised access). The dominant rationale expressed in *R v Bow Street Magistrates Court and Allison (A.P.) Ex Parte Government of the United States of America*[155] is that, when the use of authorisation to access certain information is not carried out for the purpose for which the authorisation was given, access exceeds authorisation. Consequently, in cases where a virtual sit-in targets a publicly accessible website with many users automatically reloading the page, their authorisation, although initially existing, exceeds its limits from the moment the protester's action employs this access in order to disrupt the communication, which is not why the authorisation was initially provided.

However, even the creation of this precedent has not been straightforward, since in a case preceding *Allison*, *DPP v Bignell*,[156] the court acquitted two police officers using their national police computer access for purposes unrelated to which the authorisation was given. Similarly, in another case, *DPP v Lennon*,[157] regarding the automated bombarding of an email account with thousands of emails, the court had initially found there was no case to answer as the email bombarding was not considered unauthorised modification of the email account being bombarded. However, on appeal the court convicted Lennon arguing (similarly to Allison) that the purpose of the email account was to facilitate communication and authorisation was given to other users in order to send emails for that purpose rather than to render communication actually impossible.[158]

However, although the UK case seems more straightforward, the aforementioned Directive 2013/40/EC on attacks against information systems and replacing Council Framework Decision 2005/222/JHA could have made things more complicated. It includes provisions that indicated member states should adopt an approach that would require the bypassing of technical restrictions in order for access to be unauthorised, similar to what the *Nosal I* court has argued.[159] The Directive is not binding for member states and it can be seen that the UK government actually increased the strictness of the current Computer Misuse Act 1990 by introducing the aforementioned amendments of the Serious Crime Act 2015 rather than considering a more lenient approach to punishing cybercrimes. Therefore, virtual sit-ins with the purpose of impairing rather than getting actual information from a website are also likely to be considered unauthorised acts in the UK. However, whether a similar rationale would apply for cases like the use Auernheimer made of AT&T's publicly available data is not clear. Considering the variety of interpretations regarding authorisation, it is also unclear what would happen with cross-jurisdictional cases, where depending on the courts' preferred interpretation one could be found innocent or guilty, yet with no definite answer as to what these interpretations might be.

3.6 Hacking, Hacktivism, and Cyberterrorism Laws

Another major concern that relates to the computer damage offences and hacktivism is the inclusion of these offences in a list of cyberterrorism-related offences, which further reinforce the aforementioned links between hacktivism and cyberterrorism. In the US, for example, the USA PATRIOT Act has included the intentional damage offence of the CFAA, Section 1030(a)(5)(A), in the definition of 'federal crime of terrorism.' The federal crime of terrorism is an offence that aims to influence or affect the conduct of government by intimidation or coercion, or to retaliate against government conduct. An additional requirement for including Section 1030(a)(5)(A) as a terrorist crime is the satisfying of the felony liability triggers (I) and (V).[160] Hacktions can be linked to these felony liability triggers and, thus, could easily fit the description.

Furthermore, hacktivist tactics also satisfy another element of the definition of federal crime of terrorism, which is the goal of influencing government conduct. The requirement for the act to be intimidating or coercive or retaliatory towards government conduct is also very broadly defined and can be linked to hacktivist actions against an unjust decision or policy. After all, differentiating between coercive and non-coercive protests is a very challenging process usually based on subjective assessments.

For example, the often aggressive and retaliatory hue of many of Anonymous' declarations further blurs attempts to distinguish hacktivism from cyberterrorism according to the definition given earlier. An even more direct connection was made in the case of *Fullmer*,[161] where the illegality of organising and perpetrating virtual sit-ins was considered important[162] in finding the defendants guilty of conspiracy to violate the Animal Enterprise Terrorism Act during their protests.[163]

Apart from severe increases in penalties for those accused of terrorist computer damage offences provided in the Sentencing Guidelines,[164] the implications of the link between counterterrorist laws and hacktivism are serious in terms of monitoring. As Podgor argues, the consequence of adding Section 1030(a)(5)(A) to the offences for federal terrorism is that it would essentially justify the authorities' interception of wire, oral, and electronic communications and even allow the Secret Service to engage in investigations that relate to CFAA offences that might be linked to hacktivism.[165]

Similarly, the UK counterterrorist laws also reinforce the links of computer damage offences to cyberterrorism. The Terrorism Act 2000[166] as amended by the UK Terrorism Act 2006 gives a definition of terrorism, listing the use or threat of actions designed to influence the government or an international governmental organisation *or* to intimidate the public or a section of the public and these acts are used for advancing political, religious, racial, or ideological causes. As the Electrohippies highlight, the term 'or' in Section 1.3, which was not initially part of the bill, means that actions seeking to influence the government could be considered terrorist acts without also requiring public intimidation.[167] This means the definition actually encompasses efforts to influence policy change based on political/ideological purposes—a basic goal for most protesters and hacktivist groups.

The inclusion of electronic forms of protest is further established by subsection 1.2.e of the Terrorism Act 2000, which refers to threats or actions designed to seriously interfere with or seriously disrupt an electronic system, including acts outside the UK.[168] According to the explanatory notes to the UK Terrorism Act 2000, this law is designed to cover actions which can have a devastating impact on modern networked society despite not being violent; yet, as far as explaining Section 1(2)(e), it is only added that it is meant to cover the serious disruption of key computer systems.[169] It has been argued that the term 'seriously' is adequate to differentiate between terrorism and effects that can just be a 'costly nuisance,' although others have deemed the definition wide enough to encompass traditional hacking and system impairment.[170] The act also refers to activities outside the UK or against governments abroad,[171] thus potentially criminalising hacktivists who protest against governmental or international organisations' websites in other countries.[172]

Naturally, if ECD acts are considered terrorist, those who incite such protests, such as hacktivist organisers and groups, could also be prosecuted for several inchoate offences, such as public provocation or recruitment.[173] Considering the current climate, where terrorist attacks in the UK have become more frequent and there are calls for stricter responses to terrorism by the government, there is a concern that definitions could become even more encompassing and prosecutions more aggressive.

The concerns generated from analogising hacktivism to terrorism have induced attempts to differentiate hacktivist practices from terrorism. It has been suggested, for example, that for politically motivated hacking operations to be considered as cyberterrorism, they should cause such grave harm or damage as to generate fear comparable to that of destructive, offline terrorism.[174] Denning testified before the Special Oversight Panel on Terrorism Committee on Armed Services in the US House of Representatives in 2000 that

> EDT and the Electrohippies view their operations as acts of civil disobedience, analogous to street protests and physical sit-ins, not as acts of violence or terrorism. This is an important distinction. Most activists, whether participating in the Million Mom March or a web sit-in, are not terrorists.[175]

Walker also argues that an important category of cyberterrorism is hostile activity on computer systems.[176] For Walker, defacements or DoS [denial-of-service] attacks, even if violating cybercrime laws and their potential disruption to governmental computer systems is substantial, are unlikely to have the same impact on the lives of individuals as terrorism would in order to support the analogy of hacktivism to terrorism.[177]

Even if terrorism-related prosecutions do not ensue, the legal link that exists between hacktivism and cyberterrorism could lead to further marginalisation of these protesters and the generation of more intense public censure, even for hacktivists supporting just causes and trying to take all the necessary precautions. In addition to the threatened high sanctions from the CFAA, the added fear of even higher terrorism-related penalties sanctions could also lead to proliferation and radicalisation of protests. The increased monitoring and prospects of severe punishment can lead to resentful reactions from determined hacktivists who would abandon any self-regulation limitations, leading to 'backlash' effects.[178] Some of Anonymous' activities express such a tendency of backlash or 'cumulative extremism,'[179] where apprehensions of online protesters induce more protests and lead to suggestions for more radical, covert attacks and even the design of anonymising tools for sit-ins.[180] Such responses could thus propagate a circle of radicalisation that would eventually also impact on user experience with stricter regulations and more wide-ranging surveillance being implemented from the authorities, accompanied by more disruptive activities from reacting hacktivists.

The provisions mentioned earlier in relation to the US and the UK are only core provisions serving as indicative examples, since there is an ever-increasing array of regulations expanding counterterrorist measures[181] that eventually imbue authorities with extra monitoring and enforcement powers against undesirable political/ideological groups and their supporters.[182] Although a detailed review of the very complex counterterrorist legislation could constitute a book on its own, the analysis of some basic provisions is meant to establish the potential for the legal and, thus also, the conceptual link between hacktivism and cyberterrorism and the prospective consequences of this link for hacktivists and users in general. Although terrorism-related prosecutions of hacktivist-related incidents have not happened yet (apart from the *Fullmer* case mentioned earlier), as the court in *Nosal I* argued, excessive reliance on prosecutorial discretion entails the risk that politically charged cases might tempt prosecutors to make use of their discretion in undue ways.

3.7 Expansion of Law and Lack of Consistency

One important further expansion to the scope of both cybercrime acts needs to be highlighted. An important element of Section (a)(2)(C) is the expansion of the CFAA's jurisdictional reach with the gradual broadening of the definition of the term 'protected computer,' which seems adequate to cover most unauthorised acts targeting computers within the US and abroad.[183] After the Identity Theft Enforcement and Restitution Act of 2008,[184] the definition of 'protected computers' was extended to encompass not only computers *'used in,'* but also those *'affecting,'* interstate or foreign commerce or communication—in essence, potentially every single computer online—and thus made the avoidance of US jurisdiction almost impossible for cyberdeviants globally.[185]

Similarly, for the UK, all CMA offences had to demonstrate an adequate link to the UK of either the perpetrator or the target being located in the UK.[186] However, the recent Serious Crime Act 2015 expanded the jurisdiction of UK courts in Section 43 to cover instances where UK nationals commit cybercrimes abroad, assuming that the acts constitute an offence in the jurisdiction they take place.

In addition to the extension of the jurisdictional reach of those acts, the capacity of citizens to protest against issues they might feel strongly about internationally, in combination with the difficulties of apprehending and extraditing offenders from other states, leads to a very interesting disparity that the Internet's international reach exacerbates: protesters from the UK or the US protesting against targets that are somehow linked to the US or the UK are the ones that usually get prosecuted, as documented earlier. Conversely, protesters are rarely prosecuted in cases where the protests are against another state's websites, even if originating from countries such as the US and UK, which have established liability for attacks originating from their territory against targets abroad. In fact, in many cases, international efforts, such as virtual sit-ins against Iranian or Egyptian governmental websites, would not even be investigated, if not encouraged, even when they were pre-announced with online videos by Anonymous.[187] However, when members of Anonymous protested against US-based organisations and networks, they were under investigation, if not prosecuted. This lack of uniformity in how these acts are dealt with depending on their target generates confusion as to the legitimacy and legality of hacktivist actions.

This problem of disparate legal treatment of hacktivism internationally is further exacerbated by a lack of global harmonisation of approaches and penalties for cybercrime. Despite general harmonisation efforts,[188] as already seen, even on the issue of unauthorised access, for example, serious deviations have ensued between UK and US case law. Even in the same jurisdiction, there are many different agencies that are burdened with dealing with cybercrime and, therefore, even national approaches might vary significantly, further impacting on international cooperation.[189] Moreover, the political nature of hacktivism, along with its global character, might render extraditions problematic, considering that, even between states that have very similar approaches to cybercrime, such as the US and the UK, there has been a reluctance to extradite cyberdeviants[190] or it has taken quite a long time to do so.[191] As Aas highlights, the globalising interdependence of information systems has not yet managed to impose a full homogenisation of penal approaches, with cultural specificities influencing the perception of criminality and the nature and extent of punishment.[192]

Consistent responses thus become increasingly difficult when the activities to which varying legal regimes must be applied entail elements that are morally and ideologically contested, and, hence, subject to different treatment between different regimes.[193] Essentially, this results in a general disparity in applying the law and in long delays when doing so, which further exacerbate a feeling of injustice and inefficiency on behalf of those going through the criminal justice system. This can also further reinforce feelings of illegitimacy towards these processes and even give rise to further backlash effects.

4 Conclusion

This chapter has reviewed the challenging environment within which hacktivism is realised and the potential issues of efficaciousness and fairness arising from trying to apply current cybercrime laws to hacktivist actions in the current climate. The analysis has demonstrated how the choice to deal with hacktivism using the cybercriminal law regime as a knee-jerk reaction despite its rigidity and documented inadequacies eventually intimidates moral protesters or radicalises the more determined ones and essentially generates concerns for the legitimacy of those prosecutions. These concerns for the unjust application of vague cybercrime laws and the potential for punitive responses also ends up alienating protesters further and even induces representatives from the victims' side, such as Omidyar, to speak out on behalf of the protesters. These concerns for legitimacy also potentially drive protesters underground or give rise to numerous and severe online disruptions, whilst the more principled protesters might abandon their efforts to promote more expressive and less disruptive practices. This not only compromises the deterrent effect and public interest considerations inherent in such prosecutions, but also impacts on the quality and quantity of political deliberation taking place online.

The impact of the issues highlighted in this chapter will become more obvious when we assess the role of those involved in enforcing or facilitating the enforcement of such laws within the current security-focused climate. Through this process we will be able to assess whether the problems identified in this chapter are ameliorated or potentially exacerbated. The next chapter therefore will discuss the impact of prosecutors and courts, but also the private corporations that play a very important role in regulating behaviour online as they react to the existing legislative and policy dictates, but also try to satisfy their own commercial interests.

Notes

1. Mark E. DeForrest, 'Civil Disobedience: Its Nature and Role in the American Legal Landscape' (1998) 33 Gonzaga Law Review 653, 654.
2. Juergen Habermas and Martha Calhoun, 'Right and Violence: A German Trauma' (1985) 1 Cultural Critique 125, 137.
3. Joseph Raz, *The Authority of Law: Essays on Law and Morality* (Oxford University Press, Oxford 1979); Raz (n 72) 236–237.
4. Noah Hampson, 'Hacktivism: A New Breed of Protest in a Networked World' (2012) 35 Boston College International & Comparative Law Review 511, 531–532.

5. See Habermas and Calhoun (n 2) 127–129; Stuart M. Brown Jr, 'Civil Disobedience' (1961) 58 The Journal of Philosophy 669, 672; For hacktivism, see Dorothy Denning, 'Hacktivism: An Emerging Threat to Diplomacy' (2000) 77 Foreign Service Journal 43; for recent anonymous virtual sit-ins being considered anarchist or terrorist acts, see Crosstalk, 'From Hacktivism to Wikiwarfare' (*RT*, 17 December 2010) http://www.youtube.com/watch?v=mFJa9RHAfOk; Tim Black, 'Hacktivism: The Poison Gas of Cyberspace' (*Spiked-Online*, 14 December 2010) http://www.spiked-online.com/newsite/article/10001#.Wl3fMq5l9hE.
6. For decentralised regulation, see, for example, Clifford Shearing and Jennifer Wood, 'Nodal Governance, Democracy, and the New "Denizens"' (2003) 30 Journal of Law and Society 400; Julia Black, 'Decentring Regulation: Understanding the Role of Regulation and Self-Regulation in a "Post-Regulatory" World' (2001) 54 Current Legal Problems 103; John Braithwaite, *Restorative Justice and Responsive Regulation* (Oxford University Press, Oxford 2002); for cyberspace, multi-actor regulation, see Lawrence Lessig, *Code v.2.0* (Basic Books, New York 2006); Henry H. Perritt Jr, 'Towards a Hybrid Regulatory Scheme for the Internet' (2001) 2001 The University of Chicago Legal Forum 215; Joel R. Reidenberg, 'Technology and Internet Jurisdiction' (2004) 153 University of Pennsylvania Law Review 1951.
7. Julia Black, 'Proceduralisation and Polycentric Regulation' (2005) Especial 1 RevistaDIREITOGV http://direitogv.fgv.br/sites/direitogv.fgv.br/files/rdgv_esp01_p099_130.pdf, 102.
8. Black has identified some of the most common problems for state-based regulation. She argues that law can be poorly targeted or too unsophisticated to deal with complex problems (instrument failure), there can be insufficient knowledge on behalf of state actors involved in identifying the causes of problems and generating solutions or identifying non-compliance (information and knowledge failure), and also inadequate implementation of the designated measures (implementation failure). Black, 'Proceduralisation and Polycentric Regulation' (n 7) 102; Julia Black, 'Critical Reflections on Regulation' (2002) 27 Australian Journal of Legal Philosophy 1, 2.
9. John Palfrey, 'Four Phases of Internet Regulation' (2010) Social Research 77/3 981 http://cyber.law.harvard.edu/publications.

10. Zygmunt Bauman, *Modernity and Ambivalence* (Polity Press, Cambridge 1991) 4; David Garland, *The Culture of Control: Crime and Social Order in Contemporary Society* (Oxford University Press, Oxford 2001).
11. Garland (n 10); Michael McGuire, *Hypercrime: The New Geometry of Harm* (Routledge Cavendish, Oxford 2007) 32; Jonathan Simon, *Governing through Crime* (Oxford University Press, Oxford 2007) 4; Barbara Hudson, *Justice in the Risk Society: Challenging and Re-Affirming Justice in Late Modernity* (Sage Publications, London 2003) 43–45, 49–50.
12. Cass R. Sunstein, *Laws of Fear: Beyond the Precautionary Principle* (Cambridge University Press, Cambridge 2005) 4, 15, 18, 21.
13. Garland (n 10) 18–19; Manuel Castells, *Communication Power* (Oxford University Press, Oxford 2009) 28–29.
14. Lucia Zedner, 'Pre-Crime and Post-Criminology?' (2007) 11 Theoretical Criminology 261, 265.
15. Security contractors have an interest in the intensification of security concerns and, thus, the need for security measures they offer. Moreover, governments increase their popularity by appearing strict and supportive of order and elimination of risk (ibid).
16. Naomi Klein, *The Shock Doctrine* (Penguin Books, London 2007).
17. Zedner, *Security* (Routledge, New York 2009) 117.
18. Johan Eriksson and Giampiero Giacomello, 'The Information Revolution, Security, and International Relations: (Ir) Relevant Theory?' (2006) 27 International Political Science Review 221, 222–224.
19. Garland (n 10) 134; Alex Callinicos, 'The Anti-Capitalist Movement after Genoa and New York' in Stanley Arownowitz and Heather Gautney (eds), *Implicating Empire: Globalization and Resistance in the 21st Century World Order* (Basic Books, New York 2003) 133, 140–141; Giorgio Agamben, *Means without End: Notes on Politics* (University of Minnesota Press, Minneapolis 2000) 6–7.
20. Simon (n 11) 275.
21. Dr Maximilian Forte, 'Is "Virtual" Activism Not "Real" Activism' (*Cyberspace Ethnography: Political Activism and the Internet Blog,* 29 January 2010) http://webography.wordpress.com/2010/01/29/is-virtual-activism-not-real-activism/; as Castronova has shown, even Internet role-playing games can have serious cultural and economic implications for real-world economies. See Edward Castronova, *Synthetic Worlds: The Business and Culture of Online Games* (University of Chicago Press, Chicago 2005).

22. Majid Yar, 'Public Perceptions and Public Opinion About Internet Crime' in Yvonne Jewkes and Majid Yar (eds), *Handbook of Internet Crime* (Willand Publishing, Devon 2010) 104–119, 106–107.
23. Wendy Holloway and Tony Jefferson, 'The Risk Society in an Age of Anxiety: Situating Fear of Crime' (1997) 48 The British Journal of Sociology 255, 260; Garland (n 10) 108–109; David Wall, *Cybercrime: The Transformation of Crime in the Information Age* (Polity Press, Cambridge 2007) 16.
24. Joshua B. Hill and Nancy E. Marion, 'Presidential Rhetoric and Cybercrime: Tangible and Symbolic Policy Statements' (2016) 17 Criminology, Criminal Justice, Law & Society 1–17.
25. Verizon, '2011 Was the Year of the "'Hacktivist," according to the Verizon 2012 Data Breach Investigations Report' (*Verizon,* 2012) http://newscenter.verizon.com/press-releases/verizon/2012/2011-was-the-year-of-the.html; Verizon focuses more on data breaches and information thefts rather than on more symbolically expressive tactics and, thus, manages to portray hacktivism normatively as a cybersecurity threat.

    The FBI highlighted hacktivism as a very important issue for security. Marcos Colon, 'RSA Conference 2012: Hacktivism Forcing Organizations to Look Inward' (*SC Magazine,* 29 June 2017) http://www.scmagazine.com/rsa-conference-2012-hacktivism-forcing-organizations-to-look-inward/article/230051/; Sophos security also named 2011 the year of the hacktivist to reflect the change in motives for cybersecurity breaches from purely criminal to more political. Sophos, 'Security Threat Report 2012' (*Sophos,* 2012) https://www.sophos.com/en-us/press-office/press-releases/2012/01/security-threat-report-2012.aspx.
26. McGuire (n 11) 94–95; for example, the Department of Homeland Security has defined critical infrastructure as 'the assets, systems, and networks, whether physical or virtual, so vital to the United States that their incapacitation or destruction would have a debilitating effect on security, national economic security, national public health or safety, or any combination thereof.' United States Department of Homeland Security, 'What Is Critical Infrastructure?' (undated) http://www.dhs.gov/what-critical-infrastructure; for the UK, the UK's national infrastructure is defined by the Government as 'those facilities, systems, sites and networks necessary for the functioning of the country and the delivery of the essential services upon which daily life in the UK

depends.' Centre for the Protection of National Infrastructure 'The National Infrastructure' http://www.cpni.gov.uk/about/cni/.

27. See Graham Meikle, 'Electronic Civil Disobedience and Symbolic Power' in Athina Karatzogianni (ed), *Cyberconflicts and Global Politics* (Routledge, London 2009) 184–185; the fear of crackdowns is also reflected in the views expressed by various activists and Internet freedom groups, who find that legal developments even from the beginning of 2000 would have a serious impact on the treatment of online activism. See The Electrohippies Collective, 'Cyberlaw UK: Civil Rights and Protest on the Internet' (*iwar.org*, 2000) http://www.iwar.org.uk/hackers/resources/electrohippies-collective/comm-2000-12.pdf; Electronic Frontier Foundation, 'Letter to Governor Pataki' (*Electronic Frontier Foundation*, 12 March 2003) https://w2.eff.org/Privacy/TIA/20030314_letter_to_pataki.php.
28. Meikle (n 27) 179.
29. Alexandra W. Samuel, 'Hacktivism and the Future of Political Participation' (DPhil Thesis, Harvard University 2004) 243.
30. DJNZ and The Action Tool Development Group of the Electrohippies Collective, 'Client-Side Distributed Denial-of-Service: Valid Campaign Tactic or Terrorist Act?' (2001) 34 Leonardo 269, 269.
31. Andrew Couts, 'US Gov't Ramps up Anti-Anonymous Rhetoric, Warns of Power Grid Take-Down' (*Digital Trends*) https://www.digitaltrends.com/web/us-govt-ramps-up-anti-anonymous-rhetoric-warns-of-power-grid-take-down/.
32. Holloway and Jefferson (n 23) 260.
33. Garland (n 10) 135.
34. Simon (n 11).
35. Sara S. Beale, 'What's Law Got to Do with It? The Political, Social, Psychological and Non-Legal Factors Influencing the Development of (Federal) Criminal Law' (1997) 1 Buffalo Criminal Law Review 23, 49; Garland (n 10) 7.
36. Lucia Zedner, 'Securing Liberty in the Face of Terror: Reflections from Criminal Justice' (2005) 32 Journal of Law and Society 507, 513.
37. See Giovanna Borradori, *Philosophy in a Time of Terror: Dialogues with Jürgen Habermas and Jacques Derrida* (University of Chicago Press, Chicago 2003) 40–41.
38. Katja F. Aas, *Globalization & Crime* (Sage Publications, London 2007) 164, 167; Wall (n 23) 16.

39. Ohm Paul, 'The Myth of the Superuser: Fear, Risk, and Harm Online' (2008) 41 University of California Davis Law Review 1327.
40. Ian Walden, *Computer Crimes and Digital Investigations* (Oxford University Press, New York 2007) 62, 66; McGuire (n 11) 94.
41. Kristin Finklea and Catherine Theohary, 'CRS Report for Congress: Cybercrime: Conceptual Issues for Congress and U.S. Law Enforcement' (Congressional Research Service, 2013) http://www.fas.org/sgp/crs/misc/R42547.pdf; Meikle (n 27) 184–185.
42. Skibell (n 41) 921.
43. David M. Zlotnick, 'The War within the War on Crime: The Congressional Assault on Judicial Sentencing Discretion' (2004) 57 South Methodist University Law Review 211, 247.
44. Castells, *Communication Power* (n 13) 89, 424; Beale, 'What's Law Got to Do with It?' (n 35) 44–46; Wall (n 23) 15.
45. Adam G. Klein, 'Vigilante Media: Unveiling Anonymous and the Hacktivist Persona in the Global Press' 82 Communication Monographs 3, 384–385.
46. Media increase the salience of certain sociopolitical issues by projecting these more intensely and, thus, set social agenda priorities. Subsequently, they prime audiences to believe in the increased importance of those social issues. 'Priming' is based on 'cognitive accessibility' theory, which supports that when people make judgements they employ shortcuts in the subconscious that make use of the most mentally accessible information, which is recently acquired, commonly employed, or sensational. Sara S. Beale, 'The News Media's Influence on Criminal Justice Policy: How Market-Driven News Promotes Punitiveness' (2006) 48 William & Mary Law Review 397, 441–444.
47. Aas (n 38) 155; McGuire (n 11) 89–90; Marcus J. Ranum, *The Myth of Homeland Security* (Wiley Publishing, Indiana 2004) 135; Yar, 'Public Perceptions and Public Opinion About Internet Crime' (n 22).
48. Adam G. Klein, 'Vigilante Media: Unveiling Anonymous and the Hacktivist Persona in the Global Press' 82 Communication Monographs 3, http://nca.tandfonline.com/doi/abs/10.1080/03637751.2015.1030682.
49. Sunstein, 'Laws of Fear' (n 12) 102; Aas (n 38) 155; McGuire (n 11) 116–117.
50. Beale, 'The News Media's Influence on Criminal Justice Policy' (n 46) 437–438; Yochai Benkler, *The Wealth of Networks: How Social Production Transforms Markets and Freedom* (Yale University Press, London 2006) 241–242.

51. Benkler (n 50) 245.
52. Cass R. Sunstein, *Republic.com 2.0* (Princeton University Press, Princeton 2007).
53. Moral panic ensues when 'a condition, episode, person or group of persons emerges to become defined as a threat to societal values and interests'; Stanley Cohen, *Folk Devils and Moral Panics* (Paladin, St Albans 1973) 9.
54. Aas (n 38) 167; Yar, 'Public Perceptions and Public Opinion about Internet Crime' (22) 105–106.
55. Kemshall Hazel, *Understanding Risk in Criminal Justice* (Mike McGuire ed, Open University Press, Maidenhead 2003) 6.
56. Deborah Lupton, *Risk* (Taylor & Francis E-Library, 2005) 61–62.
57. Hudson (n 11) 70.
58. Ales Zavrsnik, 'Cybercrime Definitional Challenges and Criminological Particularities' (2008) 2 Masaryk University Journal of Law & Technology 1, 4; Garland (n 10) 17.
59. Hudson (n 11) 64; Wall (n 23) 17–18, 23–24.
60. Wall (n 23) 13; Stefan Fafinski, William H. Dutton and Helen Margetts, 'Mapping and Measuring Cybercrime' (2010) OII Forum Discussion Paper No 18.
61. Ibid. 17.
62. Fafinski et al. (n 60) 14–15.
63. John Leyden, 'Webroot Guesstimates Inflate UK Spyware Problem' (*The Register*, 20 October 2005) http://www.theregister.co.uk/2005/10/20/webroot_uk_spyware_guesstimates/.
64. Wall (n 23) 23–24.
65. Sophos (n 25); Verizon (n 25).
66. Hudson (n 11) 25.
67. The rhetoric of Anonymous can often be characterised as retaliatory and threatening, with videos suggesting that governments should abide by certain standards that Anonymous designates in its declaration videos in order for the group to refrain from organising protests against those targeted. Anonymous, 'Anonymous Press Release: Open Letter from Anonymous to the UK Government' (*Anonymous*, 27 January 2011) https://www.indymedia.org.uk/en/2011/01/472905.html. In other instances, Anonymous has also publicised a code of practice for protesters who are oriented towards preventing any violence and radical tactical choices and in avoiding arrests due to provocation and illegal

acts. Anonymous, 'Anonymous—Code of Conduct' (*YouTube*, 21 December 2010) https://www.youtube.com/watch?v=-063clxiB8I.

68. Jana Herwig, 'Anonymous: Peering Behind the Mask' (*The Guardian*, 11 May 2011) http://www.guardian.co.uk/technology/2011/may/11/anonymous-behind-the-mask.
69. Couts (n 31).
70. For the views that public opinion is influencing public policy, but also for the compromising of the impact of public influence by the pressures of interest groups and strong financial actors, see many sources in Benjamin I. Page and Robert Y. Shapiro, 'Effects of Public Opinion on Policy' (1983) 77 The American Political Science Review 175, 175–176; as Burstein argues, although many theorists agree on the relationship between public opinion and public policy, the extent of the influence is often perceived differently. Paul Burstein, 'The Impact of Public Opinion on Public Policy: A Review and an Agenda' (2003) 56 Political Research Quarterly 29, 30.
71. Skibell (n 41) 910.
72. Ibid. 910–911.
73. Charlotte Decker, 'Cyber Crime 2.0: An Argument to Update the United States Criminal Code to Reflect the Changing Nature of Cyber Crime' (2007) 81 South California Law Review 959, 961.
74. The analysis of US law will focus only on federal cybercrime laws, even though there is an abundance of state laws, not only for reasons of brevity, but mainly because hacktivist actions usually relate to federal offences, as will be seen throughout the analysis.
75. 18 U.S.C., Part I, Title 47, Section 1030 (Fraud and related activity in connection with computers). Here the commonly used name of the provision as the Computer Fraud and Abuse Act 1986 (CFAA) will be used.
76. The most important amendments were introduced in 2001 with the PATRIOT Act (Uniting and Strengthening America by Providing Appropriate Tools Required to Intercept and Obstruct Terrorism Act of 2001—USAPA) 115 Stat. 272 (2001) and Identity Theft Enforcement and Restitution Act, 122 Stat. 3560 (2008).
77. Initially, 'protected computer' was defined as a computer 'used by the federal government or a financial institution' or one 'which is used in interstate or foreign commerce.' The current, considerably broader definition is 'a computer "(A) exclusively for the use of a financial institution or the United States Government, or, in the case of a computer

not exclusively for such use, used by or for a financial institution or the United States Government and the conduct constituting the offense affects that use by or for the financial institution or the Government; or (B) which is used in *or affecting* interstate or foreign commerce or communication including a computer located outside the United States that is used in a manner that affects interstate or foreign commerce or communication of the United States".' Section 1030(e)(2).

78. Eric Sinrod and William Reilly, 'Cyber-Crimes: A Practical Approach to the Application of Federal Computer Crime Laws' (2000) 16 Santa Clara Computer & High Tech Law Journal 177, 212–213.
79. United States Senate (1996) 'The National Information Infrastructure Protection Act of 1995' (Report 104–357) 6–7 cited in Charles Doyle, *Cybercrime: An Overview of the Federal Computer Fraud and Abuse Statute and Related Federal Criminal Laws* (Congressional Research Service, Report for Congress, DIANE Publishing, 2011) 16.
80. Section 1030(c)(2)(A).
81. Section 1030(c)(2)(B).
82. Section 1030(c)(2)(C).
83. Sections 1030(c)(2)(A) and (c)(2)(C).
84. Orin Kerr, 'United States v. Auernheimer, and Why I Am Representing Auernheimer Pro Bono on Appeal Before the Third Circuit' (*The Volokh Conspiracy*, 21 March 2013) http://volokh.com/2013/03/21/united-states-v-auernheimer-and-why-i-am-representing-auernheimer-pro-bono-on-appeal-before-the-third-circuit/.
85. (c.18).
86. John Worthy and Martin Fanning, 'Denial-of-Service: Plugging the Legal Loopholes?' (2007) 23 Computer Law & Security Report 194, 196; Stefan Fafinski, 'The Security Ramifications of the Police and Justice Act 2006' (2007) 2 Network Security 8, 10.
87. CMA Section 2: This section applies to offences
    a. for which the sentence is fixed by law; or
    b. for which a person of 21 years of age or over (not previously convicted) may be sentenced to imprisonment for a term of five years (or, in England and Wales, might be so sentenced but for the restrictions imposed by section 33 of the Magistrates' Courts Act 1980).
88. Richard Walton, 'The Computer Misuse Act' (2006) 11 Information Security Technical Report 39, 41.
89. Section 2(5).

90. Section 1030(e)(11).
91. Marshall Jarrett et al., 'Prosecuting Computer Crimes' (Criminal Division Computer Crime and Intellectual Property Section Criminal Division, Department of Justice, Washington D.C., undated) http://www.justice.gov/criminal/cybercrime/docs/ccmanual.pdf, 34–37.
92. Section 1030(c)(4)(A)(i)(I).
93. Section 1030(c)(4)(A)(i)(V).
94. Section 1030(c)(4)(A)(i)(VI). Harms that relate to meddling with medical records and causing physical injury and threat to public health or safety are also included but will not bother us, since hacktivists, as we have seen in Chapter 1, avoid protesting against such sensitive targets. See also Sections 1030(c)(4)(A)(i)(I-VII).
95. Jarrett et al. (n 91) 37–39.
96. Reasonable costs to any victim include the cost of responding to an offence, conducting a damage assessment, and restoring the data, program, system, or information to its condition prior to the offence, and any revenue lost, cost incurred, or other consequential damages incurred because of interruption of service; Section 1030(e)(11).
97. Section 1030(e)(11) See (n 49).
98. Gabriella E. Coleman, *Hacker, Hoaxer, Whistleblower, Spy: The Many Faces of Anonymous* (Verso, London 2014) 141.
99. Josh Halliday, 'Anonymous Hackers Jailed for Cyber Attacks' (*The Guardian,* 24 January 2013) http://www.guardian.co.uk/technology/2013/jan/24/anonymous-hackers-jailed-cyberattacks.
100. Pierre Omidyar, '*WikiLeaks, Press Freedom and Free Expression in the Digital Age*,' Huffington Post http://www.huffingtonpost.com/pierre-omidyar/wikileaks-press-freedom-a_b_4380738.html.
101. Gabriella E. Coleman, *Hacker, Hoaxer, Whistleblower, Spy: The Many Faces of Anonymous* (Verso, London 2014) 141–142.
102. Jarrett et al. (n 91) 43.
103. Fafinski et al. (n 60) 16.
104. Section 1030 (g).
105. Sections 1030(c)(4)(A), (c)(4)(D), (c)(4)(G).
106. Ohm (n 39).
107. Sections 1030(3)(2) (a-d).
108. Sections 1030(3)(6)(a-c).
109. Home Office, Serious Crime Act 2015 Fact Sheet: Overview of the Act (2015) available at https://www.gov.uk/government/uploads/system/

uploads/attachment_data/file/415943/Serious_Crime_Act_Overview.pdf.
110. Charlotte Walker-Osborn and Ben McLeod, 'Getting Tough on Cyber Crime' (1 June 2015) 57/2 ITNOW 32–33. doi:10.1093/itnow/bwv042.
111. See CMA 1990, Sections 1(3), 2(5), (3)6.
112. Section 3(3).
113. Serious Crime Act overview—Gov.uk p.2.
114. Neil MacEwan, 'The Computer Misuse Act 1990: Lessons from Its Past and Predictions for Its Future' (2008) 12 Criminal Law Review 955, 964.
115. Ibid. 964.
116. As Lord Bingham stated in *R v G and Another* [2003] UKHL 50,

> a person acts 'recklessly' with respect to: (i) a circumstance when he is aware of a risk that it exists or will exist; (ii) a result when he is aware of a risk that it will occur; and it is, in the circumstances *known to him*, unreasonable to take the risk.

117. EU Council Framework Decision 2005/222/JHA of 24 February 2005 on attacks against information systems (Framework Decision).
118. Ian J. Lloyd, *Information Technology Law* (6th edn Oxford University Press, Oxford 2011) 234; see Section 3(5)(c).
119. Council of Europe, 'Convention on Cybercrime' (ETS No. 185, Budapest, 2001) (Cybercrime Convention).
120. David Hess and Brian Martin, 'Repression, Backfire, and the Theory of Transformative Events' (2006) 11/2 Mobilization: An International Quarterly 249–267.
121. Jennifer Earl and Jessica L. Beyer, 'The Dynamics of Backlash Online: Anonymous and the Battle for WikiLeaks' (2014) 37 Intersectionality and Social Change 207–233, 209–210.
122. Ibid.
123. Ibid. 210–212.
124. See Sections 1030(b) and (c).
125. Section 206.
126. Fafinski, 'The Security Ramifications of the Police and Justice Act 2006' (86) 10.
127. (c.45).
128. Section 72.

129. See David Kravets, 'Virtual Sit-Ins Doom Online Animal Rights Activists' (*Threat Level*, 16 October 2009) http://www.wired.com/threatlevel/2009/10/animals/. See also *Us V Fullmer* 584 F.3d 132 (3rd Cir. 2009).
130. Chief Judge Stein Schjølberg, '*ITU Global Cybersecurity Agenda [GCA]*' (High Level Experts Group [HLEG] Global Strategic Report, International Telecommunications Union, Geneva 2008) http://www.itu.int/osg/csd/cybersecurity/gca/docs/Report_of_the_Chairman_of_HLEG_to_ITU_SG_03_sept_08.pdf, 26–28.
131. 'Any card, plate, code, account number, electronic serial number, mobile identification number, personal identification number, or other telecommunications service, equipment, or instrument identifier, or other means of account access that can be used, alone or in conjunction with another access device, to obtain money, goods, services, or any other thing of value, or that can be used to initiate a transfer of funds.' 18 U.S.C. Part I, Chapter 47 Section 1029 (Fraud and related activity in connection with access devices) Section 1029(e)(1).
132. See Section 2B1.1(b)(10).
133. Section 3A was introduced by Section 37 of the PJA 2006, in order to incorporate into UK law the Framework Decision (n 117).
134. Stefan Fafinski, 'Computer Misuse: The Implications of the Police and Justice Act 2006' (2008) 72 Journal of Criminal Law 53, 60–62.
135. Cybercrime Convention (n 119) Art. 6.2.
136. Peter Sommer, 'Criminalising Hacking Tools' (2006) 3 Digital Investigation 68, 71; the wide scope of the provision, especially Art. 6.2, has led Bainbridge to propose that the 'likelihood' of criminal use of the article might be construed as an objective criterion founded on the belief of a similarly knowledgeable, reasonable person; David I. Bainbridge, *Introduction to Information Technology Law* (6th edn Pearson Education Limited, Essex 2007) 463.
137. *US v Czubinski*, 106 F. 3d 1069 (1st Cir. 1997) (*Czubinski*).
138. *EF Cultural Travel BV v Explorica, Inc* 274 F.3d 577 (1st Cir. 2001).
139. Ibid. 581–582; it is also established that access is defined as the transmission of code (the Scraper software) to the publicly accessible website of the plaintiff in order to assess the exceeding of authorisation to access.
140. 318 F.3d 58 (1st Cir., 28 January 2003).
141. In addition to the previous rationales, there have been cases where the unintended use of employer information by employees has also been interpreted as eliminating authorisation, rather than exceeding it.

However, these cases are based on a duty of loyalty between employer and employee and will not be as relevant to hacktivist incidents. See, for example, *Shurgard Storage Centers, Inc. v Safeguard Self Storage, Inc* 119 F.Supp.2d 1121 (Dist. Court, Washington D.C. 2000), which follows the termination of authorisation of employees when their motives for accessing information contradict those of the authorising employer. *International Airport Centers, Llc v Citrin,* 440 F.3d 418 (7th Cir. 2006) (*Citrin*) also adopts the elimination of the authorisation approach based on the common law of agency, since the violation of the duty of loyalty of the employee towards the employer terminates their relationship and, consequently, the authorisation of access based on that relationship.

142. *United States v. Nosal,* 676 F.3d 854, (9th Cir. 2012) (en banc)(*Nosal I*).
143. *United States v. Nosal,* 828 F.3d 865 (9th Cir. 2016), reh'g denied and amended by 2016 WL 7190670 (9th Cir. 8 December 2016) (*Nosal II*).
144. For a list of cases following the Nosal rationale, see Stephanie Greene and Christine N. O'Brien, 'Exceeding Authorized Access in the Workplace: Prosecuting Disloyal Conduct under the Computer Fraud and Abuse Act' (2013) 50 American Business Law Journal 1, 22–23.
145. Rep. Zoe Lofgren (D-CA) and Sen. Ron Wyden (D-OR) have suggested the elimination of the term 'exceeding authorised access' and retention only of the term 'access without authorisation,' which will mean as introduced in the Bill suggested by Ms Lofgren '(A) to obtain information on a protected computer; (B) that the accessor lacks authorization to obtain; and (C) by knowingly circumventing one or more technological or physical measures that are designed to exclude or prevent unauthorized individuals from obtaining that information'; see Bill to amend title 18, United States Code, to provide clarification to the meaning of access without authorization, and for other purposes. (2013) 113 Congress, 1st Session, http://www.lofgren.house.gov/images/stories/pdf/aarons%20law%20-%20lofgren%20-%20061913.pdf.
146. Zoe Lofgren and Ron Wyden, 'Introducing Aaron's Law, a Desperately Needed Reform of the Computer Fraud and Abuse Act' (*Wired,* 20 June 2013) http://www.wired.com/opinion/2013/06/aarons-law-is-finally-here/. https://www.eff.org/deeplinks/2011/09/senate-committee-agrees-violating-terms-service-shouldnt.
147. *Electronic Frontier Foundation,* 'Aaron's Law Reintroduced: CFAA Didn't Fix Itself.' 29 April 2015. https://www.eff.org/deeplinks/2015/04/aarons-law-reintroduced-cfaa-didnt-fix-itself.

148. *Facebook, Inc. v. Power Ventures, Inc.*, 828 F.3d 1068, 1075–1079 (9th Cir. 2016).
149. Jamie Williams, 'Ninth Circuit Panel Backs Away From Dangerous Password Sharing Decision—But Creates Even More Confusion About the CFAA' (*Electronic Frontier Foundation*, 15 July 2016) https://www.eff.org/deeplinks/2016/07/ninth-circuit-panel-backs-away-dangerous-password-sharing-decision-creates-even.
150. See *US v Auernheimer*, Criminal No.: 2:11-cr-470 (SDW) (Dist. Court, New Jersey 2013).
151. 648 F.3d 295 (6th Cir. 2011).
152. Orin Kerr, 'United States v. Auernheimer, and Why I Am Representing Auernheimer Pro Bono on Appeal Before the Third Circuit' (*The Volokh Conspiracy*, 21 March 2013) http://volokh.com/2013/03/21/united-states-v-auernheimer-and-why-i-am-representing-auernheimer-pro-bono-on-appeal-before-the-third-circuit/.
153. US Senate Report 104-357 (n 79) 11: 'In sum under the bill, insiders, who are authorized to access a computer, face criminal liability only if they intend to cause damage to a computer, not for recklessly or negligently causing damage. By contrast, outside hackers who break into a computer could be punished for any intentional, reckless, or other damage they cause by their trespass,' cited in *US v Phillips*, 477 F.3d 215, 219 (5th Cir. 2007).
154. *US v Guzner* No. 2:09-cr-00087 (New Jersey Dist. Court) (*Guzner*); Anonymous 'Teenage Hacker Admits Scientology Cyber-Attack USA V. Guzner—Information' (*Secretdox,* 18 October 2008) http://secretdox.wordpress.com/2008/10/18/usa-v-guzner-plea-agreement-for-defendant-dmitriy-guzner/; see also *US v Mettenbrink* Case 2:09-cr-01149-GAF (Dist. Court, California 2010) (*Mettenbrink*); David Kravets 'Guilty Plea in 'Anonymous' DDoS Scientology Attack' (*Threat Level,* 26 January 2010) http://www.wired.com/threatlevel/2010/01/guilty-plea-in-scientology-ddos-attack/; in the case of Mettenbrink, the protester is charged with negligent damage and loss, while in the former, Guzner is charged with intentional damage. Both received one-year imprisonment amongst other sanctions (probation, restitution, community service), which for Mettenbrink was the maximum, while for Guzner the maximum statutory penalty was ten years.
155. [1999] All ER (D) 972 (*Allison).*
156. [1998] 1 Cr App R8 (*Bignell*).

157. *DPP v. Lennon* [2006] All ER (D) 147 (*Lennon*).
158. Ibid.
159. The changes suggested by the new Directive can be found in the guidance (Recital 17) and provisional wording of the illegal access offence (art.3) (unauthorised access in other words), which now explicitly suggest that there should be a requirement of bypassing of technological controls in order for access to be considered unauthorised. More particularly in Recital 17 we can see the following explanation:

    In the context of this Directive, contractual obligations or agreements to restrict access to information systems by way of a user policy or terms of service, as well as labour disputes as regards the access to and use of information systems of an employer for private purposes, should not incur criminal liability where the access under such circumstances would be deemed unauthorised and thus would constitute the sole basis for criminal proceedings.

    Also Art. 3 provides:

    Member States shall take the necessary measures to ensure that, when committed intentionally, the access without right, to the whole or to any part of an information system, is punishable as a criminal offence where committed ***by infringing a security measure****, at least for cases which are not minor. (Emphasis added)*

160. (I) Loss to one or more persons during any one-year period (and, for purposes of an investigation, prosecution, or other proceeding brought by the United States only; loss resulting from a related course of conduct affecting one or more other protected computers) aggregating at least $5,000 in value; (V) damage affecting a computer used by or for an entity of the United States Government in furtherance of the administration of justice, national defense, or national security.
161. *Fullmer* (n 128).
162. The protesters' behaviour also included other illegal elements, such as harassment and threats against employees of animal-testing facilities, in addition to ECD tactics.
163. 18 U.S.C. Part I, Chapter 3, Sections 43(a)–(c). The penalties provided by this act can be very high depending on the damage and losses they cause. For example, if the economic damage to the animal enterprise exceeds the amount of $10,000, the penalty could be a term of impris-

onment of up to five years. (b)(2). The definition of economic damage (d)(3)(A) here includes loss as well.

164. According to the U.S.S.G. Manual 2016 Section 3A1.4, '[i]f the offense is a felony that involved, or was intended to promote, a federal crime of terrorism, increase by 12 levels; but if the resulting offense level is less than level 32, increase to level 32.' This would actually amount to 121–151 months of incarceration and a fine of up to $175,000.
165. Ellen Podgor, 'Computer Crimes and the Patriot Act' 17 Criminal Justice, 61, 62; The USAPA also includes extended provisions, concerning surveillance and interception powers with Internet Service Provider cooperation, securing electronic communications wiretaps and intensifying jurisdiction and enforceability of federal agencies and secret services. Dana L. Bazelon, Yun J. Choi, and Jason F. Conaty, 'Computer Crimes' (2006) 43 American Criminal Law Review 259, 269, 301–302; Tara M. Raghavan, 'In Fear of Cyberterrorism: An Analysis of the Congressional Response' (2003) Journal of Law Technology & Policy 297, 304–305.
166. UK Terrorism Act 2000 (c .11).
167. The Electrohippies Collective (n 27).
168. (1)(4)(a).
169. Fafinski, 'Computer Misuse: The Implications of the Police and Justice Act 2006' (n 133) 55–56.
170. Clive Walker, 'Cyber-Terrorism: Legal Principle and Law in the United Kingdom' (2005) 110 Penn State Law Review 625, 632; Out-Law.com, 'UK Law Makes Hacking an Act of Terrorism' (*Out-Law,* 21 February 2001) http://www.out-law.com/default.aspx?page=1409; Walden (n 40) 183; The Electrohippies Collective (n 27).
171. Terrorism Act 2000, Section 1(4).
172. See account of global hacktivist protests against Mexican President Website and Frankfurt Stock Exchange website. Dorothy E. Denning, 'Hacktivism: An Emerging Threat to Diplomacy' (2000) 77 Foreign Service Journal 43.
173. Chief Judge Stein Schjølberg, '*ITU Global Cybersecurity Agenda [GCA]*' (High Level Experts Group [HLEG] Global Strategic Report, International Telecommunications Union, Geneva 2008) http://www.itu.int/osg/csd/cybersecurity/gca/docs/Report_of_the_Chairman_of_HLEG_to_ITU_SG_03_sept_08.pdf; Logan also argues that the Terrorist Act 2006 is in fact so extensive as to threaten those who express a controversial political opinion with deportation from the UK. Christina

C. Logan, 'Liberty or Safety: Implications of the USA Patriot Act and the UK's Anti-Terror Laws on Freedom of Expression and Free Exercise of Religion' (2006) 37 Seton Hall Law Review 863, 865.

174. Clay Wilson, 'Botnets, Cybercrime, and Cyberterrorism: Vulnerabilities and Policy Issues for Congress' (Library of Congress, Congressional Research Service, Washington D.C. 2008) 4; Harinda Vidanage, 'Rivalry in Cyberspace and Virtual Contours of a New Conflict Zone: The Sri Lankan Case' in Athina Karatzogianni (ed), *Cyberconflicts and Global Politics* (Routledge, Oxon 2009) 146–161, 159.
175. Cited in Ricardo Dominguez, 'Electronic Disobedience Post-9/11' (2008) 22 Third Text 661, 663.
176. Walker (n 172) 642.
177. Ibid. 643.
178. Samuel (n 29) 54–55; Ayres and Braithwaite (n 6) 25.
179. Roger Eatwell, 'Community Cohesion and Cumulative Extremism in Contemporary Britain' (2006) 77 The Political Quarterly 204.
180. Jon Leyden, 'Anonymous Unsheathes New, Potent Attack Weapon' (*The Register*, 4 August 2011) http://www.theregister.co.uk/2011/08/04/anon_develops_loic_ddos_alternative/; Sean Gallagher, 'High Orbits and Slowlorises: Understanding the Anonymous Attack Tools' (*Ars Technica*, 16 February 2012). http://arstechnica.com/business/news/2012/02/high-orbits-and-slowlorises-understanding-the-anonymous-attack-tools.ars.
181. Apart from USAPA there are also other relevant acts such as the Homeland Security Act of 2002 116 Stat. 2135 and the Intelligence Reform and Terrorism Prevention Act of 2004, 118 Stat. 3638, 2004 (IRTPA). The US Criminal Code also includes an abundance of provisions that relate to terrorism, which are out with the scope of the current analysis; also, in the UK, beyond the Terrorism Act of 2000, which is the most relevant for our case, there is an abundance of interrelated and amending counterterrorism acts, such as the Anti-Terrorism, Crime and Security Act of 2001 (c.24), Prevention of Terrorism Act 2005 (c.2), and the Terrorism Act 2006 (c.11), which all constitute a concerted effort to intensify the government's and law enforcement's capacity to monitor and punish activities which might be even remotely and inchoately related to terrorism. For more detail, see Clive Walker, 'Clamping Down on Terrorism in the United Kingdom' (2006) 4 Journal of International Criminal Justice 1137; Logan (n 175) The arbitrariness has been somehow ameliorated with the changes introduced by The Terrorism Act

2000 (Remedial) Order 2011, No.631, which requires reasonable suspicion for the stop and search powers of the authorities.

182. Logan (n 175) 869–871; Fafinski, 'Computer Misuse: The Implications of the Police and Justice Act 2006' (n 133) 56.
183. Jarrett et al. (n 91), 3–4.
184. (n 76).
185. Ibid., Section 207.
186. Richard Walton, 'The Computer Misuse Act' (2006) 11 Information Security Technical Report 39, 42; see CMA, Sections 4–5.
187. Ellinor Mills, 'Anonymous to Target Iran with DoS Attack' (*CNet,* 29 April 2011) https://www.cnet.com/news/anonymous-to-target-iran-with-dos-attack/; Mojit Kumar, 'Anonymous Hit Egyptian Government Websites as #Opegypt' (*The Hacker News,* 9 December 2012) http://thehackernews.com/2012/12/anonymous-hit-egyptian-government.html.
188. Examples of harmonisation efforts are the promulgation and ratification of the Cybercrime Convention (n 119) by many states or the Framework Decision (n 117) on attacks against information systems, criminalising denial-of-service attacks and distribution of hacking software, as well as the discussions for a new cybercrime/cyberwarfare convention and a new EU Cybercrime Directive.

    OUT-LAW, 'Commission Proposes New EU Cybercrime Law' (*The Register,* 11 October 2010) http://www.theregister.co.uk/2010/10/11/eu_new_cybercrime_law/print.html; Daniel Shane, 'Think Tank Calls for "Geneva Convention" on Cyber War' (*Information Age,* 4 February 2011) http://www.information-age.com/technology/security/1599193/think-tank-calls-for-'geneva-convention'-on-cyber-war.
189. In the US, at the congressional level, there are multiple committees with their relevant subcommittees that have jurisdiction over cybercrime decisions and different approaches and interests, consequently leading to a fragmentation of oversight and lack of uniformity in approaching issues of online criminality. See Benjamin S. Buckland, Fred Schreier, and Theodor H. Winkler, 'Democratic Governance Challenges of Cyber Security' (*Geneva Security Forum,* 2012) http://genevasecurityforum.org/files/DCAF-GSF-cyber-Paper.pdf, 19.
190. BBC, 'Gary McKinnon Extradition to US Blocked by Theresa May' (*BBC,* 16 October 2012) http://www.bbc.co.uk/news/uk-19957138; as is submitted in the APIG Report for the CMA, there has never been

an extradition of offenders to the UK. All Party Internet Group (APIG), 'Revision of the Computer Misuse Act': Report on an inquiry by the All Party Internet Group (2004) http://www.cullen-international.com/cullen/multi/national/uk/laws/cmareport.pdf, 15.

191. McGoogan Cara, 'British Hacker Lauri Love to Be Extradited to the US for "Accessing Government Computers"' (*The Telegraph*, 14:57, sec. 2016) http://www.telegraph.co.uk/technology/2016/09/16/british-hacker-lauri-love-to-be-extradited-to-the-us-for-access/.
192. Aas (n 38) 173–175.
193. Gregor Urbas, 'Criminalising Computer Misconduct: Some Legal and Philosophical Concerns' (2006) 14 Asia Pacific Law Review 95, 107; Podgor (n 167) 736; different perceptions of free speech and legal protesting could influence how these acts are perceived, while different criminal approaches with less punitive frameworks could allow for more protests.

5

Enforcing Crime Control and Hacktivism

1 Introduction

The previous chapter highlighted the potential in terms of normative sociopolitical dictates as well as legal tools and how they might have a propensity to produce inefficacious and unjust responses when dealing with hacktivism. This indicates that there is potentially a need for those implementing these legal tools and managing decisions reflecting penal policy and public interest and justice to temper the potential for excessive and populist responses that the current sociopolitical norms and legal tools facilitate.

The actors who take these decisions are the prosecutors and courts and this chapter will focus on assessing these two institutions. At the end of this chapter, the role of private actors will also be discussed, as they play a role as well in the enforcement of these norms and laws in cyberspace, directly or indirectly. Let us begin this analysis by looking at the role of prosecutors.

V. Karagiannopoulos, *Living With Hacktivism*, Palgrave Studies in Cybercrime and Cybersecurity, https://doi.org/10.1007/978-3-319-71758-6_5

2 Prosecutors and Hacktivism

2.1 The Multifaceted Role of Prosecutors

Prosecutors are dominant actors in criminal justice processes, as they have the power to decide whether to press criminal charges and what the nature of those charges should be, and to terminate prosecutions.[1] For example, the *US Attorneys' Manual* provides that prosecutors are responsible for initiating and declining prosecution, selecting charges, entering into plea agreements, opposing offers to plead nolo contendere, and entering into non-prosecution agreements in return for cooperation and participating in sentencing.[2]

Although prosecutors cannot and should not act as substitutes of the legislature and the courts, they usually retain interpretive freedom regarding legislation and influence sentencing as well.[3] Prosecutors are often perceived and expected to act, not only as law-enforcers, but as more creative agents with multiple roles, from interpreters of law and state policy facilitators to the champions of community sentiment.[4] These multiple functions are reflected in the number of elements prosecutors must assess when deciding on prosecutions. As the *US Attorneys' Manual*[5] suggests, prosecutors should take into account the priorities of federal law enforcement, the deterrent effect the prosecution will have on the offender, the nature and seriousness of the crime, and the history of the accused, his or her personal blameworthiness, his or her willingness to collaborate with the authorities for resolving other crimes, and the consequences of convicting that person.[6] If the prosecutor decides that the person was culpable only for a minor participation in a criminal conspiracy and that the motive behind such an act was morally worthy, he/she could decide that prosecution would not be the best solution.[7]

Prosecutors' wide discretion is normally unreviewable since they are considered the most knowledgeable regarding each case's details, the deterrence value, the state's enforcement goals, and the link of the case to an overall enforcement plan.[8] In the UK, for example, prosecutors decide on the adequacy of evidence for ensuring conviction and also establish that there is a serious public interest in pursuing the case and punishing the offender, while retaining the final say, even after a review process.[9] Prosecutors in the US can prosecute based on the belief that there is probable cause that a crime has been committed—an even more relaxed criterion than the UK's realistic prospect of conviction.[10] However, even for the stricter UK prosecutorial standard of requiring a realistic chance to convict, the expansion of criminal law both in terms of criminalising behaviours with overlapping provisions and extending culpability renders most prosecutions much more viable. In both jurisdictions, the prosecutors' views are considered acts of the executive that courts cannot review on the basis of the principle of separation of power.[11] Only recently, UK courts have demonstrated a tendency to more actively review prosecutorial decisions, mainly to assess whether prosecutors might have disregarded prosecutorial guidelines and policies.[12]

Prosecutorial discretion also creates serious concerns for the balance of power between the various actors of the criminal justice process. The power of prosecutors has been further extended due to the promulgation of a wide and overlapping array of criminal offences that give prosecutors the tools to pursue prosecutions as they see fit.[13] This current expansive and punitive trend in legislating, in addition to the wide, unreviewable discretion, has transformed the traditional role of prosecutors, giving them a dominant role at the expense of judges, juries, parole authorities, and defence lawyers, and, ultimately, offenders to exercise important rights.[14] The war on crime has also increased tolerance of power abuses by the authorities, presumably realised for the sake of public safety.[15] Particularly in cases that attract media attention, which could include hacktivist exploits against big corporations and governmental sites, prosecutors may be reluctant to demonstrate leniency for fear of appearing irresponsible or inconsiderate of the public's safety.[16] The cases of Aaron Swartz or 'Weev' are characteristic of such a trend.

This tendency is further reinforced by the generally accepted, yet—as research has proven[17]—controversial presumption that the public would want harsher penalties for offenders than those handed down. Prosecutors often feel the pressure to appease the potentially media-inflated, moral panics and this can lead them to avoid decisive punishment reductions or non-prosecutions, in order to satisfy the parts of society that promote securitisation and risk control, from politicians and security firms to the media or the more conservative part of the public.[18]

A related consequence of the prosecutorial trend to seek prosecutions as a public/media appeasement strategy is the frequent phenomenon of prosecuting small numbers of virtual sit-in participants quite aggressively in terms of making examples out of them and thus presumably reinforcing the deterrent effect. The prosecutorial strictness against the Paypal 14 and Aaron Swartz, which allegedly contributed to his suicide, are indicative of such polarisation between prosecutors and online activists. Moreover, although there is a definite practicality as well as 'public deterrence effect' justification in prosecuting a small number of the multiple participants who had taken part in the PayPal protests, which had seen a large number of participants in 2010, the selectiveness of these prosecutions generates serious concerns regarding fairness and attribution of overall justice. For example, as mentioned previously, Eric Rosol was fined for the full amount of $183,000 that Koch Bros decided to pay to a consulting company for advice in preparation for the virtual sit-in in which Rosol participated for only 60 seconds. As Omidyar has argued, even though he is coming from the victim's side, the selective prosecutions of a small number of protesters for protests that involve thousands of people would seem to be unjust.[19]

2.2 The Importance of Plea Bargaining

The prosecutors' widely unreviewable discretion is also combined with the proliferation of plea bargaining, which is employed to resolve the vast majority of cases in the US.[20] Facilitated by multiple overlapping laws, plea bargaining allows for prosecutors to be not only the initial assessors, but also the ultimate adjudicators, since most of the cases never reach the courtroom.[21] Alschuler, in his criticism of plea bargaining, argues that a substantial part of the actual penalty imposed relies on a tactical decision that is independent of any of the proper aims of criminal proceedings or the alleged offenders' actions or personal characteristics.[22] Considering that prosecutors become also adjudicators of facts and culpability through the process of offering guilty plea bargains to alleged offenders, the process of fact finding and contextual assessment of motivations is significantly shorter and, inevitably, not as meticulous.[23] For activities that might fit the wording of the law and for which the crucial distinction might lie in the actual context of law-breaking, such as hacktivist incidents, the reduced attention and time span devoted to assessing context and motivations might result in harsher prosecutorial assessments.

Unchecked prosecutorial discretion has led to unequal treatment of suspects and to factually innocent citizens succumbing to prosecutorial pressures to plead guilty.[24] As Davis argues, prosecutors who feel they might not be able to achieve a conviction in court will have strong incentives to induce suspects to accept plea bargains, which would guarantee them an otherwise doubtful conviction,[25] especially since in the US prosecutors can prosecute even if acquittal seems likely.[26] Prosecutors tend to favour increasingly punitive solutions because the prospect of very high penalties induces alleged offenders to accept the lower penalties that prosecutors offer for guilty pleas.[27] Alternatively, they often employ many felony charges against alleged offenders, a practice which, essentially, increases the risk of even one charge being accepted by the court, thus naturally inducing offenders to concede to plea bargains.[28] We have seen how the PayPal 14 and other Anonymous members, like Metterbrink and Guzner, have pled guilty to the charges offered during plea negotiations, despite their belief that they had not committed a serious crime for fear of risking a conviction and higher penalties in court.

In the UK, arbitrary abuses of plea bargaining are more restricted due to the many safeguards that prevent prosecutorial excesses, such as the need for a realistic prospect of conviction and the prohibiting of prosecutors from using many additional charges in order to induce pleas.[29] However, it has been argued that, both in the US and in the UK, plea bargaining has been used as a tool for increasing the prosecution of minor offenders, while more serious, resource-intensive, and hard-to-convict cases are bypassed; this has been called 'defining deviance down.'[30] Considering the usually minor nature of the offences perpetrated by hacktivists compared to everyday cybercrime, such as ransomware, and the ease with which they could be apprehended in many cases, we can see how this trend could make them ideal targets for the authorities in their efforts to demonstrate cybercrime is being dealt with.

Consequently, even though plea bargain penalties might appear milder than what sentences could be incurred in court, the fact that prosecutors often have the upper hand to convince suspects to plead guilty and the fact that many of them could be innocent or at least guilty of less serious offences than those they are charged for[31] would result in higher punishments than those deserved and would also deprive the public of hearing political disobedience cases in court. Again the US system is far more extreme, allowing the potential range of sentencing for multiple offences to be more extensive and reliant on prosecutorial desires than the more moderate UK system where guilty pleas entail more fixed reduction rates.[32]

This trend is further exacerbated by the discouragingly expensive and slow nature of court proceedings which often appears daunting and can easily exhaust defendants, financially and psychologically, and induce them to choose the faster and, on its face, less arduous and risky process of guilty pleas.[33] Hacktivists, being often young,[34] would usually wish to avoid the complications and higher sentences of an actual trial, thus agreeing to plead guilty. Even if the case does not result in an actual conviction for hacktivists, the process of being arrested and investigated, as well as being charged with a felony, can have a very serious impact on those facing these charges both practically and psychologically.[35] Consequently, the cybercrime regime, with its broad interpretations, overlapping provisions, and high penalty range is an ideal tool for prosecutors to achieve pleas, but also in portraying punitive guilty plea offers as lenient, compared to what the actual penalty could have been.

Prosecutorial trends are also influenced by the legal training of prosecutors, which is adversarial in common law jurisdictions and managerial in terms of proving efficiency through achieving convictions.[36] Prosecutors are often educated to view any hacking-related activity as generally anti-social[37] and that hinders efforts to objectively assess motivations and intentions behind controversial cyberactivities conducted at a distance.[38] As it has been argued, despite the fact that hacktivists mostly desire to shame their targets, rather than inflict actual damage, 'law enforcement officials are certainly going to want to make an example of anyone they can bring in'.[39] The same goes for the police, which wants to demonstrate maximum efficiency in dealing with the new major threat of cybercrime and thus focuses on investigations and arrests of easier-to-resolve cases. The aggressive manner with which some of the PayPal 14 hacktivists were apprehended is characteristic of such efforts as well.

In sum, the various criminal justice trends, professional mentalities, and practical concerns of prosecutors seem to reinforce the considerations identified in the previous chapter. If based on prosecutorial discretion, it seems very likely that the realisation of the concerns highlighted in relation to the sociopolitical influences and the legal landscape impacting on hacktivism would be exacerbated rather than tempered. A potential last resort for some more balance would be the judiciary.

3 The Role of Courts in Regulating Hacktivism

3.1 The General Power of the Judiciary and the Role of Sentencing Guidelines

The role of courts in ultimately enforcing and balancing the various normative and legislative policies with rule of law and justice principles is crucial in the process of assessing the importance and impact of courts when dealing with hacktivism. Courts normally shape sentencing decisions according to moral considerations as well as the offence's impact on society and decide on whether and how severely to punish.[40] Although the courts had in previous decades been a strong faction of governance, combining elements of legislative and executive power with personal expertise and neutrality, their social policymaking power has gradually been weakened.[41] Their powers have been tempered due to a rift with those exercising the executive and legislative powers, with prosecutors gradually shifting responsibility for lenient punishments of offenders to the liberal tendencies of courts and aligning with the legislature in weakening the judiciary's role.[42] Discretion has currently shifted to the executive, despite prosecutors lacking the judicial culture of neutrality, with prosecutorial decisions, as has been seen, being influenced more by managerial concerns and adversarial mentalities.[43] The weakening of courts, which are those most specialised in assessing contextual and moral elements within the criminal justice process, inevitably leads to lesser attention being given to motives and sociopolitical conditions and weaken the capacity of judges to suggest mitigation or exoneration.

Such a trend would inevitably impact on hacktivism assessments due to their nature. From the hacktivism-related cases we have discussed, only a few have gone through to a full hearing, as in many instances they have instead been resolved by guilty pleas. Considering the important role of the courts in assessing context, the resolution of most cases beforehand impacts on the independent attribution of justice by the judiciary, as is to be expected. It would have to be noted here that the results are mixed when courts actually hear hacktivist cases. For example, the case of Vogel in Germany or Weev's case in the US led to acquittals.

This tendency to detract discretionary power from courts is also exacerbated by the subordination of judicial decision-making to sentencing guidelines that, in turn, have been amended, so as to increasingly limit judicial discretion.[44] The sentencing guidelines have been considered a crucial sentencing tool in both the US and the UK, even after they were made non-mandatory in the former.[45] Irrespective of this, US courts must still consider the guidelines and are allowed to depart from them only if the sentencing council has not considered certain mitigating or aggravating factors.[46] Nevertheless, departure rates are higher in the UK than in the US as the criminal history is calculated differently and could cause departures (not factored in the guidelines, as in the US). In most cases, however, departures are upward, as sentencing guidelines tend to focus more on aggravating, rather than on mitigating circumstances.[47]

Moreover, as we have seen, cybercrime laws have focused on damage and loss, which poses challenges in terms of defining and calculating penalties, and the broadness with which both these elements are defined can often lead to very high assessments amounting to analogously high punishment.[48] For example, after 2001, in addition to eliminating the need to prove intent for causing a specific amount of loss, courts in the US have gradually extended the range of types of losses that could be calculated in order to assess the felonious character of the offences and the extent of the penalties.[49] Even in cases where protesters might take precautions to minimise damages, prosecutors can decide to accept the inclusion of various unforeseeable damages/losses in their assessment, which will eventually increase potential sanctions. US courts have also exacerbated the tendency to accommodate victims, having often accepted with little challenge the victims' damage and loss assessments.[50] The case of Weev is important here, since the defendant was found guilty on the basis of a claimed loss of AT&T caused by the company deciding to send out letters to all it customers regarding the breach of privacy, even though it had done so successfully via email already.[51] Similarly, Rosol was asked to pay the full $183,000 as a fine for his participation in a virtual sit-in in addition to two years of probation.

Moreover, the US Sentencing Guidelines have recently included pecuniary losses that do not even have to satisfy the criterion of reasonable predictability.[52] The guidelines also distinguish penalty ranges based mainly on economic criteria, and they disregard instrumental concerns in relation to potential benefits from benign hacking.[53] Mitigating factors are much less explicit and less numerous than aggravating factors, which are by contrast very detailed.[54] Despite the contextual criteria introduced by the sentencing guidelines, in the US, these guidelines contain many more aggravating than mitigating circumstances, eventually allowing for multiple increases in punishment ranges through similar criteria.[55] For example, in Weev's case, his sentence range was increased for use of both sophisticated means and a special skill, which were considered overlapping factors.[56]

In the UK, there are also similar concerns with the Sentencing Guidelines,[57] which constitute mandatory guidance for UK courts,[58] as they demonstrate an increasing importance given to culpability, the limits of which have been extended, but also to foreseeable harms, which can include loss assessments.[59] More particularly, Section 143(1) of the UK Criminal Justice Act 2003 clarifies that seriousness should be assessed based not only on already caused harms, but also on any intended or foreseeable harms. The Guidelines on Seriousness Section 1(11) provide that, where no actual harm has occurred, courts will assess the relative dangerousness of the offender's conduct in relation to the likelihood of harm occurring and the gravity of the potential harm.[60] However, it is provided that assessments should be tempered by the level of culpability, which would be determined by the nature of motives, the premeditation or spontaneity of the act, or the existence of a relationship of trust between the victim and the offender.[61] It is unclear, though, how the court would be able to confidently assess such abstract concepts, that is, the likelihood and gravity of the potential harm, especially when these assessments might involve abstract information and network resources and elaborate technical detail.

A guidelines-based calculation of sentences in addition to the open-ended calculation of abstract concepts such as damage and loss for immaterial property such as information/data creates generalised and also vague criteria for assessing punishment severity. Reliance on general guidelines for sentencing is, of course, a wider issue with the current structure of the criminal justice system, but can also be very detrimental for hacktivists, resulting in higher penalties, even if these are to be hypothesised when discussing guilty pleas. This is because the existence of pre-defined, generalised mitigating and mainly aggravating circumstances creates a more mechanistic way of assessing punishment ranges and, therefore, would often generate problems for assessing deviant acts, the moral elements of which might not be translatable into fixed sentencing criteria. It is, however, exactly these elements that highlight the distinction of moral hacktivist actions from criminal cybersecurity compromises and support the hacktivists' claim to more lenient responses by the courts.

3.2 The Influence of Judicial Culture

The above-mentioned concerns become even more pertinent when one considers how trends in judicial decision-making and legal reasoning can strongly influence the judiciary.[62] As Holmes has argued,

> [t]he felt necessities of the time, the prevalent moral and political theories, intuitions of public policy, avowed or unconscious, even the prejudices, which judges share with their fellow men, have a good deal more to do than the syllogism in determining the rules by which men should be governed.[63]

Research has also demonstrated that dominant rationales are bound to influence decisions in a discriminatory way against those labelled as anti-social.[64] Therefore, the prominent normative and legal trends of security and risk control will, according to what Holmes describes, influence judges' perceptions of risk-generating behaviours, with hacktivism being one such category of risk-rich activities. As Garland clarifies,

> the social and economic determinants of 'the outside world' certainly affect the conduct of penal agents (police officers, judges, prison officials, etc.), but they do so indirectly, through the gradual reshaping of the rules of thought and action within a field that has what sociologists call a 'relative autonomy.'[65]

Moreover, judges are also influenced by their ideologies and the socio-political specificities in which they live, work, and develop.[66] Consequently, in addition to established social norms directly influencing judicial decision-making, the documented lack of trust of the public towards the judiciary and the calls for more punitive sentences could have an impact on judges' sentencing choices, especially for high-profile cases.[67] The aforementioned stereotyping of hacktivists as criminals or terrorists, subconsciously internalised and integrated in decisional patterns, is also likely to influence judicial responses and judges would inevitably have to exercise additional effort to remain unbiased.[68]

A potential implicit bias could also be connected with the ideological influences flowing from the usually high socio-economic background of judges trying such serious cases.[69] The background of judges could impede their understanding and acceptability of radical and innovative protesting of marginalised minorities, for which, however, electronic civil disobedience (ECD) might often be one of the few feasible and accessible dissent tactics. Moreover, the understanding of online activist tactics will also be hindered by the judges' level of familiarisation with new technologies, as their cognitive background is important for justifying their ultimate decision.[70] Judges might not be in tune with the latest technological advances and cyberspace debates, and the confusion that is often evident in disparate cybercriminal law interpretations and decisions inevitably impacts on the justness and applicability of judicial decisions.[71] The shaping of judicial opinions on technical issues also becomes more reliant on security experts' and victims' assessments, which can often exaggerate the dangers and implications of the offence in question for their own interests.[72]

3.3 The Role of the Jury

The jury is also a fundamental part of the judicial system. Juries operate as the voice of the community and since criminal trials are evaluations of culpability, jurors can decide on the suspect's blameworthiness by assessing the actual facts of each case.[73] Juridical assessments, apart from echoing the public sentiment towards an offence, normally provide a limitation to overcriminalisation, governmental excesses, and the enforcement of obsolete laws,[74] while also informing the legislature, the executive, and the courts of current moral perceptions towards certain behaviours.[75]

Sentencing decisions can be influenced by the jury's power to acquit, even against law and fact or, more moderately, to return a verdict for a lesser offence.[76] The power of the jury to acquit, despite condemning facts, has been named 'jury nullification,' because juries ultimately nullify the law they have declined to enforce—a power relating to the ancient precedent of juridical powers and due process rights.[77] In instances of nullification acquittals, jurors usually consider the law supporting the prosecution unjust or regard the specific case as out of the scope and purpose of the law, and thus applying it would be against their conscience and beyond their role of assessing guilt and attributing justice.[78] Nullification or mitigation could also happen in cases where none of these elements pertains, but the jury thinks the offender had overwhelming moral reasons for his or her actions.[79] As West argues, in the US, constitutional amendments and rules protecting jury verdicts allow the jury to acquit a defendant without explaining its decisions and without the decision being appealable due to the double-jeopardy clause.[80] Therefore, the judiciary has the potential, in theory, to facilitate more procedurally consistent and substantively just processes and decisions. This would be important for hacktivists attempting to avoid sanction by promoting their moral motivations should their cases reach the court.

Jury nullifications, however, are extremely rare and juries are also influenced by tendencies that dominate the contemporary sociopolitical realities and discourses and, subsequently, shape their cognitive experience and common symbolisms from which they can draw analogies.[81] Therefore, public beliefs about crime online and publicised, salient events can greatly influence jurors' perceptions with a great likelihood of a negative predisposition towards hacktivism in accordance with the pertaining moral panics about cybercrime. Any potential jury bias will also be harder to overcome, since the majority will be lacking the strong disciplined education for objectivity and reliance on the legal principle that judges have.[82] To make matters worse, prosecutors can also exert a strong influence on jurors. As Chief Judge Wachtler said humorously, juries could be convinced to even indict a ham sandwich.[83]

Even if juries could be sympathetic to the protesters' causes, the fact that the courts have generally precluded the hearing of defences on behalf of political protesters in the past further restricts the ability of hacktivists to present and explain their case to a jury in more detail.[84] The contemporary trend to prevent the necessity/higher law defences from being heard by the juries is especially important for political protesters' cases, since research has aptly demonstrated that juries will often use their nullification powers if they are allowed to hear these defences.[85] Consequently, the elimination of that prospect for the jury and the defendants deprives political protesters of a potentially mitigating solution. This becomes more important when considered in conjunction with research showing that the public tends to be more lenient when allowed to hear the specific details of a criminal case and allowing the above-mentioned defences could provide an extensive account of the motives and the whole context of the protest. In fact, as research has shown, jurors are prone to find a person less blameworthy if he or she has a good motive or generally good character.[86] In addition to general trends to consider motivation-related evidence as irrelevant,[87] this rejection becomes even more important, particularly since juries have demonstrated leniency when familiarised with the facts of a political protest, despite its controversy.[88]

The denial of the opportunity to assess culpability more holistically often leads to a more mechanistic application of laws and again seems to disregard crucial contextual differentiations between *prima facie* similar offences and leaves the jury bound by judicial instruction and prosecutorial influence. In the case of hacktivism, bypassing the opportunity for juries to express their views on the contextual and moral elements that influence the protesters' ultimate blameworthiness could result in sentencing that is inconsistent with public perceptions and, thus, more likely to be disproportionate. As discussed previously, this can lead (and has already led) to further protests in the form of backlash, which decrease rather than increase online safety for the public overall.

4 Private Actors, Law Enforcement, and Hacktivism

4.1 Private Corporations and Collaboration with the Authorities

The importance of private actors in regulating online behaviours has been documented even from the early debates between cyberlaw theorists, as an inevitable reality of the structural nature of the medium. Private actors have gradually attained a prominent role in regulating cyberspace. They can do this directly through a combination of infrastructure control, private terms of use, and code-based tools, or indirectly, through lobbying governments for policies[89] or as proxies for enforcing political decisions.[90] The current focus on risk minimisation and information control has eventually resulted in incentivising private actors, mainly those creating and managing Internet networks and software, into abiding or contributing to the current crime and information control trends.

The creation of software that facilitates control has been a result not only of direct but mostly indirect ordering. The promulgation of regulations by the legislatures and regulatory bodies influences other stakeholders, such as code writers and corporate actors, and induces changes in software and hardware functions and Internet structures.[91] Governments thus employ incentivising or coercive mechanisms to steer code-making and corporate policy towards facilitating information control.[92] The opaque and automated nature of code-based solutions that do not need to go through a public legitimisation process as laws and public policies do[93] can further exacerbate the danger of imposing unreviewable restrictions on speech and privacy through private actors employing technological controls or contractual conditions on users.[94]

The influence of private actors' actions and policies in accordance with the crime control policies that current norms and laws dictate can, thus, impact on hacktivism, both in terms of organising and communicating their message and also in terms of facilitating their surveillance. As McNamee suggests, for example, although some measures might be taken in order to prevent the potential for excessive or arbitrary policing by private actors, the political pressures, the increasing legislated obligations for such companies, the lack of strict procedural safeguards, and the fact that the preservation of rights is not a task for private actors result in invasions of free speech and privacy.[95]

Current legislative initiatives have had an impact on Internet service and content providers, transforming them into police enforcers by enabling or forcing the unaccountable and extensive information exchange between the authorities and the private corporations managing information production and exchange platforms. For example, the US government passed a law that granted legal immunity to many US telecommunications companies, thus protecting them from lawsuits that had arisen from the role of these companies in warrantless surveillance of online activities of users.[96] The recent revelations by Edward Snowden regarding the US National Security Agency Prism project, which involves generalised surveillance of online communications is indicative of the extent of the collaboration of governments with private telecommunications companies in policing.[97] The European Court of Human Rights in *KU v Finland*[98] has also accepted that legislation legitimises Internet Service Providers' (ISPs') data retention and sharing with the authorities, especially for reasons relating to crime prevention.[99] More recently, the new Investigatory Powers Act 2016 in the UK expects that ISPs will preserve all user-browsing information for a year and make it available to the authorities, if necessary. Therefore, despite an expectation that private companies which have an important role to play in facilitating speech and privacy rights of citizens online would have some obligation to preserve the rights of their users,[100] in many cases the current climate, legislation, and political pressures make this obligation far harder to abide by.

Even when companies want to prioritise user privacy, opposing the authorities might be hard to achieve in the current climate of crime control and terrorist fear. The recent debate between Apple and the FBI over the provision of a tool for bypassing password encryption on iPhones in relation to a terrorism-related investigation is indicative of the heavy pressure that governments can put on even the most powerful technological corporations. Although Apple proved resilient in this recent situation, other companies have not managed to fend off such pressures. Twitter, for example, had initially declined to disclose data of its users, but was eventually forced to comply with a decision by a San Francisco court requesting the private details of bloggers, even if the illegal act was realised from citizens abroad using the service.[101] The difficulties for users to preserve their privacy rights here is evident as they would be required to access the San Francisco courts, which would make the review of these decisions very costly and inaccessible for most users.[102] Additionally, as Levy reports, Google or Comcast, for example, customarily avoid asking any questions or provide notice to customers when they are served subpoenas to disclose customer information regarding a criminal investigation and instead focus only on whether the form has been filled out correctly and has been issued by courts of competent jurisdiction.[103] He acknowledges, though, that ISPs, as opposed to Google, would not have access to the speech they transmit and, hence, they could not check on the potential reasonableness of the subpoena claim.[104]

Considering these issues, online activists cannot rely on private actors to protect the privacy of protesters against governmental requests and challenge the authorities, since most companies will want to avoid coming into conflict with state agencies. After all, large online conglomerates have collaborated even with the most oppressive of regimes at times. The case of Yahoo, Microsoft, Google, or Cisco collaborating with the Chinese regime that expects the companies operating in China to filter politically controversial communications, police content, and even allow the authorities access to private user accounts is the most characteristic example.[105]

4.2 Private Regulators and Hacktivist Speech

Having an impact on hacktivist expression does not have to rely solely on preventing the protest itself or criminalising it, but on a more preventive level, private actors can weaken the impact of the political collective and its speech and organising efforts by hindering their audience access. Legislation relating to the management of content in online communications encourages ISPs to censor controversial speech and activities based on notices for the takedown of alleged illegal content. For example, the Communications Decency Act[106] and the Digital Millennium Copyright Act[107] in the US and the E-commerce Directive in the EU,[108] which has been transposed into UK law by the Electronic Commerce (EC Directive) Regulations of 2002,[109] all include 'safe harbour' provisions that incentivise companies hosting online content to expeditiously take down postings, groups, or even websites that they have been notified are illegal, often without examining the validity of the claim.[110]

As McNamee discusses,

> [c]ompanies such as Facebook come under intense pressure in relation to individual incidents that attract the interest of politicians and/or the press. These create strong pressure for private companies to regulate their clients in order to prevent possibly illegal activities (and this will be exacerbated by any weakening of the intermediary liability regimes), it also creates pressure to regulate any activity that creates a liability or public relations risk for the company. Intermediaries design their terms and conditions in order to prepare for exactly such an eventuality.[111]

One can easily infer from these comments that if political expression was considered controversial or if a group was considered to be in the government/police spotlight, large Internet companies would prefer to take them down rather than be considered to be contributing or supporting controversial groups and political speech.

Furthermore, intermediaries usually manage their services based on contract terms and conditions that are non-negotiable. These 'terms of use' establish certain standards of allowable speech, which are mainly enforced with the help of software that automatically assesses the existence of those standards and by responding to user notifications. The usual vagueness and arbitrary nature of the terms regarding allowable speech enable content-managing companies to discretionarily limit expression and user interaction to what they would consider acceptable.

Moreover, as Nunziato submits, Google and other companies, based on their sponsored advertisements regulated by their terms of service, have consistently declined to host advertisements of controversial political advocacy groups with a politically or religiously critical content.[112] Due to the dominant market position of such prominent content- and service-providing companies, private policies can result in the censoring of a great amount of protectable political or social criticism, which will not be accessible on prime search engine spaces or popular websites.[113]

In this risk-averse climate, activist groups' views that could often entail much controversy would thus be in greater danger of facing censorship, either as a result of code-based, opaque enforcement of terms of use or because of more conservative user flagging. For example, both Twitter and Facebook have censored Anonymous' accounts regarding various operations or blocked the hashtag of Anonymous.[114] Legislation is, essentially, structured in such a way that it encourages and justifies as safe corporate practice wholesale infringements on speech and privacy so that online corporations may avoid the potential of liability. Simultaneously, these aforementioned safe harbour provisions and the policies they encourage fail to promote the potential for more stakeholders to engage in democratic deliberation and thus ignore their implicit human rights responsibilities for promoting speech and association in a generally privatised cyberspace.

On the same note, online money-processing services, such as PayPal or Visa, have similarly demonstrated a tendency to succumb to political pressures, if not pre-empt them. The most typical example is the events surrounding Operation Payback/Avenge Assange, where these companies declined to offer their services to WikiLeaks regarding the processing of donations, despite there being no criminal charges against the latter's activities at the time.[115] The CEO of eBay (parent company of PayPal), Pierre Omidyar, has explicitly highlighted the following regarding the withdrawal of services to WikiLeaks during the 2010 revelations:

> Today, it appears, notification of a criminal investigation is enough to force businesses whose cause is not the First Amendment to cut off a publisher the way Amazon, PayPal, Visa and MasterCard each have done WikiLeaks. … Unlike the press barons of old, the executives of these businesses cannot tell their shareholders that it will hurt their company more to cave on a matter of principle than to drop a customer.[116]

WikiLeaks won the case against Visa a few years later for its decision to stop processing donations. Such policies, as the case of WikiLeaks demonstrates, further exacerbate the problem, leading to additional protests and radicalisation of the victimised users and their supporters in addition to restricting contestational democratic deliberation online. Eventually, these censoring acts also impact not only on the rights of the protesters and the websites they restrict support for, but on the companies' security and the public's online experience due to the backlash protests these unjustified censoring acts could generate.

Therefore, subordinating corporate actors to legislative and political dictates in addition to creating risk-averse processes for regulating speech online can have indirect, but equally important, negative impact on user rights generally and hacktivists as well. Current processes can hinder the organisational capabilities of political/hacktivist groups and weaken their actions by obscuring their online presence and reducing the opportunities for critical and politically controversial expression in ways that can often be arbitrary and excessively restrictive of users' rights. The potential lack of prioritisation regarding users' speech and privacy rights or a weakness to safeguard those rights against interference from the authorities generates reactions, though, that further reinforce online insecurity and risk. Laidlaw highlights that even beyond the implicit human rights responsibilities that companies can have, at the moment, private companies that are important for the preservation of privacy and democratic speech online operate in a 'governance lacuna' that allows them to arbitrarily decide the kind of speech that would be promoted.[117] Taking it even further, McNamee argues that, although private actors on the Internet were initially given self-regulatory powers, the concept of self-regulation has now taken the form of 'devolved enforcement, surveillance and extra-judicial punishment of allegedly illegal activities.'[118] Inevitably, the subordination of many private actors to the dictates of a crime control/ security mentality towards online activity restricts any positive regulatory potential for reinforcing civil liberties online. Furthermore, it detracts from democratic progress by compromising the interests of controversial political groups, thus reducing political diversification and minority participation in democratic deliberation processes.

5 Conclusion

This chapter has built upon the previous chapter on cybercrime-related norms and legislation in relation to hacktivism and has discussed how the different stakeholders that are called to enforce and support such security-focused rationales and legislative choices might be in a position to ameliorate the concerns highlighted regarding the impact of the dominant norms and applicable laws in relation to how hacktivism would be dealt with under this framework.

Having looked at the powers and practices of prosecutors, courts, as well as private corporations offering services online, this chapter further reinforces the view that the effects flowing from the current focus on security and risk-averse policies, in addition to an over-reliance on a punitive and overtly broad cybercriminal law regime, are exacerbated rather than ameliorated. This would, in turn, result in the usual responses to hacktivism as they are highly likely to produce problematic results similar to those highlighted throughout this book regarding the attribution of proportionate and efficacious punishments, but also in terms of enhancing democratic deliberation and preserving public online safety.

More particularly, the conditions shaping the current enforcement environment seem to be encouraging more punitive and managerial policies that prioritise results rather than fairness, and risk prevention rather than balanced approaches between security and civil liberties. Especially for hacktivists' legally ambiguous activities that relate to the exercise of civil liberties online in an era where the limits of such liberties are hazy at best, the stakes are much higher. Second, the fact that hacktivists will be processed through a criminal justice system that is just coming to grips with the intricacies of Internet crime and its stakeholders are primarily educated to operate on adversarial and managerial standards also appears to be generating inefficacious or excessive responses, which propagate a vicious circle of backlash and radicalisation between the protesters and the authorities. Furthermore, where additional stakeholders are employed, such as Internet intermediaries, these do not seem to be in a position to induce more balanced approaches. Instead, they also seem to be incentivised, directly or indirectly, to act as proxies for facilitating surveillance and censoring of controversial political entities rather than maintaining an objective stance that would reflect their crucial role as information gatekeepers.

Considering the above, there seem to be good reasons for trying to identify ways in which more just and efficacious results could be produced with the aim of reducing conflict-based radical responses and preserving important democratic rights and civil liberties as well as enhancing overall cybersecurity. The next chapter will attempt to address the problems identified from a theoretical and practical perspective and provide suggestions towards achieving more legitimate responses. The main aims are to manage to break the radicalisation circle and generate more productive processes for democratic deliberation and contestation online, in addition to eliminating excessively harmful hacktivist practices and increasing overall online safety.

Notes

1. Amie N. Ely, 'Prosecutorial Discretion as an Ethical Necessity: The Ashcroft Memorandum's Curtailment of the Prosecutor's Duty to Seek Justice' (2004–5) 90 Cornell Law Review 237, 242–243; Kent Greenawalt, *Conflicts of Law and Morality* (Oxford University Press, New York 1989) 350–351.
2. United States Department of Justice, 'United States Attorney's Manual' (1997) http://www.justice.gov/usao/eousa/foia_reading_room/usam/ Chapter 9-27.110 A; for UK, see Crown Prosecution Service, 'The Code for Crown Prosecutors' (2010) http://www.cps.gov.uk/publications/code_for_crown_prosecutors/.
3. Ely (n 1) 244–246.

4. Greenawalt (n 1) 352; Crown Prosecution Service (n 2) 3.
5. US Department of Justice (2) Chapter 9-27.110.
6. Ely (n 1) 244.
7. US Department of Justice (2) Chapter 9-27.230 Section B.4.
8. Courts seldom review the prosecutors' decisions based on allegations of improper charges and usually only when there is a constitutional challenge behind the allegation, such as racial discrimination. There is also a lack of review of prosecutorial decisions in relation to overcharging defendants to obtain plea agreements, pre-textual charges, and failures to disclose exculpatory material to juries. In the UK, courts could suggest to the Crown Prosecution Service to reconsider a decision to prosecute or not, but the decision ultimately lies with the CPS. Crown Prosecution Service, 'Appeals: Judicial Review of Prosecutorial Decisions' (21 May 2009) http://www.cps.gov.uk/legal/a_to_c/appeals_judicial_review_of_prosecution_decisions/; the courts in England have reflected the tendency to impose a very light review to prosecutorial discretion, accepting reviews mostly for cases of abusive use of discretion. Yoav Dotan, 'Should Prosecutorial Discretion Enjoy Special Treatment in Judicial Review?: A Comparative Analysis of the Law in England and Israel' (1997) 3 Public Law 513, 513–515.
9. Crown Prosecution Service (n 2).
10. Nick Vamos, 'Please Don't Call It "Plea Bargaining"' (2009) Criminal Law Review 617, 620.
11. Dotan (n 8) 515; Rebecca Krauss, 'The Theory of Prosecutorial Discretion in Federal Law: Origins and Developments' (2009) 6 Seton Hall Circuit Review 1.
12. Dotan (n 8) 518–519.
13. Glenn Reynolds, 'Ham Sandwich Nation: Due Process When Everything Is a Crime' (Legal Studies Research Paper 206, University of Tennessee, Tennessee 2013) http://ssrn.com/abstract=2203713.
14. Jonathan Simon, *Governing through Crime* (Oxford University Press, Oxford 2007) 35, 38–39.
15. Even though federal prosecutors are more detached from particular local incidents, than regular state prosecutors, being elected in country-wide elections, they still have to make similar considerations. Ibid. 42–43, 72–73.
16. Kenneth J. Melilli, 'Prosecutorial Discretion in an Adversary System' (1992) Brigham Youth University Law Review 669, 688; Paul

Rosenzweig, 'Overcriminalization: An Agenda for Change' (2004) 54 American University Law Review 809, 811.

17. Researchers have found that, when the public is actually informed of specific cases of criminality and of alternative, more lenient and less costly forms of punishment than custodial sentences, many tend to prefer more lenient penalties and methods of punishment than those handed down by courts for similar incidents. F. Cullen, B. Fisher, and B. Applegate, 'Public Opinion About Punishment and Corrections' (2000) 27 Crime and Justice, 10–13, 16–17; Mike Hough and Julian V. Roberts, 'Sentencing Trends in Britain: Public Knowledge and Public Opinion' (1999) 1 Punishment & Society 11, 17–18; Majid Yar, 'Public Perceptions and Public Opinion About Internet Crime' in Yvonne Jewkes and Majid Yar (eds), *Handbook of Internet Crime* (Willand Publishing, Devon 2010) 104–119, 106.
18. Anonymous, for example, has argued about there being a political bias in decisions to prosecute hacktivists, which can be perceived by the lack of interest by prosecutors in finding the perpetrators of denial-of-service attacks against the WikiLeaks website, which is also a serious network compromise. Anonymous, 'Anonymous Press Release: Open Letter from Anonymous to the UK Government' (*Anonops*, 27 January 2011) https://www.indymedia.org.uk/en/2011/01/472905.html.
19. Pierre Omidyar, 'WikiLeaks, Press Freedom and Free Expression in the Digital Age' (*Huffington Post*, 2 February 2014) http://www.huffingtonpost.com/pierre-omidyar/wikileaks-press-freedom-a_b_4380738.html.
20. Russell L. Christopher, 'The Prosecutor's Dilemma: Bargains and Punishments' (2003) 72 Fordham Law Review 93.
21. Krauss (n 11) 7–9.
22. Albert Alschuler, 'Implementing the Criminal Defendant's Right to Trial: Alternatives to the Plea Bargaining System' (1983) 50 University of Chicago Law Review 931, 932.
23. Krauss (n 11) 8–9.
24. See examples in Samuel R. Gross et al., Exonerations in the United States 1989–2003, (2005) 95/2 Journal of Criminal Law and Criminology 523; Angela J. Davis, *Arbitrary Justice: The Power of the American Prosecutor* (Oxford University Press, Oxford 2007) 48–52.
25. Davis (n 24) 44.

26. Vamos (n 10) 621.
27. Sara S. Beale, 'The News Media's Influence on Criminal Justice Policy: How Market-Driven News Promotes Punitiveness' (2006) 48 William & Mary Law Review 397, 422–423.
28. Reynolds (n 13) 3–4.
29. Ibid. 622–623.
30. Garland (n 10) 117–119.
31. Ibid.
32. Vamos (n 10) 623.
33. Fawzia Cassim, 'Formulating Specialised Legislation to Address the Growing Spectre of Cybercrime: A Comparative Study' (2009) 12 Potchefstroom Electronic Law Journal 35, 45. Prosecuted protesters on multiple felonious charges have lost their jobs or have been unable to find one while awaiting trial, even threatening to commit suicide. Gerry Smith and Ryan J. Reilly, 'Alleged 'Paypal 14' Hackers Seek Deal to Stay out of Prison after Nearly 2 Years in Limbo' (*Huffington Post*, 18 May 2013) http://www.huffingtonpost.com/2013/05/18/paypal-14-hackers_n_3281768.html; see also discussion about Aaron Swartz in Lawrence Lessig, 'Prosecutor as Bully' (*Lessig Blog, v2*, 12 January 2013) http://lessig.tumblr.com/post/40347463044/prosecutor-as-bully.
34. For example, the four members of Anonymous prosecuted for the PayPal attacks in the UK were between 16 and 25 years old when the offence was perpetrated. Brid-Aine Parnell, 'Brit Mastermind of Anonymous Paypal Attack Gets 18 Months' Porridge' (*The Register*, 24 January 2013) http://www.theregister.co.uk/2013/01/24/uk_anonymous_hackers_sentencing_payback/.
35. Some of the consequences can be pre-trial incarceration, loss of employment, social stigmatisation, criminal defence costs, as well as emotional stress: Melilli (n 16) 672; protesters have talked about the impact their prosecution has had with many being unable to find work until the case is resolved and one even threatening to commit suicide if he is convicted: Smith and Reilly (n 33); Douglas Lucas, 'Exclusive: The Legendary #Anonymous Paypal 14 Speak Out Post-Sentencing' (*The Cryptosphere*, 31 October 2014) https://thecryptosphere.com/2014/10/31/exclusive-the-anonymous-paypal-14-speak-out-post-sentencing/.
36. Melilli (n 16) 686, 694.

37. DJNZ and The Action Tool Development Group of the Electrohippies Collective, 'Client-Side Distributed Denial-of-Service: Valid Campaign Tactic or Terrorist Act?' (2001) 34 Leonardo 269, 270; civil disobedience had been compared with plain street criminality in the US ever since the 1960s and 1970s, when crime was emerging as a core policy interest. See Sara S. Beale, 'What's Law Got to Do with It? The Political, Social, Psychological and Non-Legal Factors Influencing the Development of (Federal) Criminal Law' (1997) 1 Buffalo Criminal Law Review 23, 40–41; UK and US officials have expressed their perspective on the members of Anonymous as socially detached hackers who have unavoidable criminal and antisocial tendencies, characterising them even as terrorists. Jaikumar Vijayan, 'Anonymous' Arrests Tied to Paypal DDoS Attacks, FBI Says' (*Computer World*, 20 July 2011).
38. Trevor Thompson, 'Terrorizing the Technological Neighborhood Watch: The Alienation and Deterrence of the White Hats under the CFAA' (2008) 36 Florida State University Law Review 537, 567.
39. Jaikumar Vijayan, 'Anonymous' Arrests Tied to Paypal DDoS Attacks, FBI Says' (*Computer World*, 20 July 2011) http://www.computerworld.com.au/article/394256/_anonymous_arrests_tied_paypal_ddos_attacks_fbi_says/.
40. Carl Cohen, 'Civil Disobedience and the Law' (1966) 21 Rutgers Law Review 1, 16–17.
41. Simon (n 11) 111–112.
42. However, judges have often been blamed as overtly lenient. Zlotnick (n 43) 247–249; Mike Hough and Julian V. Roberts, 'Sentencing Trends in Britain: Public Knowledge and Public Opinion' (1999) 1 Punishment & Society 11.
43. Zlotnick (n 43) 212–214.
44. Ibid. 232–238; Michael A. Wolff, 'Evidence-Based Judicial Discretion: Promoting Public Safety through State Sentencing Reform' (2008) 83 New York University Law Review 1389, 1398–1400; Julian V. Roberts, 'Sentencing Guidelines and Judicial Discretion' (2011) 51 British Journal of Criminology 1, 5–6.
45. See *US v Booker,* 543 U.S. 220 (2005) (*Booker*) rendering the guidelines advisory after 2005, but still considered basic for sentencing: however, as the U.S.S. Manual 2016 explains, departures are allowed only when the court finds 'an aggravating or mitigating circumstance of a kind, or to a degree, not adequately taken into consideration by the

Sentencing Commission in formulating the guidelines that should result in a sentence different from that described.' 18 U.S.C. Section 3553(b); reliance on sentencing guidelines with binding effect is now common in the UK (after the Coroners and Justice Act of 2009). Roberts (n 44) 5–6, 13–14; however, especially in the UK, there is a qualification in the duty of the courts to follow the guidelines based on whether such a decision would be contrary to the interests of justice. Coroners and Justice Act 2009 Section 125(1)(b).

46. Alexa Chu Clinton, 'Taming the Hydra: Prosecutorial Discretion under the Acceptance of Responsibility Provision of the US Sentencing Guidelines' (2012) 79 The University of Chicago Law Review 1467, 1471–1472.
47. See Roberts (n 44) 7–8.
48. Jarrett et al. (n 91) 34–35.
49. Ibid. 37–39; reasonable costs to any victim include the cost of responding to an offence, conducting a damage assessment, and restoring the data, program, system, or information to its condition prior to the offence, and any revenue lost, cost incurred, or other consequential damages incurred because of interruption of service; Section 1030(e)(11); this definition could include the prorated salary of system administrators, the wage of web-security personnel, the expense of recreating lost work, the cost of re-installing system software and security measures. See *US v. Middleton* 231 F.3d 1207 (9th Cir. 2000); *EF Cultural Travel BV v Explorica, Inc* 274 F.3d 577 (1st Cir. 2001); loss could also include harms like lost advertising revenue or sales and the salaries of employees who are prevented from working due to systems inoperability. The Honourable Marshall Jarrett et al., 'Prosecuting Computer Crimes' (Criminal Division Computer Crime and Intellectual Property Section Criminal Division, Department of Justice, Office of Legal Education Executive Office for United States Attorneys, Washington D.C.) http://www.justice.gov/criminal/cybercrime/docs/ccmanual.pdf.
50. Skibell (n 41) 930–934.
51. Orin Kerr, 'United States v. Auernheimer, and Why I Am Representing Auernheimer Pro Bono on Appeal Before the Third Circuit' (*The Volokh Conspiracy*, 21 March 2013) http://volokh.com/2013/03/21/united-states-v-auernheimer-and-why-i-am-representing-auernheimer-pro-bono-on-appeal-before-the-third-circuit/.

52. See the commentary to the 2016 Guidelines Manual where it is stated that 'actual loss *includes* the following pecuniary harm, *regardless of whether such pecuniary harm was reasonably foreseeable:* any reasonable cost to the victim including the cost of responding to an offense, conducting a damage assessment, and restoring the data, program, system, or information to its condition prior to the offense, and any revenue lost, cost incurred, or other damages incurred because of interruption of service.' See United States Sentencing Commission, 'United States Sentencing Commission Guidelines Manual' (2016) 96.
53. Anonymous, 'Immunizing the Internet, Or: How I Learned to Stop Worrying and Love the Worm' (2006) 119 Harvard Law Review 2442, 2453–2454; considering how PayPal claimed losses of $5.5 million from operation Payback/Avenge Assange, it would not be surprising to have such great increases in sentences for protesters on the basis of their attacks having compromised the financial security of those companies.
54. According to the 2016 USSC Guidelines Manual, any damage above $6,500 would incur an incremental increase in the penalty range.
55. See United States Sentencing Commission, '2011 Federal Sentencing Guidelines Manual' Chapter 2B1.1. Also see the more recent 2016 Guidelines Manual.
56. *US v Auernheimer*, Criminal No.: 2:11-cr-470 (SDW) (Dist. Court, New Jersey 2013) Defendant's Sentencing Memorandum http://www.scribd.com/doc/130262013/u-s-v-auernheimer-def-sentencing-memo.
57. Sentencing Guidelines Council, 'Sentencing Guidelines' http://sentencingcouncil.judiciary.gov.uk/guidelines/guidelines-to-download.htm.
58. Criminal Justice Act 2003, c.44, Section 170(9).
59. Sentencing Guidelines Council, 'Overarching Principles: Seriousness' (2004) http://sentencingcouncil.judiciary.gov.uk/docs/web_seriousness_guideline.pdf.
60. Ibid.
61. Ibid.
62. Ian McLeod, *Legal Theory* (2nd edn Palgrave Macmillan, New York 2003) 137; Frank B. Cross, 'Decisionmaking in the US Circuit Courts of Appeals' (2003) 91 California Law Review 1475, 1464.
63. Oliver Wendel Holmes Jr., *The Common Law* (Paulo J.S. Pereira and Diego M. Beltran (eds), University of Toronto Law School Typographical Society, Toronto 2011) 5.

64. See Daniel L. Real and Honorable John F. Irwin, 'Unconscious Influences on Judicial Decision-Making: The Illusion of Objectivity' (2010) 43 McGeorge Law Review 1, 3–4, 6.
65. Garland (n 10) 24.
66. Donald Nicolson, 'Ideology and the South African Judicial Process-Lessons from the Past' (1992) 8 South Africa Journal on Human Rights 50; see analysis of various researches on the influence of ideology and the factors that influence ideology itself in Joel Grossman, 'Social Backgrounds and Judicial Decision-Making' (1966) 79 Harvard Law Review 1551, 1556–1557.
67. Mike Hough and Julian V. Roberts, 'Sentencing Trends in Britain: Public Knowledge and Public Opinion' (1999) 1 Punishment & Society 11, 14–20.
68. Real and Irwin (n 64) 6–7.
69. Nicolson (n 66) 285; Grossman (n 66) 1553–1554.
70. Cross (n 62) 1477–1478.
71. Skibell (n 41) 926–927; Gregor Urbas, 'Criminalising Computer Misconduct: Some Legal and Philosophical Concerns' (2006) 14 Asia Pacific Law Review 95, 104, 106; the imposition of a Twitter ban on PayPal 14 in relation to the trial for the PayPal attack as a bail condition is indicative of this lack of understanding, since the convergence of platforms and the multitude of platforms Anonymous is using are numerous, even excluding Twitter: The Smoking Gun 'Judge Lifts Twitter Ban on "Anonymous" 14' (*The Smoking Gun,* 19 March 2012) http://www.thesmokinggun.com/documents/judge-lifts-anonymous-twitter-ban-145792.
72. Wall (n 23) 17–18, 23–24; Jennifer Granick, 'Faking It: Calculating Loss in Computer Crime Sentencing' (2005) 2 I/S: A Journal of Law and Policy 207, 218.
73. Michael Cahill, 'Punishment Decisions at Conviction: Recognizing the Jury as Fault-Finder' (2005) University of Chicago Legal Forum 91, 95.
74. Richard Myers, 'Requiring a Jury Vote of Censure to Convict' (2009) 88 North Carolina Law Review 137, 152.
75. Ibid. 142–143.
76. Martin C. Loesch, 'Motive Testimony and a Civil Disobedience Justification' (1990) 5 Notre Dame Journal of Law, Ethics & Public Policy 1069, 1099–1100; Greenawalt (n 1) 360–361.

77. Robert Hall, 'Legal Toleration of Civil Disobedience' (1971) 81 Ethics 128, 135, 137; Bernard D. Lambek, 'Necessity and International Law: Arguments for the Legality of Civil Disobedience' (1987) 5 Yale Law & Policy Review 472, 479.
78. Greenawalt (n 1) 365–366. In the UK, the case of *R v Ponting* [1985] Crim. LR 318 is a characteristic example of jury nullification, where the jury accepted the argument of the defendant that revealing confidential information was in the public interest and acquitted him contrary to the directions of the court.
79. Greenawalt (n 9) 365.
80. Jessica L. West, 'Is Injustice Relevant? Narrative and Blameworthiness in Protester Trials' Vermont Law School Research Paper No. 11-13, 2013) http://ssrn.com/abstract=2247518, 47.
81. Dennis J. Devine et al., 'Jury Decision Making: 45 Years of Empirical Research on Deliberating Groups' (2000) 7 Psychology, Public Policy and Law 622, 636; Beale, 'The News Media's Influence on Criminal Justice Policy' (n 9) 402, 448–449.
82. Freda Adler, 'Socioeconomic Factors Influencing Jury Verdicts' (1973) 3 New York University Review of Law and Social Change 1, 1–2; Real and Irwin (n 64) 1–3, 7–8.
83. Reynolds (n 13) 4–5; the phrase is attributed to US Chief Judge Sol Wachtler, who advocated abandoning grand juries, as they were very prone to prosecutorial influences and to let judges decide, so that prosecutorial excesses could be tempered. Marcia Kramer and Frank Lombardi, 'New Top State Judge: Abolish Grand Juries & Let Us Decide' (*New York Daily News,* New York 1985) 3.
84. J.L. Cavallaro, 'The Demise of the Political Necessity Defense: Indirect Civil Disobedience and United States v. Schoon' (1993) 81 California Law Review 351, 356–357.
85. Devine et al. (n 81) 629–630.
86. West (n 80) 40–41.
87. West (n 80).
88. James L. Cavallaro, 'The Demise of the Political Necessity Defense: Indirect Civil Disobedience and United States v. Schoon' (1993) 81 California Law Review 352, 360–361.
89. A typical example is the cases of big studios in relation to copyright protections, where lobbying for new, stricter, and more expansive laws has been persistent. See the example of the Sonny Bono Copyright

Extension Term Act. Krystal E. Noga, 'Securitizing Copyrights: An Answer to the Sonny Bono Copyright Term Extension Act' (2007) 9 Tulane Journal of Technology & Intellectual Property 1, 9–10.
90. The example of the Chinese government, which has passed numerous policies obliging ISPs and even Internet cafés to participate in policing cyberspace, is characteristic of how the state can employ private actors for indirect regulation. See Vasileios Karagiannopoulos, 'China and the Internet: Expanding on Lessig's Regulation Nightmares' (2012) 9 SCRIPTed 150.
91. Lessig, *Code v.2.0* (n 6) 62–67, 72, 80.
92. Ibid. 133. The policies of large corporations towards WikiLeaks are characteristic of an implicit political pressure from the US government. Another example would be the collaboration of the UK government with ISPs in terms of putting into effect the retention of user browsing data in accordance with the new Investigatory Powers Act 2016.
93. Emily Laidlaw, Regulating Speech in Cyberspace' (Cambridge University Press, Cambridge, 2015) 40–41; Christoph B. Graber, 'Internet Creativity, Communicative Freedom and a Constitutional Rights Theory: Response to "Code Is Law"' (Lucerne: i-call, The Research Centre for International Communications and Art Law, University of Lucerne, Working paper 03, 2010) 6.
94. Jody Freeman, 'Real Democracy Problem in Administrative Law' in David Dyzenhaus (ed), *Recrafting the Rule of Law* (Hart Publishing, Oxford 1999) 335.
95. Joe McNamee, 'The Slide from "Self-Regulation" to Corporate Censorship' (*European Digital Rights*, Brussels 2011) http://www.edri.org/files/EDRI_selfreg_final_20110124.pdf, 8–11.
96. Elana Schor, 'Telecoms Granted Immunity in US Wiretapping Probe' (*The Guardian*, 20 June 2008) http://www.guardian.co.uk/world/2008/jun/20/georgebush.usa.
97. Stephen Braun et al., 'Secret to Prism Program: Even Bigger Data Seizure' (*Associated Press*, 15 June 2013) https://www.yahoo.com/news/secret-prism-program-even-bigger-140403980.html; Kim Dotcom, 'Prism: Concerns over Government Tyranny Are Legitimate' (*The Guardian*, 13 June 2013) http://www.guardian.co.uk/commentisfree/2013/jun/13/prism-utah-data-center-surveillance.
98. (2008) ECtHR 2872/02.

99. Benjamin S. Buckland, Fred Schreier, and Theodor H. Winkler, 'Democratic Governance Challenges of Cyber Security' (*Geneva Security Forum,* 2012) http://genevasecurityforum.org/files/DCAF-GSF-cyber-Paper.pdf, 19, 22; additionally, antipiracy legislation and judicial decisions, often demonstrate the intention to engage ISPs into actively deterring, if not monitoring, users regarding copyright infringement and potentially even imposing penalties in the form of blacklisting or imposing connectivity restrictions. In the case of the Digital Economy Act 2010 in the UK, it even lead major ISPs to challenge, unsuccessfully, the imposition of such obligations upon them. See case comment in Sam De Silva and Faye Weedon, 'A Future Less Certain for the Digital Economy Act?' (2011) 17 Computer and Telecommunications Law Review 149. Despite some of these legislative dictates eventually failing to coming to fruition, the trend to engage service and content providers in policing efforts is generally evident in modern cyberlaw.
100. Laidlaw (n 93) 47–48.
101. See Nigel Green and Josh Halliday, 'Twitter Unmasks Anonymous British User in Landmark Legal Battle' (*The Guardian,* 29 May 2011) http://www.guardian.co.uk/technology/2011/may/29/twitter-anonymous-user-legal-battle; the same was done in a New York case for an Occupy Wall Street protester account. Cyrus Farivar, 'NY Judge Compels Twitter to Reveal User's Data' (*Ars Technica,* 2 July 2012) http://arstechnica.com/tech-policy/2012/07/ny-judge-compels-twitter-to-reveal-user-data/.
102. See Green and Halliday (n 101).
103. Paul A. Levy, 'Responding to Prosecutors Seeking to Identify Anonymous Bloggers—Google and Other ISPs Could Learn from the Mainstream Media' (*Consumer Law and Policy Blog,* 17 November 2010) http://pubcit.typepad.com/clpblog/2010/11/responding-to-prosecutors-seeking-to-identify-anonymous-bloggers-google-and-other-isps-could-learn-f.html.
104. Ibid.
105. Amnesty International, 'Undermining Freedom of Expression in China: The Role of Yahoo!, Microsoft and Google' (*Amnesty International,* 2006) http://web.amnesty.org/library/pdf/POL300262006ENGLISH/$File/POL3002606.pdf.
106. 47 U.S.C. Section 230(c).
107. 17 U.S.C. Section 512.

108. Council Directive (EC) 2000/31 on certain legal aspects of information society services, in particular electronic commerce, in the Internal Market (E-commerce Directive)[2000] OJ L 178, art. 14.
109. No.2013, art.19.
110. Frank Pasquale, 'Trusting (and Verifying) Online Intermediaries' Policing' in Berin Szoka and Adam Marcus (eds), *The Next Digital Decade: Essays on the Future of the Internet* (Techfreedom, Washington D.C. 2010) 360. See analysis in Organisation for Economic Co-Operation and Development, *The Economic and Social Role of Internet Intermediaries* (*OECD*, 2010) http://www.oecd.org/internet/ieconomy/44949023.pdf, 10–11.
111. McNamee (n 95) 34.
112. Dawn C. Nunziato, 'The Death of the Public Forum in Cyberspace' (2005) 20 Berkeley Technology Law Journal 1115, 1123–1124.
113. Ibid.
114. Sn Vikas, 'Anonymous' Operation India Removed from Facebook and Twitter' (*The Next Web,* 12 June 2011) http://thenextweb.com/in/2011/06/12/anonymous-operation-india-removed-from-facebook-and-twitter/.
115. Deanna Zandt, 'Are the Cyber Battles with the Enemies of Wikileaks the New Civil Disobedience?' (*Alternet,* 13 December 2010) http://www.alternet.org/story/149183/are_the_cyber_battles_with_the_enemies_of_wikileaks_the_new_civil_disobedience.
116. Pierre Omidyar, 'WikiLeaks, Press Freedom and Free Expression in the Digital Age' (*Huffington Post*, 2 February 2014) http://www.huffingtonpost.com/pierre-omidyar/wikileaks-press-freedom-a_b_4380738.html.
117. Laidlaw (n 93) 59.
118. McNamee (n 95) 7.

6

Moving from Conflict to Symbiosis

1 Introduction

The analysis so far has demonstrated that hacktivists' link to civil liberties and user norms, such as privacy and freedom of information and speech, as well as its often global and legally ambiguous character, significantly challenge, morally and practically, attempts to regulate these acts through the criminal justice regime. In many cases, hacktivism underscores and exacerbates existing flaws of the current cybercrime regime, such as the excessive attention on risk and security and its increasing vagueness, broadness, and punitive nature. Reliance on the criminal justice system as the main tool for dealing with hacktivist incidents was shown to often produce unjust results through disproportionate penalties and discretionary policing and sentencing processes. In addition to that, current responses tend to lack in efficaciousness, as they compromise the expression of dissent and at the same time end up generating backlash effects, which in turn increase harmful online political disruptions. Furthermore, the focus on low-level cases of hacktivism also fails to deter dangerous cybercriminals and encourage less harmful practices. All these results are far from the underlying rationales that the current responses are meant to reinforce, which ultimately gives rise to a legitimacy deficit. Essentially, this deficit is premised on the lack of efficaciousness

V. Karagiannopoulos, *Living With Hacktivism*, Palgrave Studies in Cybercrime and Cybersecurity, https://doi.org/10.1007/978-3-319-71758-6_6

and justness that flows from adopting conflict-inducing responses in order to deal with activities that are born out of social conflict anyway.

The alternative rationale suggested here will thus focus on remedying the highlighted legitimacy deficits by suggesting an active and constantly evolving engagement of all interested stakeholders in a holistic effort to achieve more balance through symbiotic methods and tools. The next section will provide some criteria for assessing legitimacy and will discuss the necessary focal points required for facilitating more legitimate responses and how these could be achieved through the adoption of symbiotic rationales.

2 The Need for a More Holistic Understanding

2.1 Understanding the Legitimacy Deficit

Reed argues that in order for laws to be considered legitimate in cyberspace they would have to either be consistent with established user norms, or at least, be able to command the respect of citizens, which would involve demonstrating certain qualities.[1] These qualities are the promotion of valuable social aims, the reasonableness of complying with them, feasible enforceability, and also the production of the rules by a legal authority.[2] Similarly, Baldwin attempts to formulate a process for developing legitimate regulatory solutions by identifying five criteria for assessing legitimacy. These are efficiency; the existence of a legislative mandate from the democratically elected state organs; accountability; reaching decisions through fair and open procedures of due process and basing solutions on objective expertise.[3] As he argues, irrespective of the multiple, often conflicting, political views that might have different focal values regarding legitimacy, there are certain principles, such as those he identifies, that constitute a common ground on which discussions and assessment of legitimacy could, at least, be based.[4]

In addition to suggesting these criteria, Baldwin, perhaps even more importantly, highlights the crucial need, when developing regulatory suggestions, to maintain a balance between the legitimising criteria, always taking into account the concepts of legitimacy that other affected parties might have.[5] This is considered crucial for ensuring that it is considered legitimate by everyone influenced and thus there is less or no resistance to it. These required compromises regarding the development of legitimate solutions inevitably portray the relativity inherent in assessments of legitimacy when regulating, where legitimacy can never be perceived as an absolute condition.[6] Shaping a more legitimate framework when dealing with a particularly diverse issue, such as hacktivism, is, thus, also a contextual process that should take into account multiple elements of justifiability and also the particular context to which the solutions relate. Finding ways to balance these legitimacy criteria in existing and new processes where many parties interact is, therefore, a crucial step for shaping appropriate alternatives and improving existing processes.

2.2 Balancing Multi-actor Regulation and the Need for Symbiosis

The previous chapter demonstrated that additional actors beyond the state are engaged in the process of impacting how hacktivism as a movement and a cluster of practices is dealt with, from organising to active protest stage. It also highlighted the importance of the reaction of hacktivists to those regulatory efforts, which themselves inform how the various stakeholders operate and interact. However, it simultaneously unveiled how existing prominent rules, symbolisms, and political demands influence, and even subordinate, additional actors, such as private online companies, to the dominant dictates of a 'command and control' regime. At the same time, the criminal justice system—by nature a slow-moving, bureaucratic system—lacks the mechanisms for timely assimilation of the counter-responses from all those impacted upon by the regulatory decisions and the flexibility to quickly adopt to the particular trends that its regulatory efforts are generating. The example of Aaron's law for reforming the Computer

Fraud and Abuse Act (CFAA) is characteristic of how slow the legislative processes can be in effecting change.

Relying on legislative developments effectively negates the potential benefits of the flexibility and adaptability that can be facilitated by a network of interacting regulatory influences, such as decentralisation of power and increased accountability, more informed and democratised decision-making, and more efficient, specialised enforcement.[7] Mutual acknowledgement and effort to understand the considerations of all parties involved in the process are even more important in the current era, where interconnectivity and globalisation make problems pervasive and important for all sides and thus render regulatory challenges usually irresolvable by top-down, single-actor efforts.[8]

However, the suggestion of multi-actor regulatory processes is not panacea in itself, since it could end up instead in an undesirable smorgasbord, allow implicit domination of the process by incumbent actors through subordination of weaker actors, or even involve alliances between actors to marginalise other factions. This is mainly because regulators often have conflicting methodologies and goals that make regulatory collaboration and progress difficult.[9] Therefore, discussing symbiotic solutions also entails managing multiple tug-o-wars between conflicting forces. In this case, the conflicts are between factions that promote maximisation of control of information and factions that want more freedom of information, which is the core underlying conflict.

Moreover, conflicts can also be internal between different sub-actors, with public authorities, for example, being torn between satisfying the regulatory suggestions of private actors, preserving constitutional processes, and/or giving in to punitive populist influences. Undeniably, hacktivists also have their philosophical, organisational, and tactical tensions and diverse practices which influence their self-regulation and their reactions to external influences.

This is further explained by the theory of 'autopoiesis,' which perceives society as made up of separate systems that are self-referential, closed normatively, but cognitively open and constituted by many subsystems that themselves self-define meaning and create unique identities.[10] This means that even though systems produce their own norms, structures, and procedures, which they recognise as valid, through their cognitive openness, they can observe other systems and be influenced by them indirectly.[11] It appears that the cognitive openness of systems can gradually relax their strict autonomy, since systems need to relate to other systems and actors if they ever were to influence their environment and impact on other actors/systems.[12] Consequently, regulation takes a more reflective, developmental form, as it is expressed as the parallel co-evolution of the various subsystems, which happens through the indirect influence they gradually exert on each other.[13] Contemporarily, this mutual co-evolution is further reinforced by the new technologies which have made information and interactions between actors much more immediate and large-scale due to the minimisation of distance and maximisation of communication speeds.

This constructive cognitive interaction between multiple stakeholders reinforces their developmental process. This happens since every party is induced to document the norms and functions of other actors and use the acquired knowledge to develop more acceptable responses to their influences that would take into account diverse interests and views.[14] Teubner argues for indirect regulatory interventions because he believes that direct interventions/impositions of one system upon another, considering their normative differences, are bound to lead to the indifference of the 'target' system to the intervention, the destruction of the 'target' system itself, or the destruction of the intervening system.[15] Through the various examples we have seen, the direct interventions on hacktivists for enforcing cybersecurity norms have caused a mix of reactions, from abandoning the practice altogether to going underground and becoming more radicalised, bypassing regulatory efforts, to generating backlash effects that lead to more protests from the activists and their public supporters alike.

Murray suggests that creative interactions between different stakeholders could lead to more acceptable regulation and less conflict by promoting the notion of 'symbiosis'. He develops his theory also based on autopoiesis, which he applies to cyberspace interactions, considering every stakeholder a subsystem in the regulatory processes.[16] Symbiosis theory suggests that 'the best regulatory model is not one built upon an active intervention into the settled regulatory environment, the result of which is likely to be extremely disruptive, rather it is one that harnesses, as best as possible, the relationships already in place between the actors.'[17] Self-reflection as well as open communication between actors here play a crucial role, with regulators gathering information from the various stakeholders and making viable regulatory suggestions. This is based on the information gathered through the processing of constant feedback expressed by the other actors through compliance or disruption.[18] As Teubner aptly argues, through the combination of the processes of developing internal norms and of interfering with other systems that indirectly impose reciprocal restraints to law, the law regulates society by regulating itself.[19]

The minimisation of conflict and the simultaneous effort for gradual compromises are very important for dealing with online civil disobedience as a phenomenon arising primarily out of regulatory and political conflicts. Therefore, symbiosis seems to more appropriately describe the way multi-actor regulation could work in an environment that inevitably incorporates an established regulatory system with concrete actors' roles and modus operandi (criminal justice system), but also has integral norms, actors, and even structural elements (technologies like encryption) that can often challenge traditional, one-dimensional perceptions of control. Moreover, the model of symbiosis and gradual, informed, and multifaceted change is consistent with the principle of hacktivism, as a symbolic, sensitising practice, which is principally performed to initiate change through the setting of smaller changes in motion rather than immediate and radical paradigm shifts.

An important aspect of symbiosis that should be highlighted is the active role of the presumed regulatees. Regulation in a network of active nodes does not entail passive regulatees and active regulators. Consequently, in addition to being a main target of regulatory influences, hacktivists are indeed a regulating force within the wider struggles of regulating speech and privacy online, which also impacts on how they are eventually treated as well. In our case, hacktivists partly shape and influence the responses to their actions through their reactions to the interventions they receive as well as through their self-regulation, which in turn influences how they operate and are perceived and dealt with by the criminal justice system, private actors, and the public.

Before proceeding to analyse symbiotic processes relating to our case in more detail, it needs to be made clear that the following regulatory suggestions inevitably entail a certain degree of patient consideration and self-reflection in order to facilitate this paradigm shift from conflict to symbiosis. Parts of what is suggested in principle and in practice, although potentially consistent with basic principles of law and accepted social values and practices, could prove challenging to apply in the current security-focused and risk-averse climate and could only happen gradually and through indirect, slow processes of interaction between stakeholders.

The symbiotic theory of indirect, gradual co-evolution shows us that, even if suggestions might initially appear controversial, through symbiotic process, interacting parties might gradually become more accepting of diverse views. Indeed, there have been cases where suggestions that were initially considered extraordinary and impossible have gradually become tested and accepted. For example, restorative justice solutions had been considered difficult to promote in theory and practice, yet steps have been taken gradually towards that direction with interesting results.[20] Moreover, civil disobedience has gradually become morally acceptable as seen in the works of Habermas and Calhoun or Rawls as well as in practice with the black rights movement or Gandhi.[21] Another example is the gradual legal acceptance of same-sex marriage, whereas even a relationship would have been considered criminal in the past. These changes did not happen overnight, but through a realisation that took multiple levels of effort from a variety of stakeholders implementing formal and informal processes. Experience has shown that perceptions in ethics, law, and criminal justice processes can shift with time and thus a more holistic, openly interactive rationale regarding hacktivism could provide an ideological basis for enriching our regulatory perceptions.

Shaping more appropriate solutions is a slow process of acquisition of information and transforming it to knowledge and then action. What follows then is a network of constant micro-interventions involving a diverse mix of actors and tools that will impact on hacktivism directly or indirectly. Having discussed the challenges posed by the current legal framework and its application, let us first focus on interventions that aim to ameliorate these processes.

3 Building Symbiosis from Within the Criminal Justice System

Irrespective of the many criticisms towards it, the criminal justice system still maintains its importance as an established process that would inevitably be employed to deal with law-breaking activities and also as a source for normative dictates and processes that guide the regulation of citizen behaviours.[22] Moreover, the introduction of the Internet into already established, state-focused legal regimes makes it very hard to perceive regulation of criminality online as independent from already existing norms, established laws, and judicial decision-making processes.[23] After all, as Goldsmith and Wu argue, even if our lives are dominated mostly by social norms and symbolisms, market influences, or even technological measures in cyberspace, rather than laws, an underlying system of territorial government and physical coercion is also needed in order for these controls to function properly.[24]

The importance of the legal system, even for systems that promote network-based regulatory structures, does not just lie in the shaping of social behaviours, but also in its usefulness as a tool, which is meant to institutionalise security and justice values, and normally provides procedures, if not paradigms, of accountability for other regulating actors.[25] As Lessig argues, for example, in a society where corporations define code and influence behaviours online, state-originating controlling mechanisms can offer negative and positive normative and practical examples, and infuse novel regulatory developments with important values.[26]

Considering the current situation with its focus on criminalisation and prosecution of hacktivism as cybercrime, the first stage of transition into a more symbiotic model should, therefore, relate to enabling law and law enforcement to interact, learn, and progressively integrate more interactive, just, and efficient processes when dealing with hacktivism. One way to achieve this would be to promote the education of those involved in creating and enforcing the laws and processes of the criminal justice system regarding new technologies consistently with the benefits and potential risks.

3.1 Informed Processes in the Criminal Justice System

Symbiotic approaches would assume that holistic information-gathering before any prosecutorial or judicial decision-making would be a crucial step in the right direction.[27] A common weakness of law-based responses to fast-paced and law-challenging technological phenomena is the lack of specialised knowledge and clear understanding on behalf of the enforcers.[28] This could be facilitated by engaging not just with media reporters and security firms, but with advising bodies that provide diverse and objective information on the topics in question and individuals who have participated in such activities. Even more crucial is to cross-pollinate the criminal justice system with individuals who have an awareness of cyberspace as a social space and not just as a technical tool that can be used to perpetrate crimes in an obfuscated manner.

A shift to how knowledge is shaped and acquired regarding cybercrime and hacktivism more specifically will enable a better understanding of the activities in question and their implications. This can, in turn, facilitate less adversarial attitudes—a change that could then result in more proportionate reactions.[29] The achievement of more educated and balanced decision-making will, in turn, increase the informed consideration of prosecutions and also legitimise their justification, thus making them more publicly acceptable and reducing backlash effects. The proliferation of less sensationalised information regarding hacktivism is also very important for dispelling the moral panics generated by the media and the cybersecurity sector,[30] and putting the problem of cyber-insecurity within a more realistic context.

An understanding of new digital technologies would allow prosecutors and judges to consider the fact that laws and norms as they are applied in cyberspace are influenced by other actors and communities, which stretch beyond national borders, thus supporting a need for a more cosmopolitan viewing of Internet-related problems.[31] The direct implication of such a critique is that judges, through their familiarisation with the nature of the phenomena they adjudicate, will gradually become more capable of assessing the knock-on effects of their decisions, which are often quasi-legislative in nature.[32] Increasing technological education and social discourse regarding cyberdeviance and the relevant political challenges that are also intrinsic to cyberspace and its communities could, therefore, produce more legitimate and more generally acceptable decisions and sentences by those communities impacted upon as well. Informed prosecutors and, more importantly, judges could also provide better guidance and clarifications for juries, thus making them more capable of understanding and adjudicating on the nature of complex issues such as online civil disobedience. These elements would, in turn, increase compliance with the decisions and would also reduce social conflict and radicalised responses.

3.2 Reconsidering the Focus on Damage and Loss

By deciding to focus on losses for assessing liability and penalty extents, current laws and sentencing guidelines reflect an almost 'strict liability standard' that criminalises even benign hacking aimed at exploration and innovative uses of technology.[33] This is especially so since the threshold of unacceptable damage is either easily reachable by low harmfulness actions and reliance on victim assessments or the damage extent is irrelevant for incurring high penalties.[34] The realisation of this imbalance would consequently suggest that there would be adequate leeway to moderate the attention on damage and loss, or at least define it more narrowly. Legislators and prosecutors could also attempt to establish more accountable ways of assessing damage and loss than just relying on victims' assessments reinforced by cybersecurity firms' predictions. A realisation of the fluidity of these assessments regarding network and information resources is required in order for exaggerated claims to be tempered by more realistic assessments. As Fafinski et al. suggest, '[i]t is difficult to decide at what point to draw the line in respect of consequential losses. Guidelines as to remoteness of damage, a concept used to limit quantum of damages in, for instance, breaches of contract and negligence actions would be required.'[35]

The importance of these factors (loss/damage) could be moderated indirectly by introducing more objective processes for the damage and loss assessments through third-party assessors appointed specifically by the courts or even during plea-bargain procedures. More restrictive, yet adequately inclusive, definitions of loss/damage could also minimise the influence of abstract elements in calculations relating to loss that would not be directly caused or predicted by the allegedly offensive protesters. For example, it has been suggested that the costs of re-securing should not be included in damage/loss calculations, since security and the patching of systemic weaknesses are considered a given obligation of all organisations to update their cybersecurity consistently.[36] Moreover, it is suggested that reputational harms, system improvements, and forensic expenses should also be excluded from the general assessments.[37] Creating a more realistic framework for damage and loss calculations is thus very important, since, as has been seen, such assessments might never be tested in courts, but would be commonly used by prosecutors when offering plea agreements. Although this reconsideration is relevant to cybercrime in general, it is of particular interest to hacktivists, since the damage/loss incurred is usually secondary to the political message and not the actual purpose of their impairing acts.

3.3 Offering Safe Harbour for Cooperative Behaviour

An alternative suggestion for reducing harmful political disruptions online and also actively improving overall collaboration and cybersecurity is the promulgation of incentives and rewards for efforts that help improve cybersecurity.[38] Tactics that relate to the provision of incentives have been commonly employed, mostly in the form of financial incentives provided to companies in exchange for compliance and cooperation.[39] However, even within the context of the criminal justice process, informants and those collaborating with the police have traditionally been treated more leniently. Following this rationale one could introduce incentives that will have an impact on hacktivism and will not be linked to financial incentives, but to penalty mitigation or exoneration offers.

However, the provided information here could relate to cybersecurity risks and poor information security policies that hacktivists identify. Such rewards could induce protesters to behave in less harmful and more legitimate ways. Based on rewarding such behaviours, more lenient, specialised penalties could be promoted in cases where common goals between the hacktivists and the authorities exist, such as the protection of consumer privacy and online safety. For example, hacktivists often protest against lax security regarding how companies store and safeguard customer data in their systems or how secure is the software they create. Unless their intrusions are accompanied by misuse of the information obtained and hacking of existing technological restrictions, their acts should be considered less worthy of punishment if the sole aim is the exposure of a company's disregard for user security.[40] Moreover, if the ultimate goals are socially beneficial, then the rehabilitative element of imposing strict punishment is also weakened to an extent. Such examples have existed from the Back Orifice tool of the cDc to the more modern case of Weev and AT&T. As it stands, the current system can end up punishing such efforts as felonious, which impacts on the benefits flowing from highlighting the potential insecurities.[41]

Punitive measures do not educate citizens to behave responsibly online and to avoid or reduce damaging/loss-inducing behaviours that could increase their penalties. Instead, protesters, as has been seen, could respond to aggressive persecution by resorting to methods that help them avoid identification and liability for their law-breaking, for example, by masking their identities. The opportunity to motivate citizens to be responsible when participating in socially beneficial hacktivist efforts would thus be reinforced if political hackers highlighting security problems knew they will not be prosecuted as plain criminals, but consistently with the potential harmfulness of their actions, which could lead to more well-thought out actions.

If such safe harbour agreements become more commonplace instead of the counterproductive plea bargains, the authorities could avoid punishing hacktions, such as web defacements, redirects, and virus distributions. The precondition would again be that the security weaknesses used for realising these protests are revealed to the website administrators or the authorities, or are publicised, generally perhaps with ways to patch these problems if they relate to weaknesses inherent in commonly used software. Safe harbour provisions would thus be based on avoiding the harsh punishment of morally motivated users, while increasing overall security by providing information about network weaknesses in addition to the actual protest having taken place.[42]

The provision of such mitigation/exoneration opportunities could be reliant either on prosecutorial discretion or even more explicitly established as a mitigating circumstance in sentencing guidelines. The consistent employment of these safe harbour opportunities would also shift the focus from damage and loss to the motivation of protesters and their ultimate result regarding cybersecurity. Consequently, the protesters' restorative reaction would establish a defence mitigating their culpability and/or sentence. Promoting safe harbour provisions for ethical, collaborative hackers would serve the purpose of increasing overall security by preventing more harmful compromises in the future for the targeted websites by cybercriminals with no moral motivations. It would also allow morally sensitive and security-considerate cyberdeviants to avoid high penalties for exploits that ultimately aim to improve security and protect citizen rights against state or corporate excesses or negligence.

The adoption of such approaches would also remedy the problem of targeted companies resorting to courts for compensation for the offences, only to find that protesters' funds are inadequate, which has negative implications for both parties or that the cases are unenforceable due to jurisdictional hurdles. The security advice and the eventual prevention of important breaches and consequent lawsuits in the future by disgruntled users could substitute for civil compensation. Of course, it should come as no surprise if protesters decline to collaborate and assist in securing corporate or state networks due to their anti-establishment ideologies.[43] However, no single, particular solution can be totally successful, and although in some cases such reactionary sentiments might prevail, in other cases, the general social benefit could also outweigh the ideological barriers to collaboration.

Potential cooperation between ethical hackers and law-enforcement and information-managing organisations in need of more secure systems would also be a step towards increasing the understanding of society and law-enforcement agencies of the beneficial aspects of moral hacking, which could gradually lead to less punitive and more understanding responses towards everyone employing such techniques, including hacktivists.[44] Moreover, as Thompson argues, avoiding the harsh punishment of ethical hacking would benefit moral hackers, without actually having an impact on the deterrence and treatment of purely criminal ones, as these safe harbour provisions would be inapplicable to those who act with criminal motives, cover their tracks, and employ destructive tactics.[45] The need to engage more with ethical hackers for promoting cybersecurity has also been acknowledged in the UK Cybersecurity agenda 2011 although no similar reference to the ethical hacking community exists in the respective 2016 agenda document.[46]

3.4 Promoting Technology-Based and Community-Focused Penalties

The goals of efficient prevention and deserved, proportionate punishment as justifying reasons of criminal punishment, which would, in turn, increase the legitimacy of criminal sanctions, could also be promoted by employing specialised Internet restrictions and community service penalties for hacktivists. Well-balanced penalties relating to the potential abuses that hacktivists might have perpetrated would increase the acceptance of sanctions, as they would be considered more consistent with the protesters' specific context, but also usually less harmful and socially beneficial and more cost-effective than imprisonment. Therefore, they would be consistent with the protesters' declared ultimate purpose, which is the promotion of community welfare. This also links with the aforementioned need for more knowledgeable and informed responses, since the designation of such penalties would need to be consistent with current norms and practices regarding the use of technology in order to be considered proportionate and useful.

Penalties for cyberdeviants could range from a partial ban on Internet access to the monitoring of use after the imposition of restrictions or even the forfeiture of IT hardware and software. Moreover, penalties can entail the provision of actual IT services to the community through supervised teaching of computing in youth centres or helping in the securing of networks and covering other IT needs of public services, a goal which would be consistent with governmental policies to increase cybersecurity awareness overall. Even from the early years, the courts have found that for delinquency, which can exist only online, much like electronic civil disobedience (ECD), relating the penalty to the restrictions of use of the medium can be an efficacious and proportionate penalty[47]; therefore, such solutions could be further encouraged.

These penalties, though, ought to be assessed in relation to the nature of the offence, the technology involved, and the potential of the sanctions for preventing recidivism,[48] as they are more personalised and more lenient than incarceration and actively socially beneficial. When community service is included, these penalties would better reflect the potentially socially considerate intentions behind hacktivist initiatives. These alternative penal choices also express a renewed focus on rehabilitation and not on sterile, punitive retribution, and for these reasons they have been suggested by Supreme Court Judge Wolff in the US as a solution to the problem of increased punitiveness.[49] Similar sanctions have also formed part of official suggestions regarding the UK Cybersecurity Agenda in 2011 in the form of community sanctions or Internet restrictions to be monitored using cybertags.[50] The enrichment and choice of case-specific penalties regarding each offender could potentially further produce a dialogue of the needs and desires of the offenders, the victims, and society more generally, thus promoting a more symbiotic process between hacktivists, the legal system, and society.

A concern is the balancing of the penalties in relation to the offenders' rights of access to technology and information. Even when such penalties are attached to a release as conditions, there are specific factors that courts should consider that are reasonably related to the nature and characteristics of the offence and the history and characteristics of the defendant, the deterrence of further criminal contact, or the protection of the public. Although there are many examples of such restrictions—mainly linked to cases of online sexual exploitation of children—the courts have argued that these restrictions must not unreasonably deprive the offender of their liberties.[51] The increasing need of citizens to use digital technologies in order to participate in everyday economic and political functions generates questions as to the proportionality and predictability of harms flowing from such restrictions.[52] For example, in the PayPal 14 case, an access ban on Twitter, as a bail condition, was lifted on the basis of restricting free speech, with monitoring of the medium being considered adequate to prevent further offending.[53]

The increasing importance of Internet connectivity for everyday lives also needs to be reflected in the wording of such technology-based sanctions. The United Nations (UN) Human Rights Rapporteur found that total disconnection measures are disproportionate and has emphasised the need to preserve access, even during times of unrest.[54] In 2016, a non-binding UN resolution acknowledged the need to apply a 'comprehensive human rights-based approach in providing and in expanding access to Internet and requests all States to make efforts to bridge the many forms of digital divides.'[55]

Given the importance attributed to connectivity, courts ought to consider the duration and broadness of the restrictions imposed. In various cases, a complete ban on Internet access was not accepted by the court with the justification that it would prevent the offender from participating in everyday basic functions, from filing in tax reports to shopping online.[56] Other cases, however, have accepted full bans even for less serious offences, creating confusion as to the existence of a consensus in this area.[57] However, courts could moderate general bans through the introduction of temporal limitations.[58] As Fredrickson argues, though, there are various stands taken by the various circuit courts that to seek to establish a consensus is probably impossible.[59] Therefore, decisions for imposing such penalties, and their extent and duration, ought to be the result of careful assessment for structuring the penalty appropriately to the offender's personal and professional needs.[60]

These are only a few suggestions as to how the criminal justice system could promote more just and efficacious responses that would be considered more well-thought-out and proportionate. Such solutions would help reduce any backlash that current responses seem to generate, while also offering back to the community and increasing overall security and a more balanced functioning of the cybercriminal law regime overall. As discussed, though, this is only one of the aspects that symbiosis should be focusing on and there is more to be said regarding micro-interventions and how these could be achieved beyond the criminal justice system and in relation to various stakeholders as well as the hacktivists themselves. Let us see some of these suggestions in the following section.

4 Moving Beyond the Criminal Justice System

4.1 Facilitating Spaces and Processes of Dialogue

The legal ambiguity of hacktivism partly reflects the speech deficit that cyberspace, as a milieu of privately controlled islands online, creates. With that lack of public space online as one of the generating causes of ECD, the need to resort to expressive disruptions could be partly alleviated through the provision of additional deliberative processes and spaces. These could allow for more expressive freedom and also facilitate inclusive and equal dialogue conditions between speakers, rather than preserve the dominant relations of power that the current media scene often supports.[61] Consequently, efforts should not just focus on bringing diverse political views and forces together, but on the conditions that this dialogue is being realised. The dialogic process would benefit from open and critical fora that could allow reconsideration of the participants' views without power inequalities steering discussions and decision-making.[62] In order to facilitate the dialogic assessments and decision-making in ways that also respect already established processes, regulators ought to reconsider multi-stakeholder processes as the first level to decentralising regulation and power.

We could begin by assessing the institutional background within the context of which the dialogue takes place, the efficiency of the processes as they are structured in relation to achieving the goals of decentralised, equal, and accountable deliberation and the problems the current methods might involve.[63] For example, procedures giving priority to already incumbent actors compared to civil society, in terms of how the forum is institutionally constructed to prioritise states, would be of interest to assess. Of similar importance in terms of restructuring deliberative fora would be whether the participation and dialogue processes are resource-demanding, and thus, excluding financially weaker parties. Even the process of defining civil society and its representatives can involve exclusionary processes. This reassessment would be particularly useful, especially since even the current example of multi-stakeholderism, such as the Internet Governance Forum (IGF), has been criticised as failing to promote equality, diversity, and global representation.[64]

As early as 2005, Lovink and Rossiter emphasised the need for more inclusive processes:

> [T]he people benefiting from such endeavours as the World Summit of the Information Society are, for the most part, those on the speaking and funding circuits, not people who are supposedly represented in such a process. Networks call for a new logics of politics, one based not just on a hand-picked collection of NGOs that have identified themselves as 'global civil society.'[65]

There are constant critiques of multi-stakeholder efforts being too bureaucratised to be appealing or easy to join and operate under for groups that do not have ample resources, a process which already exacerbates the inevitable 'asymmetries of power' within organisations with a diverse mix of members.[66] As Hofmann argues, although there is a romantic perception regarding the processes and efficaciousness of multi-stakeholderism, unfortunately, the reality is not as it is usually portrayed, that is, as a multifaceted, balanced democratising force.[67]

Other researchers have highlighted the problems of formalism and state-focused structures in official fora, such as the IGF, where talks take place under the UN control; the majority of seats are held by governments, and meetings are content-filtered to avoid controversial topics being recorded.[68] One could easily see how the multitude of organisations and collectives might feel under-represented or misrepresented and resort to more disruptive ways of communicating their political message, especially since the discussions rarely take on challenging policy issues.[69]

Multi-stakeholder models could gradually be structured in less formal ways and with more direct, interactive deliberative processes and engaging more with digital technologies in order to allow groups from around the globe to voice their views and suggestions. Generalising distance-participation would facilitate more accessible, inclusive, and accountable decisions and, consequently, more democratically legitimised decisions, which could help reduce conflicts and protests. Informal deliberative processes enable more substantive and inclusive discussions for a wider spectrum of civil society actors, especially since hacktivist collectives, as a more informal part of civil society, would avoid formal organisational models or their 'members' might be part of a diversity of collectives as well.[70] The informal interaction structures, which could be characterised as 'everyday multi-stakeholderism,' should thus facilitate a more dynamic and constant interaction between actors, on a more frequent and informal basis. This will, in turn, establish an ongoing flow of information and opinion-exchange mechanisms between regulators, thus facilitating more productive symbiotic processes.[71]

The diversity of protesting modes of organising can be seen in the Anti-Counterfeiting Trade Agreement global protests. The multiplicity of vectors of lobbying and active protesting on behalf of a variety of civil society organisations and protest collectives are indicative of the diversity of the dialogic processes that online interactions can facilitate. These actions were organised within the confines of specific fora, but also encompassed coordinated, but independent expressive actions.[72] Participation in the formalised fora might be a challenge for advocacy groups due to either the exclusionary nature of the forum in question or their choice of alternative communicational tools and processes rather than those the forum adopts. However, speech opportunities can still be enhanced through institutional advocacy processes. This can involve 'gaining some degree of insider status in institutions or in organizations that initiate, prepare, legislate, or execute policy change'.[73] It can be done through a process of providing expertise to policymakers or lobbying, or essentially operating as a communicational link between different stakeholders, from users to policymakers.[74] Therefore, membership is not a prerequisite to promoting creative dialogue, and in some cases, the quasi-external status of such processes could allow organisations to communicate their concerns and messages through actors who are more established and influential within certain fora, rather than trying to claim such a space for themselves.

It has been argued that in order to proceed with attempts to create functional dialogic fora, there would have to be a consensual normative base, where some basic presumptions in relation to governance will inform further policy discussions.[75] But how could we achieve normative consensus in an environment where actors with different normative backgrounds and interests interact within these processes? We would potentially need to adopt a pre-procedural agreement that no norms would be imposed. As Castells argues, a common culture and understanding between the networked societies today does not rely on homogenising social values, but on sharing the value of communication.[76] This can allow different groups with diverse cultural backgrounds and interests to come closer. But this will not be done by agreeing on the content of the communication, as this could exclude dissent. Instead, it should primarily rely on the processes of communication, consequently allowing diversity and dissent to play a co-evolutionary role in more legal and efficient ways and processes than network disruptions.[77]

The introduction of new norms and processes could be further facilitated by engaging more with the technical/hacker community in general, which is often more informed, specialised, and has realistic practical perceptions about the needs and possible regulatory solutions applied to Internet-related problems. Even through formalised processes, deliberative fora, such as the IGF, are gradually transfusing values of the online communities, such as freedom of information in the Internet governance processes.[78] The multiplication of the sources and processes through which 'netizen' norms and values can be integrated into policy-making discussions will also eventually increase the legitimacy of the policies promulgated, allowing the wider civil society to feel included in the construction of broader political decisions.[79] This, in turn, would reduce conflict and the need for more forceful expression through symbolic, disruptive protest. Even if hacktivist groups do not join such processes, hacktivists are often also part of other collectives that could be included in the new, more creative, informal processes, thus reducing the need to resort to illegal disruptions.

Irrespective of efforts to increase deliberative opportunities, hacktivist actions would not be eliminated, since the problems they relate to are so numerous and the conditions of speech inequality and social injustice so pervasive that there will often be potentially justifying reasons for CD protests offline and online. However, that does not mean that we should not attempt to find more ways to increase deliberation and reduce disruptive protests in a creative manner that addresses the deeper causes of the disruptions. Consequently, the proliferation of more inclusive fora should not be seen as the co-opting of hacktivism by groups, tactics, and purposes that are more conventional. Instead, it should be seen as an attempt to open up deliberation in acknowledgement of what hacktivism represents and demands, and to reduce the speech deficits that generate the need for more hacktivist protests.

4.2 Counter-notices and Pop-up Protests

Another way for service and content providers, such as PayPal, Facebook, or YouTube, to influence the regulation of hacktivist groups and activities is through the use of terms of service as discussed previously. The serious implications for the privacy and speech rights of controversial political groups and hacktivists could be made more proportionate by finding ways to increase the accountability of their decisions in ways that would reflect their gatekeeper role and responsibilities. This could be done by establishing opportunities for second-level review by users against censoring decisions that violate their rights of privacy, speech, and access. On that basis, processes of resolution that promote the interaction between the publisher of allegedly problematic material and those requesting to take it down will be a very positive step. In the US, for example, the Digital Millennium Copyright Act (DMCA) includes a provision that relates to countering take-down notices of materials that are considered to infringe copyright.[80] The rationale behind the counter-notice is to assess whether the complainant who requested that certain content be removed has indeed a legitimate interest in this act and is willing to pursue it in courts, rather than just acting in bad faith towards speech he/she finds unpleasant or contrary to their beliefs.[81]

Counter-notices have not been employed extensively, as most people are ignorant of their existence.[82] However, this provision could constitute a guiding example of how the appeal processes for arbitrary decisions to remove content on behalf of content providers could be countered. Allowing users to appeal take-down decisions through quick arbitration processes provided by the website administrators would produce more legitimate decisions by providing a more transparent and validated process for service and content providers to eventually proceed with the filtering of requests.[83] These changes will impact not only on hacktivists, but also generally on citizens' expression and interaction online. However, since hacktivists often employ controversial speech, the regulatory benefits will be even more relevant in these cases. Such practices could perhaps induce content providers to reconsider their initial take-down decisions, bearing in mind the potentially increased costs of take-down reassessments.

In addition to keeping controversial speech online, this would not remedy the fact that the protesting speech would be expressed on particular sites that would not satisfy a need for reaching a wide enough audience in relation to a space that is relevant to the protested cause. Li attempts to provide an alternative which he feels could remedy those concerns, by suggesting cyberattacks that would have the form of pop-up windows, essentially creating a 'cybersidewalk,' where the protest could take place without losing its claim to a free speech/expression protection.[84] As Li claims, the pop-up uses the attack not as a form of obscure expression in itself, as in the case of virtual sit-ins, but as a means for delivering the message, and if the message is relevant to the protested space, then it could be analogised to an offline picket protest.[85] This form of protest would allow the protested side to offer counterarguments and in fact further democratic deliberation.[86]

Although such an act would still be a violation of the laws discussed in the previous chapters regarding unauthorised access and impairment, at least such attacks avoid the criticisms regarding censorship and loss of operational income that is burdening the usual protest techniques, such as virtual sit-ins or defacements. Essentially, here the political protest still takes place, but more symbiotically with the speech and presence of those the protest is aimed at. Such solutions demonstrate how we could reconceptualise protests by looking at the history of activism on private space and attempting to find ways to translate the court findings and the rationales behind those decisions into cyberspace protests in a way that compromises the concerns of most of the parties involved.

4.3 The Prospect of Technological Countermeasures

Following an early example against the EDT's Zapatista protests by the US government, an alternative, but not risk-free way for dealing particularly with virtual sit-ins would be for those targeted by the protesters to engage in some form of counter-disruption against the protesting computer systems. Such tactics, though, can generate further legitimacy concerns.[87] However, the expansion and importance of digital technologies and information networks has increased exponentially since that first example in the late 1990s. Consequently, actors employing counterattacking tools would have to take into account moral and practical challenges, since counterattacks could cause undue damage to innocent users and even induce retaliation from protesters.

As this would essentially be an actively defensive action against the incoming traffic generated by multiple computer sources, in cases of virtual sit-ins, the main concerns flowing from the employment of counter-attacking software are maintaining the proportionality of harms between the protest and the counterattack. This would be assessed by gauging the potential side effects of the counterattacks, the nature of the targets, and the accountability of the counterattackers. Accountability concerns are even more pertinent due to the potential for disruption of compromised computers engaged in the protests, since it has not been uncommon that botnets are employed to enhance the effect of virtual sit-ins despite this being against the core principle of public engagement intrinsic in such online protests. Computers in a botnet might belong to providers of critical infrastructure services, for example, a hospital network.[88] Even if state agencies or private companies can legitimately argue for compromising the functionality of computers belonging to individual user-protesters, the risk of indiscriminate counterattacking could impact on the integrity of an important computer network. Therefore, the moderation of the impact of such countermeasures based on such a risk ought to be an adequately serious concern, which should in turn induce considerate deployment of aggressive technological countermeasures.

Criteria for assessing proportionality and preserving legitimacy during the use of countermeasures could be drawn from traditional legal processes that justify actions relating to necessary preventive acts against an imminent harm and shouldering liability for potential excesses. Reidenberg, for example, argues for the need to prescribe strict authorisation criteria that are consistent with democratic societies' rule of law values.[89] In these cases of attack and counterattack, proportionality is the first principle that comes to mind. Aggressive countermeasures ought to be employed, for example, after assessing the origin of the targeted computers, or if that is not possible within the short space that the counterattack should be deployed, counterattackers should try to moderate the designated disruptions in order to minimise the risks of undue harms. For example, a hackback that is aimed to destroy the hard-drives of protesters participating in a short-term virtual sit-in would not be justifiable as it would be disproportionate to the harm of the original attack. Brenner, in justifying counterattacks, also employs the right to defend one's property if the defender can prove that there was no alternative means of protection in a timely manner that would entail less force than a code-based counter-strike.[90] Justification will, of course, rely on assessments regarding the nature, imminence, and potential disruptiveness of the attack and impact on the counterattacking party.

For private actors, accountability could also be assessed on the basis of self-defence, which could legitimise the private use of reasonable force, even if force and counterforce in hacktivism are expressed in forms of technological disruption.[91] In cases where counterattacking organisations mistakenly or excessively employ potentially damaging disruptive countermeasures that exceed the limits of a reasonable mistake, they would also be liable in court for failing to abide by proportionality standards and could compensate those harmed from unjustifiably disproportionate counterattacks.[92] However, it is not hard to imagine why bringing a lawsuit against a protested company on the basis of it trying to counter the protest that would have impacted on its networks might be beyond the financial capabilities of the protesters the counterattack has impacted upon.

The moderation of the effects caused by the countering tools should also be proportionate in order to prevent an escalation of counter protests. Considering the backlash effects discussed previously, avoiding protester retaliation would be easier to achieve if the counterattacks demonstrate the intention of those employing those tools to act defensively rather than vindictively. A legitimate aim would be to weaken the initial protesting attack and not to aim to destroy the protesters' computer resources. After all, protests are usually based on the use of elementary tools for targeting websites with information requests or use non-harmful viruses and are not by themselves meant to maximise damage. Consequently, countermeasures ought to reflect the threat that hacktivist tools and tactics usually pose and also respond to the nature of those attacks.

In addition to employing counterattacking measures, those targeted could also opt to employ technical defences that would absorb/redirect the traffic generated by a virtual sit-in. This more passive way of defence would avoid any issues relating to the balancing of consequences from a counterattack and would allow those targeted to mitigate the effects of an unwanted protest.

This could also be done in conjunction with the blocking of traffic from blacklisted IP addresses that are linked with botnets or other malicious sources.[93] One would consider such a defensive solution to be a very effective way of dealing with virtual sit-ins, especially if considered in conjunction with defensive software absorbing or redirecting traffic or filtering it based on a constantly updated blacklist of IP addresses. This can become gradually easier since it has been argued that there will be a general need for telecommunications service providers to employ harmonised and standardised trace-back tools and subsequently even IP listing, as part of a general forensic tracing obligation regarding crime prevention.[94]

5 The Role of Hacktivists

5.1 Hacktivists as Communities and Self-regulation

The hacktivist community has an important role to play in shaping how hacktivism is viewed and dealt with as a political practice, since their organising, rhetoric, and tactical choices influence the way hacktivists themselves are perceived and treated by other actors. The opaque structure and diverse tactical orientation and the gradual radicalisation of the protests after the initial era, with the inevitable disregard of traditional moral safeguards, have further justified crackdowns by the authorities on hacktivists. Moreover, some more damaging and less politically expressive hacktions, mainly done under the banner of Anonymous, have served to delegitimise hacktivism as a practice by making the protesters' efforts appear more retaliatory/vigilantist and less politically justifiable.[95]

In order to mitigate these issues, a retrospective self-reflection process with reference to current practices and their deviation from the more self-regulated first era of hacktivism would appear helpful. This will be particularly important currently when hacktivism has become popularised, but at the same time much more diverse in terms of the activities it is linked with. Although the intensification of cybercrime laws means that prosecutions will be more forthcoming anyway, the changes in accountability that Anonymous has brought with its structural opaqueness and tactical diversification make the need for introspection significant for all those engaging in such activities. Even though hacktivism organically changes with time and responds to the more restrictive conditions that cyberprotesters have to face, it is important to acknowledge that there is a degree of responsibility that hacktivists themselves must shoulder in terms of keeping their practices morally justifiable by following healthy examples, rather than a race to the bottom in a chase purely for more disruptiveness and lulz. After all, one cannot expect or hope for a reconsideration of the current responses from the state without the parallel demonstration of more socially considerate behaviours by the protesters. It is these practices that will attract public attention and support and thus put more pressure on the government to ease its approach towards hacktivists.

Self-regulation is 'the situation of a group of persons or bodies, acting together, performing a regulatory function in respect of themselves and others who accept their authority.'[96] Hacktivist communities often demonstrate a mix of 'voluntary self-regulation,' with no link to a governmental influence, which usually involves the potential threat of prosecution by the state.[97] The stricter the regulation by the state, the more that voluntary self-regulation subsides, giving way to coerced self-regulation or radical deregulation, leading protesters underground. However, coerced behaviours are less guaranteed to survive, especially when the behaviour in question is already a reaction to a socially coercive phenomenon and can, thus, easily turn to radicalisation and disobedience of community self-regulation norms as pointless. For example, openness about the identity of hacktivists was an initial voluntary choice of the protesters. However, the high penalty risks that current legislation can entail for those protesting openly, along with the harsh prosecutorial line adopted, have weakened the insistence on openness, so Anonymous has been discussing various anonymity-enhancing tactics, such as the new Pyloris protest tool.

Governance would be impossible if the systems and subsystems regulated do not also have the willingness and the organisational capacity to moderate their behaviours and force compliance through internal mechanisms.[98] Many hacktivist groups have, however, demonstrated a measure of organisational concreteness and ability to self-regulate in terms of promulgating basic rules of behaviour and tactical guidelines.[99] The difficulties regarding self-regulation arise mainly when we try to discuss more loose collectives, such as Anonymous. One should, however, bear in mind that Anonymous is only one aspect of the hacktivist movement and we should not be restricted in our suggestions for self-regulation on the basis of what could be achieved through the structures and practices of Anonymous. Even though this discussion focuses more on the practices that are available to every political entity and less on trying to justify one particular group or collective, it is important to discuss self-regulation taking into account the full organisational spectrum that exists.

There are two challenges regarding the self-regulation of hacktivist communities. The first relates to the organisational structures of the particular group in question, which can be more amorphous than traditional online communities and, therefore, often appear to lack a central authority that would designate and impose tactical and moral standards. The second is that hacktivist groups have no concrete membership. Therefore, any sanctions for violation of norms could be hard to impose efficiently, either for lack of any impact on members, who might not have formal relations with the collective or due to the difficulty of locating those deviating from the organisational and tactical guidelines set. Let us then discuss how these challenges impact on the setting of normative standards and the imposition of these sanctions.

5.2 Establishing Tactical Standards

In the process of maintaining the moral standards of protesting and minimising radicalisation, protesters must make efforts to articulate and preserve the moral and tactical characteristics that support the legitimacy of hacktivist actions, particularly by increasing fairness, proportionality, and accountability practices.[100] This effort will allow for the reinforcement of the moral character of hacktivist protests and will also set the criteria for imposing community sanctions when communal norms are disregarded. This first stage is crucial because, without the designation of prescribed moral guidelines by the protester community, the activities could more easily deteriorate into plain criminality or vigilantism. This in turn would result in alienating the public and delegitimising future protest efforts. Without public support, the hacktivists' actions would often be pointless, since their actions are meant to recruit the public to their causes and not to alienate them.

An important aspect of demonstrating and preserving the moral character of hacktivist practices is the use of rhetoric that does not feel immature or extremist by adopting a warring or vigilantist disposition, as often occurs with Anonymous. The tone of the rhetoric used is crucial as it should link to overarching struggles in a manner that expresses dissent and disaffection, but also ideologically reflects the tactical and moral standards that politically justify the hacktivists' actions. As Meikle argues,

> promoting an emergent cyberspatial politics as 'hacktivism' means dealing with the baggage of the 'hack' component of the term. This term may make it all too easy for electronic civil disobedience to be marginalized and demonized in turn. One challenge for activists, then, is not just to formulate new strategies and tactics appropriate to a shifting mediascape, but to recognize the ongoing need to create a careful vocabulary for discussing those tactics and strategies.[101]

Although different expressive styles and uses of language are inevitable, the use of different language should aim at opening up dialogue, rather than expressing sterile condemnation and retaliatory tendencies, which would induce a counter-offensive or condemning response from the other actors and potentially alienate parts of the public. As Gardiner argues, even for proponents of more dramatised and alternative ways of using ironic or paradoxical language and symbolisms as a politically contestational tool, not unlike the hacktivist culture-jamming language,[102] reaching some sort of agreement in dialogue must be seen as an important goal.[103] Therefore, even if the protesters' hacktions manage to subvert the language of their targets during the event, the language employed before and after the event is also important in making actual political use of these expressive hacks,[104] integrating hacktivist performances into concrete political arguments.

Naturally, the norms and language of hacktivists cannot be fully changed solely through the use of more politically mature rhetoric. However, hacktivists can, at least, demonstrate publicly through their argumentation that their disruptive tactics are not solely done for the sake of disruption or the lulz, but are targeted interventions that link with their deeper political motivations and messages. After all, when one considers the rhetoric of groups before Anonymous, such as Electronic Disturbance Theater (EDT) or the Electrohippies, it becomes obvious that a more concretised political argumentation is not inconsistent with the hacktivist tradition.[105]

However, the designation and preservation of such normative and tactical safeguards as well as the development of a mature, if contestational, political rhetoric also demonstrates the usefulness of supervision of the use of hacktivist tools and the realisation of their protests. The most appropriate participants for shouldering this responsibility would be the more senior, technically adept hacktivists or groups distributing the tactical software or coordinating any actions. Even in self-regulatory models, there must be some form of 'authority' which could suggest or highlight the existence of tactical and moral standards that participants would accept.[106] Although cyberpolitical movements, such as hacktivist groups, are often ideologically diverse, mobilised masses that mostly converge to fight for specific goals,[107] hacktivist groups, even Anonymous, have some members who are more experienced and are accorded seniority in the relevant online spaces where protesters congregate.[108] As Coleman highlights, there is a sense of soft leadership in Anonymous that allows the introduction of new members and challenges the cliques of traditional political party structures.[109] Since the organisers of the various protests could be charged with serious conspiracy charges, community members wishing to avoid such serious liability would have to explicitly demonstrate a willingness and actual effort to maintain the legitimacy of the acts they organise.

Examples of promoting more legitimate practices could include the avoidance of destructive/very harmful software (damaging viruses—defacements where data are destroyed) or targeting sites offering infrastructural services, and even potentially an attempt to get permission from the authorities for a virtual sit-in where the law might entail such a provision for offline marches.[110] Efforts to simulate the requirements of offline protests could increase legitimacy by placing the online protests into a more familiar, offline context of legitimacy and could potentially be a direction that hacktivists should consider.

Publicising moral standards and inducing members and supporters to abide by them could also be realised by the integration of those standards into the code-based tools employed during the protests. Since organisers often have control of, or at least can suggest to participants, the software tools to be employed for particular protests, such as virtual sit-in tools or viruses, a way of preserving legitimacy would be promulgating software that shapes protesters' behaviours accordingly. Principles such as openness of identity and damage minimisation have already been integrated into hacktivist tools in the past.[111] Consequently, self-regulating online collectives could support the use of such tools more persistently and discourage the use of any incompatible protest tools.

5.3 Identifying Deviants and Imposing Sanctions

Even if supervisory agents can exist within the hacktivist mobilisations/collectives, as Murray argues, a community can only regulate itself through the monitoring of consensus and, therefore, defining its membership is a crucial step in these regulatory processes.[112] Regulators should assess whether the moral dictates could actually impact on the casual protesters who will often maintain weak links with the communities, even if deviants could be identified in the first place. Murray warns that communities which lack a particular structure and are formed only on a temporary consensus over specific actions and goals can be so expansive and have such decentralised power structures that community regulation would ultimately be impossible.[113] Hacktivist communities can indeed find it challenging to impose sanctions, such as flaming or banishment from the group,[114] since their members only converge for specific protests, and hence lack a predefined sociopolitical identity and develop meanings and norms as they evolve.[115] At the same time, though, as Coleman reports, within the Anonymous Internet Relay Chat (iRC) channels, operators have excluded from the groups those who suggest tactics that are inconsistent with the usual practices, such as using botnets in virtual sit-ins.[116]

Considering these points, there indeed seem to be differences between the structural characteristics of regulable communities and the way hacktivist collectives are formed and operate. For hacktivists, although a sense of common ideologies and goals might exist within those protesting collectives, political backgrounds and tactical preferences will often vary. The problem of lacking concrete community bonds and membership is also exacerbated by the anonymity often adopted. The turn of many online protesters from open identity or traceable pseudonymity to actual anonymity could thus further increase the difficulty of identifying and sanctioning protesters.[117] Consequently, in addition to actually promoting conditions allowing the identification of deviant members, hacktivist communities will have to deal with the question of whether they produce enough links with their members and supporters for any potential identification of deviance and sanctioning to be possible.

Although, prima facie, it appears that hacktivist collectives are totally amorphous and anonymous, there are certain elements that could facilitate, at least to an extent, the identification of members and, thus, also the imposition of sanctions. In the first type of hacktivist groups, those having a specific, identifiable core of organising members, such as the first generation of hacktivist groups, for example, EDT, the Electrohippies, or Hacktivismo, a violation of the group's norms by these core members could have more specific implications. Norm violation could, for example, mean the expulsion or shaming of the violator by the other group members or the denial of followers to support some of the group's actions, from participation in protests to even publicisation of causes and donations to support the group. Moreover, for such groups with a relatively obvious hierarchy between core organisers and simple participants, most non-organising participants would not be in a position to violate the designated norms, since the parameters of the protests, such as the target, time, duration, notification, and tools for the protest would usually be set by the organising protesters.[118] In these cases, the organisers are often an identifiable authority, not so much in the sense of being acknowledged as such, but more in the sense of initiating and coordinating protests and designating the software required. Consequently, sanctions could be imposed in the micro-community of organisers, even if irrelevant for casual participants who lack group attachments. Inevitably, for virtual sit-ins there might be the case of participants engaging with the protest through the use of a botnet in order to enhance their actions. This would probably be a deviation that would be hard to monitor, unless the user of the botnet is known to the rest of the community or specifically declares it.

However, even in more difficult cases to regulate, there could be a way for community sanctions to be employed if efforts are made to more actively exploit existing, or develop new points of, centralisation within the collective. This could potentially be realised through the use of iRC channels where users interact, or any other website or forum that might constitute a meeting space for hacktivists and supporters. Although participation in those channels can be anonymous, the linking of these channels and the hacktivist collectives to social media could result in many supporters interacting with the groups by logging in using their, often identifiable, social network identities.[119] Even if that is not the case, most users will often adopt pseudonyms that they link to their accounts and are known by them within the online fora. This could facilitate the identification of participants, at least within the community, since people will use a single identity for their various interactions. The risks for privacy here are important and regulatory actors, such as private online content providers who would manage such projects, should make efforts to assure that user identities will not be permeable during the use of their accounts in various online platforms.[120] For the adoption of such measures, stricter controls should be employed regarding surveillance and private information exchanges between private actors and state authorities, so that citizens are not coerced into anonymity to avoid overtly punitive sanctions and undue surveillance.

But even if anonymity trends persist, this would not mean that intra-community identification would be impossible, at least for more consistent participants. The online community relations between users could be employed more actively in order for more identification to be facilitated within the community. Information made voluntarily available by deviant users bragging to peers in the groups they frequent[121] or through more traditional online community gossip could eventually lead community members to identify norm violators. With online communities expansively taking over our everyday time and even emulating real-life ones,[122] community members could potentially uncover the online identities of deviant peers. Consequently, at least at the level of frequent participants, some sense of identifiability and loose community-building could enable a meaningful imposition of sanctions or, if that is not possible, at least a debate on suggested best practices.[123] Perhaps a more traditional basic group structure would support self-regulation better, but could be very risky in situations where identifiable members and particularly organisers are arrested and given serious penalties.[124]

A related concern is the potential bypassing of community sanctions that are imposed technologically by the sanctioned users. For example, banned members could return under another pseudonym, rendering their banishment essentially moot. However, in communities where users have been active for long and have an established status under a certain alias, reappearing with another name could have similar consequences to abandoning one's real-life name, assuming, of course, that the user was an active community member. As it has been argued, distinctions between real-life and online communities are artificial[125] and the more our lives are lived online, the more important and similar to offline communities online communities become.[126] Therefore, expelled users returning with different names will not be able to reconnect with their old contacts and retain their previous group status and, if uncovered, could be banned again.

The success of sanctions is, therefore, a matter of how important participation in a specific group is for users and also how strict the group is at enforcing its rules. Consequently, expulsion from an online community, even if loosely constituted, will be analogously costlier for frequent rather than casual participants due to the existence of genuine links with other members and the habit of belonging to and interacting with a collective.[127] In that sense, Anonymous would be more of a community than first-era groups, which did not originate from an online community, as Anonymous has from 4chan, thus lacking common spaces of convergence where established relationships could be originating from and transitioning into the protest spaces as well.

In sum, one could argue that community self-regulation is a challenging prospect for hacktivist collectives, but one that is also important for corresponding to the challenges for moral legitimacy that such practices entail. This discussion establishes that, for self-regulatory mechanisms to work, there would at least have to be some form of central gathering space and/or command centre, and some sense of consistency in participation on behalf of the protesters. Moreover, the more active employment of code within those communities, together with the establishing of more interactive communicative processes between participants, could increase the bonds of protesters with the community and facilitate community regulation.

Considering the difficulties in the self-regulation of hacktivist communities, one of the main reasons that multi-actor approaches have dominated regulatory discussions and have been adopted in this book is the fact that no particular, one-sided suggestion is absolutely effective on its own or fitting for every context. In fact, even the synergy of all the solutions suggested in this chapter would not achieve permanent and absolute efficaciousness. However, the deficiencies of hacktivist community self-regulation do not make it undesirable. Irrespective of the degree of success, such solutions should be encouraged, since they generally facilitate discussion and norm-building within and between the online communities, and constitute an important initial level of accountability that educates online activists and the public overall regarding online protest norms. Additionally, self-regulatory mechanisms increase the levels of prevention of harmful activities and can thus enhance the legitimacy of the protests, the quality of democratic deliberation, and the avoidance of harsh punishments for protesters.

6 Conclusion

This chapter has highlighted that dealing with hacktivism involves tackling elements that exacerbate the legitimacy deficit highlighted in the previous chapters, which generates issues such as disproportionate punishment and backlash protests, protester radicalisation, qualitative and quantitative reduction of political deliberation, and lower overall cybersecurity. We then proceeded to suggest how such a deficit in terms of just and efficacious responses could be remedied through a switching of rationales from conflict to symbiosis that actively involve multiple parties, from governmental agencies and private companies to the hacktivists themselves. Although the suggestions offered are by no means an exhaustive list, they are indicative of the rationales that need to be followed in order for the effect of the deficit in legitimacy to be ameliorated.

Some core conclusions were drawn from the discussion in this final chapter. First, regulation of online phenomena and especially phenomena as complex as hacktivism require the creative and symbiotic interplay between all related actors in order to achieve the best possible results. No actor and no response alone could achieve an adequately efficient or just result, since the challenges are overwhelming and multifaceted. Nevertheless, as Lessig has argued, regulatory controls need not be perfect, since the combination of smaller influences towards the achievement of our goals can provide us with an adequately successful, overall end-result.[128] A core understanding in this last chapter is exactly the fact that each suggestion independently might appear to be insignificant in dealing with the problem, yet it is the synergy of all these efforts that could lead to a more just and efficient regulatory approach towards hacktivist incidents.

However, perhaps the most important conclusion relevant to achieving a more efficient, just, and democratic way to deal with ECD is that it is a practice that moves across the spectrum of political legitimacy and criminal activity depending on the context. In principle and in many incidents that we have reviewed, hacktivism cannot be seen as a purely criminal activity, nor do we achieve any ultimately beneficial results by treating it as purely criminal in most cases. At the same time, we would have to acknowledge that it falls outside the scope of traditional forms of protected speech and has the potential to be corrupted into a damaging and vigilantist practice. Nevertheless, we should not be plagued by the rigidity of dualism in perceiving hacktivism as either good or bad. This will entrap us in a vicious circle of attempting to apply this binary conceptualisation to the responses we try to develop. And this will usually be fruitless within an online social space that itself redefines traditional, hierarchical conceptions and structures in relation to a political practice that challenges binary assessments of morality/legality.

Irrespective of positive or negative categorisations, what is more important is to acknowledge hacktivism as a new organically developed mode of protest that flows from political struggles that are expressed online. It essentially expresses the new cyberspatial ways that conflict and political deliberation can be realised. If we want a healthier, safer online environment, it is up to competing actors and interests to adopt behaviours that reduce sterile conflict and promote symbiotic solutions to problems in an environment where multiple actors can intervene and collaborate. This requires concerted effort from all actors involved in order for a more harmonious interplay to be achieved.

Acknowledging the importance of promoting symbiotic solutions to problems could eventually become obvious as a potentially better way forward, not only for hacktivism, but for every conflict in cyberspace. Perhaps the case of hacktivism is an example of how cyberspace interactions could improve on the basis of switching from conflict to symbiosis. After all, symbiosis might be harder to achieve, but it is always better than just monistic survival. In fact, it safeguards survival.

Notes

1. Chris Reed, *Making Laws for Cyberspace* (Oxford University Press, Oxford 2012) 17–26.
2. Ibid. 20–26.
3. Robert Baldwin, *Rules and Government* (Clarendon Press, Oxford 1995) 41–46.
4. Ibid. 52–53.
5. Ibid. 55–56.
6. Ibid. 48–54.
7. Julia Black, 'Critical Reflections on Regulation' (2002) 27 Australian Journal of Legal Philosophy 1, 3–4.
8. Mathias Klang, 'Disruptive Technology: Effects of Technology Regulation on Democracy' (DPhil, Goeteborg University 2006) 20.
9. Andrew D. Murray, *The Regulation of Cyberspace: Control in the Online Environment* (Routledge, London 2007) 25, 27–28; Klang (n 8) 29.
10. Julia Black, 'Constitutionalising Self-Regulation' (1996) 59 The Modern Law Review 24, 44; Murray (n 9) 244. Much like the legal system produces and reinforces its norms and structures through its legal acts, corporations define their norms and structures through market policies, while online users and hacktivists shape their own norms and ways of communicating and acting, demonstrating their tendency for a prima facie autonomy.
11. Ibid.
12. Gunther Teubner, *Law as an Autopoietic System* (Blackwell, Oxford 1993) 71.
13. Ibid. 61; Murray (n 9) 245.
14. Julia Black, 'Constitutionalising Self-Regulation' (n 10) 44–45.
15. Gunther Teubner, 'Juridification: Concepts, Aspects, Limits, Solutions' in Gunther Teubner (ed), *Juridification of Social Spheres: A Comparative Analysis in the Areas of Labour, Corporate, Antitrust and Social Welfare Law* (De Gruyter, Berlin 1987) 3–48.
16. Murray (n 9) 243–245.
17. Ibid. 243–244.
18. Ibid. 247–248.
19. Teubner, *Law as an Autopoietic System* (n 12) 65.
20. For the gradual introduction of restorative justice processes into mainstream criminal justice practice, see Andrew von Hirsch et al. (eds),

Restorative Justice and Criminal Justice: Competing or Reconcilable Paradigms? (Hart Publishing, Oxford 2003); John Braithwaite, *Restorative Justice and Responsive Regulation* (Oxford University Press, Oxford 2002).

21. Juergen Habermas and Martha Calhoun, 'Right and Violence: A German Trauma' (1985) 1 Cultural Critique 125.
22. Brownen Morgan and Karen Yeung, *An Introduction to Law and Regulation: Text and Materials* (Cambridge University Press, Cambridge 2007) 95.
23. Suart Biegel, *Beyond Our Control?: Confronting the Limits of Our Legal System in the Age of Cyberspace* (The MIT Press, London 2003) 52.
24. Jack Goldsmith and Tim Wu, *Who Controls the Internet? Illusions of a Borderless World* (Oxford University Press, Oxford 2006) 181.
25. Morgan and Yeung (n 22) 228, 236.
26. Lawrence Lessig, *Code v.2.0* (Basic Books, New York 2006) 77–78.
27. Julia Black, 'Proceduralisation and Polycentric Regulation' (2005) Especial 1 RevistaDIREITOGV, 99 http://direitogv.fgv.br/sites/direitogv.fgv.br/files/rdgv_esp01_p099_130.pdf, 109.
28. Many critics of the inefficiencies of state regulation have focused on the capacity of private actors and more specialised agencies to better understand and have the know-how for dealing with problems that require specialised knowledge. See Black, 'Critical Reflections on Regulation' (n 7).
29. Kenneth J. Melilli, 'Prosecutorial Discretion in an Adversary System' (1992) Brigham Youth University Law Review 669.
30. Ales Zavrsnik, 'Cybercrime Definitional Challenges and Criminological Particularities' (2008) 2 Masaryk University Journal of Law & Technology 1, 8.
31. Allan R. Stein, 'Parochialism and Pluralism in Cyberspace Regulation' (2004) 153 University of Pennsylvania Law Review 2003, 2004.
32. Ibid. 2006.
33. Trevor Thompson, 'Terrorizing the Technological Neighborhood Watch: The Alienation and Deterrence of the White Hats under the CFAA' (2008) 36 Florida State University Law Review 537, 559–560.
34. Ibid. 557; both the felony requirements in the US and the Computer Misuse Act 1990 in the UK have a small interest in the extent of damage for establishing liability and focus more on assessing damage and loss for sentencing.

35. Stefan Fafinski, William H. Dutton, and Helen Margetts, 'Mapping and Measuring Cybercrime' (2010) OII Forum Discussion Paper No 18, 17.
36. Reid Skibell, 'Cybercrime and Misdemeanors: A Reevaluation of the Computer Fraud and Abuse Act' (2003) 18 Berkeley Technology Law Journal 909, 941–944.
37. Jennifer Granick, 'Faking It: Calculating Loss in Computer Crime Sentencing' (2005) 2 A Journal of Law and Policy 207, 208, 228; Pierre Omidyar, 'WikiLeaks, Press Freedom and Free Expression in the Digital Age' (*Huffington Post*, 2 February 2014) http://www.huffingtonpost.com/pierre-omidyar/wikileaks-press-freedom-a_b_4380738.html.
38. Martin Krygier, 'Ethical Positivism and the Liberalism of Fear' (1999) 24 Australian Journal of Legal Philosophy 65, 89.
39. Morgan and Yeung (n 9) 82.
40. Hacktivist groups have also often supported crime prevention purposes, such as exposing software vulnerabilities or monitoring and exposing child pornography websites and offenders. Violet Blue, 'Anonymous Attacks Child Porn Websites and Publish User Names' (*ZDnet Blog*, 21 October 2011) http://www.zdnet.com/blog/violetblue/anonymous-attacks-child-porn-websites-and-publish-user-names/757.
41. For example, Auernheimer, a self-proclaimed troll, was sentenced to 41 months in prison for having obtained email accounts of users by taking advantage of weak data security practices by AT&T. See *US v Auernheimer*, Criminal No.: 2:11-cr-470 (SDW) (Dist. Court, New Jersey 2013); he was eventually acquitted, but for reasons unrelated to the aspect of computer misuse.

    Another alleged member of Anonymous, who claims to have helped expose two rapists in the Steubenville, Ohio, rape case by legally obtaining and publishing online information, was threatened with high penalties as well based on charges of hacking into a website to post such materials, an act for which another collaborating hacker has claimed responsibility. See Nancy Goldstein, 'Steubenville's Tangled Web of Injustice' (*The Guardian*, 12 June 2013) http://www.guardian.co.uk/commentisfree/2013/jun/12/steubenville-tangled-web-injustice. This case resulted in a guilty plea on behalf of Eric Lostutter for conspiring to access a computer without authorisation and lying to an FBI agent. Although his efforts helped bring the Steubenville rape to the fore and initiated a discussion regarding the issue on a national level, Lostutter was considered a bully by the court for having targeted and exposed personal data and email information of the football team's website administrator during the campaign with other Anonymous members. He was sentenced to two years in prison for his actions, which is as high a penalty as one of the rapists got and twice as much as that of the second rapist. See http://www.washingtontimes.com/news/2017/mar/8/deric-lostutter-hacker-sentenced-2-years-prison-cr/.

42. Trevor Thompson, 'Terrorizing the Technological Neighborhood Watch: The Alienation and Deterrence of the White Hats under the CFAA' (2008) 36 Florida State University Law Review 537, 574.
43. Mary M. Calkins, 'They Shoot Trojan Horses, Don't They-an Economic Analysis of Anti-Hacking Regulatory Models' (2000) 89 Georgia Law Journal 171, 205–206.
44. Michael Lee et al., 'Electronic Commerce, Hackers, and the Search for Legitimacy: A Regulatory Proposal' (1999) 14 Berkeley Technology Law Journal 839, 872; Thompson (n 33) 575.
45. Thompson (n 33) 578–579.
46. Cabinet Office, *The UK Cyber Security Strategy: Protecting and Promoting the UK in a Digital World* (London 2011) https://www.gov.uk/government/uploads/system/uploads/attachment_data/file/60961/uk-cyber-security-strategy-final.pdf, 29; Cabinet Office, National security and intelligence, HM Treasury, and The Rt Hon Philip Hammond MP, '*National Cyber Security Strategy 2016 to 2021*' (London 2016) https://www.gov.uk/government/publications/national-cyber-security-strategy-2016-to-2021.
47. Reid Skibell, 'Cybercrime and Misdemeanors: A Reevaluation of the Computer Fraud and Abuse Act' (2003) 18 Berkeley Technology Law Journal 909, 944; Jessica Habib, 'Cyber Crime and Punishment: Filtering out Internet Felons' (2003) 14 Fordham Intellectual Property Media & Entertainment Law Journal 1051, 1054–1055. See, for example, *US v Mitnick*, 145 F.3d 1342 (9th Cir. 1998); *US v Crandon*, 173 F.3d 124 (3rd Cir. 1999).
48. Gabriel Gillett, 'A World without Internet: A New Framework for Analyzing a Supervised Release Condition that Restricts Computer and Internet Access' (2010) 79 Fordham Law Review 217, 220.
49. Michael A. Wolff, 'Evidence-Based Judicial Discretion: Promoting Public Safety through State Sentencing Reform' (2008) 83 New York University Law Review 1389, 1416–1417.
50. Cabinet Office (n 46) 30.

51. See relevant cases in Matthew Fredrickson, 'Sentencing Court Discretion and the Confused Ban on Internet Bans' (June 2014) 9 Wash J.L. Tech. & Arts 349 https://digital.lib.washington.edu:443/dspace-law/handle/1773.1/1343.
52. Gillett (n 48) 227–228; examples are *US v Sofsky*, 287 F.3d 122 (2nd Cir. 2002) (*Sofsky*); *US v White*, 244 F.3d 1199 (10th Cir. 2001) (*White*).
53. The Smoking Gun, 'Judge Lifts Twitter Ban on "Anonymous" 14' (*The Smoking Gun*, 19 March 2012) http://www.thesmokinggun.com/documents/judge-lifts-anonymous-twitter-ban-145792.
54. Frank La Rue, 'Report of the Special Rapporteur on the Promotion and Protection of the Right to Freedom of Opinion and Expression. VI. Conclusions and Recommendations' (*United Nations General Assembly*, 16 May 2011) http://www2.ohchr.org/english/bodies/hrcouncil/docs/17session/a.hrc.17.27_en.pdf.
55. United Nations General Assembly, Human Rights Council, 'Oral Revision Document Regarding the Promotion, Protection and Enjoyment of Human Rights on the Internet' (30 June 2016) https://www.article19.org/data/files/Internet_Statement_Adopted.pdf.
56. See *White* (n 52) and also *US v Holm*, 326 F.3d 872 (7th Cir. 2003) *(Holm); US v Heckman*, 592 F.3d 400 (3rd Cir. 2010).
57. See, for example, *United States v. Paul*, 274 F.3d 155 (5th Cir. 2001); *United States v Brigham*, 569 F.3d 220 (5th Cir. 2009).
58. Gillett (n 48) 246; See *US v Walser*, 275 F.3d 981 (10th Cir. 2001).
59. Fredrickson (n 51) 355–356.
60. The state should not impose technological use restrictions, if these would render the finding of work impossible. See *US v Russell*, 600 F.3d 631 (D.C. Cir. 2010) (stressing that McDonald's and PETCO require computer use to complete job application and duties, respectively); *Holm* (n 56).
61. Manuel Castells, *Communication Power* (Oxford University Press, Oxford 2009) 72–74.
62. Morgan and Yeung (n 22) 36–37.
63. Similar characteristics are the focus of regulatory assessments in responsive models of regulation articulated by Black and Baldwin, trying to demonstrate the need for a more holistic understanding of the context and the effects of regulatory solutions. Robert Baldwin and Julia Black, 'Really Responsive Regulation' (2008) 71 The Modern Law Review 59.
64. Arne Hintz, *Deconstructing Multi-Stakeholderism: The Discourses and Realities of Global Governance at the World Summit on the Information Society (WSIS)* (Central European University, Budapest 2007) 3–4;

Rebecca Mackinnon, *Consent of the Networked: The Worldwide Struggle for Internet Freedom* (Basic Books, New York 2012) 208.
65. Geert Lovink and Ned Rossiter, 'Dawn of the Organised Networks' (2005) 5 Fibreculture Journal http://five.fibreculturejournal.org/fcj-029-dawn-of-the-organised-networks/.
66. Jeanette Hofmann, 'Multi-Stakeholderism in Internet Governance: Putting a Fiction into Practice' (2016) 1 Journal of Cyber Policy 1 http://www.tandfonline.com/doi/full/10.1080/23738871.2016.1158303, 33–34.
67. Ibid. 34–35.
68. Dmitry Epstein, 'The Duality of Information Policy Debates: The Case of the Internet Governance Forum' (DPhil, Cornell University 2012) 115–116; Milton Mueller, 'IGF 2015: Running in Place' (2015) http://www.internetgovernance.org/2015/11/16/igf-2015-running-in-place/.
69. Hofmann (n 66) 37–38.
70. Arne Hintz and Stefania Milan, 'At the Margins of Internet Governance: Grassroots Tech Groups and Communication Policy' (2009) 5 International Journal of Media & Cultural Politics 23, 34.
71. Ibid.
72. Losey, James, 'The Anti-Counterfeiting Trade Agreement and European Civil Society: A Case Study on Networked Advocacy' (2014) 4 Journal of Information Policy 205–227. doi:10.5325/jinfopoli.4.2014.0205.
73. Sabine Lang, *NGOs, Civil Society, and the Public Sphere* (Cambridge University Press, New York 2013). P. 22 cited in Losey (n 72) 220.
74. Losey (n 72) 220.
75. Milton Mueller, John Mathiason, and Hans Klein, 'The Internet and Global Governance Principles and Norms for a New Regime' (2007) 13 Global Governance 237.
76. Castells (n 61) 39.
77. Ibid.
78. Epstein (n 68).
79. Castells (n 61) 12.
80. 17 U.S.C. Section 512 (g)(3).
81. See Sections 512(g)(2)(B) and 512(g)(2)(C). See also Lydia P. Loren, 'Deterring Abuse of the Copyright Takedown Regime by Taking Misrepresentation Claims Seriously' (2011) 46 Wake Forest Law Review 745, 757–758.

82. Ibid.
83. Benoit Frydman and Isabelle Rorive, 'Regulating Internet Content through Intermediaries in Europe and the USA' (2002) 23 Zeitschrift für Rechtssoziologie 41, 52 analyses the US approach, which adopts such interactive processes.
84. Xiang Li, 'Hacktivism and the First Amendment: Drawing the Line between Cyber Protests and Crime' (2013) 27 Harvard Journal Law & Technology, 301, 327.
85. Ibid.
86. Ibid.
87. Dorothy E. Denning, 'Activism, Hacktivism, and Cyberterrorism: The Internet as a Tool for Influencing Foreign Policy' in Jon Arquila and David Ronfeldt (eds), *Networks and Netwars: The Future of Terror, Crime, and Militancy* (RAND Corporation 2001) 265.
88. Curtis Karnow, 'Launch on Warning: Aggressive Defense of Computer Systems' (2004) 7 Yale Journal of Law & Technology 87, 93; Counterstrike-software companies do not exclude the chance of small, collateral damage to innocent parties. It is, however, suggested that if the exact address of the attacker cannot be verified as not being of such critical nature, less aggressive measures should be preferred, expressing the need to minimise risk. Bruce P. Smith, 'Hacking, Poaching, and Counterattacking: Digital Counterstrikes and the Contours of Self-Help' (2005) 1 Journal of Law Economy & Policy 171, 181.
89. Joel R. Reidenberg, 'Technology and Internet Jurisdiction' (2004) 153 University of Pennsylvania Law Review 1951, 1964.
90. Susan W. Brenner, *Cybercrime: Criminal Threats from Cyberspace* (Praeger Publishers, Oxford 2010) 212–214.
91. Jay P. Kesan and Ruperto Majuca, 'Optimal Hackback' (2010) 84 Chicago-Kent Law Review 831–833.
92. Reidenberg, 'Technology and Internet Jurisdiction' (n 89) 1965; Consideration of proportionality and accountability have also been based on the defences of choice of evils or necessity. Smith (n 88) 191–192.
93. CISCO, for example, compiles lists of domain names and IP addresses related to malign web traffic and spamming email servers, facilitating filtering of such traffic. CISCO, 'Combating Botnets Using the CISCO Asa Botnet Traffic Filter' (*CISCO White Paper,* 2009) http://www.cisco.com/en/US/prod/collateral/vpndevc/ps6032/ps6094/ps6120/white_paper_c11-532091.html; see also the relevant project Spamhaus.org, 'Spamhaus Botnet Controller List,' https://www.spamhaus.org/bcl/.

94. Malcom Shore, Yi Du, and Sherali Zeadally, 'A Public-Private Partnership Model for National Cybersecurity' (2011) 3 Policy & Internet 1, 18.
95. Anonymous has gone beyond symbolic protests by hacking into corporate and police networks and exposing credit card information or personal addresses of policemen involved in protest arrests that have been considered purely retaliatory, with low politically expressive quality. Adam G. Klein, 'Vigilante Media: Unveiling Anonymous and the Hacktivist Persona in the Global Press' 82/3 Communication Monographs http://nca.tandfonline.com/doi/abs/10.1080/03637751.2015.1030682, 397.
96. Black, 'Constitutionalising Self-Regulation' (n 10) 26–27.
97. Ibid.
98. Julia Black, 'Decentring Regulation: Understanding the Role of Regulation and Self-Regulation in a "Post-Regulatory" World' (2001) 54 Current Legal Problems 103, 125–126.
99. Examples are the guidelines by the Electrohippies regarding their actions and the use of their virtual sit-in tools, or the user licence created by Hacktivismo regarding the use of their tools for non-criminal purposes.
100. Earlier groups have been more eloquent in suggesting safeguards. In groups with an organising core, such as EDT, the realisation of the various protests entailed specific tactical guidelines in order for the actions to be as harmless as possible and demonstrate their moral motives. Even with less structured collectives like Anonymous, similar guidelines have been often deliberated and even publicised with online videos for online and offline protests: Anonymous, 'Anonymous – Code of Conduct' (*YouTube*, 21 December 2010) https://www.youtube.com/watch?v=-063clxiB8I.
101. Graham Meikle, 'Electronic Civil Disobedience and Symbolic Power' in Athina Karatzogianni (ed), *Cyberconflicts and Global Politics* (Routledge, London 2009) 182–183.
102. Leah A. Lievrouw, 'Oppositional and Activist New Media: Remediation, Reconfiguration, Participation' (Proceedings of the Ninth Participatory Design Conference, Trento 2006) https://dl.acm.org/citation.cfm?id=1147279 6; Jordan, *Activism!: Direct Action, Hacktivism and the Future of Society* 103.

103. Gardiner Michael E. Gardiner, 'Wild Publics and Grotesque Symposiums: Habermas and Bakhtin on Dialogue, Everyday Life and the Public Sphere' (2004) 52 The Sociological Review 28, 39.
104. Tim Jordan and Paul A. Taylor, *Hacktivism and Cyberwars: Rebels with a Cause?* (Routledge, London 2004) 158.
105. See examples in DJNZ and The Action Tool Development Group of the Electrohippies Collective, 'Client-Side Distributed Denial-of-Service: Valid Campaign Tactic or Terrorist Act?' (2001) 34 Leonardo 269; Ricardo Dominguez, 'Electronic Disobedience Post-9/11' (2008) 22 Third Text 661.
106. Jacob van Kokswijk, 'Social Control in Online Society–Advantages of Self-Regulation on the Internet' (International Conference on Cyberworlds, Singapore 2010) 240.
107. Robert S. Jansen, 'Populist Mobilization: A New Theoretical Approach to Populism' (2011) 29 Sociological Theory 75, 82–83.
108. For example, Moot is the founder of 4chan, and despite the lack of formal authority, he would be acknowledged as someone many in Anonymous would at least listen to: Adrian Crenshaw, 'Crude, Inconsistent Threat: Understanding Anonymous' (*Irongeek,* 2011) http://www.irongeek.com/i.php?page=security/understanding-anonymous.
109. Gabriella Coleman, *Hacker, Hoaxer, Whistleblower, Spy: The Many Faces of Anonymous* (Verso Books, 2014) 76.
110. Hacktivists in Germany resorted to such legitimisation means, such as prior notification and request of permission from the authorities, which played a role in their countering the prosecutor's charges for coercion: see European Digital Rights, 'Frankfurt Appellate Court Says Online Demonstration Is Not Coercion' (*European Digital Rights*, 7 June 2006) https://edri.org/edrigramnumber4-11demonstration/.
111. Virtual sit-in tools usually do not mask the identity of users, while viruses employed do not cause undue harms to computer systems.
112. Murray (n 9) 128.
113. Ibid. 163–164.
114. The most commonly used sanctions would be banishment from the online collectives and strong censure or shaming mechanisms on behalf of the community through public, online criticism (flaming) or the exposition of personal details of the norm violators, demonstrating the community's disapproval (doxing).

115. Christian Fuchs, *Internet and Society: Social Theory in the Information Age* (Routledge, New York 2008) 308, 314–315.
116. Coleman (n 109) 95.
117. Kevin Rawlinson, 'Activists Warned to Watch What They Say as Social Media Monitoring Becomes "Next Big Thing in Law Enforcement"' (*The Independent*, 1 October 2012) http://www.independent.co.uk/news/uk/crime/activists-warned-to-watch-what-they-say-as-social-media-monitoring-becomes-next-big-thing-in-law-enforcement-8191977.html; Cyrus Farivar, 'NY Judge Compels Twitter to Reveal User's Data' (*Ars Technica*, 2 July 2012) http://arstechnica.com/tech-policy/2012/07/ny-judge-compels-twitter-to-reveal-user-data/.
118. EDT, for example, was organising its protests through its ECD web page calling protesters to participate and setting the standards beforehand. Ricardo Dominguez, 'Electronic Civil Disobedience' (*thing.net*, undated) http://www.thing.net/~rdom/ecd/ecd.html.
119. The concept of identity portability, where people can join many networks and websites through their Facebook accounts, for example, is characteristic of this phenomenon and is becoming increasingly popular with many websites offering the opportunity to use one's established identity from affiliated websites. For the functions and spread of portable identities, see Daniel Kahn, 'Social Intermediaries: Creating a More Responsible Web through Portable Identity, Cross-Web Reputation, and Code-Backed Norms' (2010) 11 Columbia Science & Technology Law Review 176.
120. Ibid.
121. Paul A. Taylor, *Hackers: Crime in the Digital Sublime* (Routledge, London 1999) 6–10; a characteristic example is Mafiaboy, who managed to take large corporate websites offline and was caught after he bragged about it in a hacker forum. Wikipedia, 'Mafiaboy' (2011) http://en.wikipedia.org/wiki/MafiaBoy. See a recent example: Mary C. Long, 'Anonymous' Hacker Brags on Twitter and Gets Caught' (*Adweek*, 17 April 2012) http://www.adweek.com/digital/hacker-brags-on-twitter/.
122. Murray (n 9) 146–147.
123. Indicative of the imposition of sanctions is the extensive censuring of one alleged Anonymous member, who presented himself publicly as a spokesperson, thus violating an important norm of the collective which prides itself upon not having leaders or official spokesmen: Coleman (n 109) 184–186.

124. The Electrohippies stopped their virtual sit-in and other hacktivist actions due to their fear of high penalties. The Electrohippies Collective, 'Cyberlaw UK: Civil Rights and Protest on the Internet' (*iwar.org*, 2000) http://www.iwar.org.uk/hackers/resources/electrohippies-collective/comm-2000-12.pdf.
125. van Kokswijk (n 106) 239.
126. Murray (n 9) 146–147.
127. Ibid. 141–142.
128. Lessig, *Code v.2.0* (n 26) 73.

7

Final Conclusions

Having reached the end of this book, it is necessary to highlight the most important points that have been distilled. There were three main questions posed in the course of this discussion. The first point related to whether we should be interested in how hacktivism is dealt with as a law-breaking activity that combines negative and also positive elements for networked societies. The next was whether the current framework of responses towards hacktivism is adequately achieving the desirable goals of security, crime prevention, justice, and promoting democratic deliberation. The third major question was whether changing or improving the current conflict-focused structures is possible and in what ways could Western democratic societies move closer to a more just and efficacious way of dealing with hacktivist incidents through a different rationale of symbiosis.

In relation to these major interrelated questions, there have been three major conclusions, which are also interrelated and are constituted by smaller conclusions that are relevant not just for hacktivism, but also to more general issues regarding the regulation of cyberspace activity.

The first complex conclusion has evolved from the chapters analysing the various aspects of hacktivism and its role and importance within

V. Karagiannopoulos, *Living With Hacktivism*, Palgrave Studies in Cybercrime and Cybersecurity, https://doi.org/10.1007/978-3-319-71758-6_7

cyberspace power conflicts and the development of the Internet as a social space. Hacktivism is a cluster of practices of political expression in cyberspace which have evolved since its popularisation, fusing two intrinsic activities that have been prevalent in cyberspace as a novel social space, namely hacking and political activism. Hacktivism is a law-breaking practice that can entail security risks and harmful consequences, but also has the potential to demonstrate elements of political usefulness. Hacktivism has seen different degrees of popularity throughout different eras, with perhaps the most popular and the most chaotic period being the current one. However, its consistent presence throughout the years in various forms and on a global scale renders hacktivism something more than just a passing trend that will recede on its own or through oppression. It rather appears to be manifesting in waves and, as a natural form of expression for countercultural tendencies, it is bound to appear each time the sociopolitical conditions call for it in its various shapes and forms.

The establishment of the special nature and role of hacktivism, but also its potential for being corrupted into undesirable forms of coercion and vigilantism, also becomes evident through our discussion of free speech and civil disobedience. Particularly through linking and analogising hacktivist practices to civil disobedience, we can better see its utility and potential harmfulness for contemporary democratic online politics, which informs the critique of hacktivist practice itself, but also of the current responses to it.

The second major conclusion is that dealing with hacktivism is a demanding process that is currently often fraught with inefficiencies and inadequacies in bringing out its positive dimensions and mitigating its negative potential. What we mainly see today as a response is a very selective and punitive treatment of easy-to-apprehend hacktivists by the criminal justice system. This often causes backlash from other hacktivists and supporters in terms of more protests as well as radicalisation of more determined protesters going underground. At the same time, the more moderate hacktivists who would follow more principled and politically more beneficial practices move away from the practice for fear of persecution. The overall result is more potentially harmful acts, disproportionate penalties for those apprehended and less productive democratic contestation online.

Drawing from this second conclusion, the third major conclusion is that there is a need to reconsider our responses to hacktivism more particularly, but also towards controversial online expression and cyberdeviancy more generally. The realisation flowing from the discussion above is that the conflicts that propagate the vicious circle of punitiveness and radicalisation are mainly caused by a lack of understanding of cyberspace as a social space where different power structures clash or an unwillingness to do so, which is reinforced by a persistence on conflict-based solutions. These conditions result in each party involved in the conflict resorting to potentially more intensified, retaliatory reactions or withdrawal from the political arena. Consequently, more cooperative and inclusive approaches based on deliberation and mutual understanding are discouraged, which impacts on the preservation of moral standards in online political contestation and reduces democratic deliberation. This book acknowledges that this persistence on conflict-based responses to the challenges posed by a phenomenon that is born out of conflict will keep generating more problems than those it seems to be resolving. Consequently, this book attempts to find the solution in more multifaceted and reconciliatory conceptions of problem-solving by adopting a theory focused on symbiosis.

This work suggests that there is a need for a more interactive, multi-actor regulatory structure that can gradually begin to remedy the problems that hierarchical, conflict-focused responses introduce. Symbiosis is not achieved through major, wholesale changes. It rather works better through well-thought-out micro-interventions in various areas in which conflict-inducing perceptions and actions are identified. It supplements existing, yet reconceptualised, responses with novel suggestions as well, in providing some examples of how better results could be achieved overall. These can range from reconsidering criminal justice processes and trends to creating more open communicative processes for productive democratic deliberation and responsibilising hacktivists in relation to their aims, rhetoric, and consequences of their actions.

An overarching concern is that the current prevailing trends of security, risk, and information control suggest that a shift towards symbiosis will be hard to promote, since the conflict-based rationales are seemingly intensifying. However, the inefficacious and unjust results the recent responses often entail could gradually induce the different stakeholders to reconsider their approaches and rationales. Even if rights-related concerns could not be strong enough to induce a policy reconsideration, security and crime prevention considerations for the state and corporations could facilitate a gradual realisation of the failure of more punitive and restrictive policies and gradually lead to a shift towards more symbiotic approaches. The same goes for hacktivists, who could see the moral concerns and legal risks in adopting a more radical rhetoric and harmful tactics and shift towards less retaliatory and more expressive practices.

This book has suggested changes, some minor and some more important, without, however, opting for a total break with the current political system or the main principles supporting policymaking. Nonetheless, the analysis does not aim to just reproduce the dominant ideas of the status quo without making an effort to suggest a different route in policymaking within that dominating framework, since the hacktivism example demonstrates that perhaps a deeper reconsideration is required on how to generally approach deviance online.

I hope that the arguments made here will serve as guidance for future researchers, policymakers, and even hacktivists for implementing a different approach, not only for hacktivism, but also in relation to the wider issue of cybersecurity and Internet civil rights. The voices of change exist and come from different areas even beyond the hacktivist core. This book has tried to identify these voices and demonstrate how they might facilitate a gradual change in perspectives, acknowledging the difficulties, but also the fact that thinking and acting only based on established norms and perceptions has rarely brought about any significant social improvement. My aim is that this discussion will provide food for thought for supporters of symbiosis as a conceptual paradigm with theoretical arguments and practical suggestions that could facilitate their efforts. However, I hope that perhaps this work will also induce critics to reconsider and readjust some of their arguments or consider new, hybrid ones. As cyberspace has hybridised our everyday lives, it is only natural that we start to think in hybrid ways as well. And hacktivism, being a hybrid practice in itself, at least forces us to start doing exactly this.

Bibliography

Table of Cases

European Court of Human Rights

Appleby v United Kingdom (2003) 37 EHRR 38
Gorzelik and others v Poland (2005) 40 EHRR
KU v Finland (2008) ECtHR 2872/02

Germany

OberlandesGericht Frankfurt am Main v Thomas Vogel (No. 1 Ss 319/05)

United Kingdom

City of London v Samede & Ors [2012] EWHC 34 QB
DPP v Lennon [2006] All ER (D) 147
R v Jones (Margaret) [2005] QB 259

V. Karagiannopoulos, *Living With Hacktivism*, Palgrave Studies in Cybercrime and Cybersecurity, https://doi.org/10.1007/978-3-319-71758-6

R v Bow Street Magistrates Court and Allison (A.P.) Ex Parte Government of the United States of America [1999] All ER (D) 972
R v Weatherhead, Rhodes, Gibson and Burchall, Southwark Crown Court, 24 January 2013
R v G and Another [2003] UKHL 50
R v Howe [1987] 1 AC 417
R v Ponting [1985] Crim LR 318
R v Saibene and others [2010] Lewes Crown Court

United States

Amalgamated Food Employees Union Local 590 v Logan Valley Plaza, Inc., 391 U.S. 308 (1968)
America Online, Inc. v IMS et al. 24 F.Supp.2d 548 (E.D.Va. 1998)
America Online v National Health Care Discount, Inc., 121 F. Supp. 2d 1255 (N.D. Iowa 2000)
Chicago v Streeter, No. 85-108644 (Cir. Court, Cook County, Ill. 1985)
Citizens United v Federal Election Commission 558 U.S. 310 (2010)
Cyber Promotions, Inc. v America Online, Inc., 948 F. Supp. 436 (E.D. Pa. 1996)
EF Cultural Travel BV v Explorica, Inc., 274 F.3d 577 (1st Cir. 2001)
EF Cultural Travel BV, et al. v. Zefer Corporation, 318 F.3d 58 (1st Cir., January 28, 2003)
Hudgens v. NLRB 424 U.S. 507, 96 S. Ct. 1029, 47 L. Ed. 2d 196, 1976 U.S
Hogan v. Twp. of Haddon, 278 F. App'x 98, 102 (3d Cir. 2008)
Illinois v Jarka, No. 002170 (Cir. Court Ill. 1985), reprinted in 42 GUILD PRAC. 108–10 (1985)
International Airport Centers, Llc v Citrin, 440 F.3d 418 (7th Cir. 2006)
LVRC Holdings v Brekka, 518 F.3d 1127 (9th Cir. 2009)
Massachusetts v Carter, No. 8745-JC-0091A (Dist. Court, Hampshire County, Mass. 1987)
People of the State of New York v Gray, 150 Misc. 2d 852 (N.Y. Co. 1991)
Register.com, Inc. v Verio, Inc., 126 F.Supp. 2d 238, 255 (S.D.N.Y. 2000)
State v Allen, 917 P.2d 848 (Kan. 1996)
Storage Centers, Inc. v Safeguard Self Storage, Inc., 119 F.Supp. 2d 1121 (Dist. Court, Washington D.C. 2000)
Sutliffe v. Epping Sch. Dist., 584 F.3d 314, 333–34 (1st Cir. 2009)
United States v Aguilar, 883 F.2d 662, 693 (9th Cir. 1989)

United States v American Library Association, 539 U.S. 194 (2003)
United States v Auernheimer, Criminal No.: 2:11-cr-470 (SDW) (Dist. Court, New Jersey 2013)
United States v Berrigan, 283 F. Supp. 336 (Dist. Court, Maryland, 1968)
United States v Booker, 543 U.S. 220 (2005)
United States v Cassidy, 616 F.2d 101 (4th Cir. 1979)
United States v Crandon, 173 F.3d 124 (3rd Cir. 1999)
United States v Czubinski, 106 F. 3d 1069 (1st Cir. 1997)
United States v Dorrell, 758 F.2d 427 (9th Cir. 1985)
United States v Guzner, No. 2:09-cr-00087 (Dist. Court, New Jersey 2009)
United States v Heckman, 592 F.3d 400 (3rd Cir. 2010)
United States v Holm, 326 F.3d 872 (7th Cir. 2003)
United States v Kroncke, 459 F.2d 697 (8th Cir. 1972)
United States v Marley, 549 F.2d 561 (8th Cir. 1977)
United States v Maxwell, 254 F.3d 21 (1st Cir. 2001)
United States v May, 622 F.2d 1000 (9th Cir. 1980), cert denied, 449 U.S. 984 (1980)
United States v Mettenbrink, Case 2:09-cr-01149-GAF (Dist. Court, California 2010)
United States v Middleton, 231 F.3d 1207 (9th Cir. 2000)
United States v Mitnick, 145 F.3d 1342 (9th Cir. 1998)
United States v Morris, 928 F.2d 504 (2nd Cir. 1991)
United States v Nosal, 676 F.3d 854 (9th Cir. 2012)
United States v. Nosal, 828 F.3d 865 (9th Cir. 2016), reh'g denied and amended by 2016 WL 7190670 (9th Cir. Dec. 8, 2016)
United States v Phillips, 477 F.3d 215 (5th Cir. 2007)
United States v Russell, 600 F.3d 631 (D.C. Cir. 2010)
United States v Schoon, 22 Ill.971 F.2d 193 (9th Cir. 1991)
United States v Sofsky, 287 F.3d 122 (2nd Cir. 2002)
United States v Walser, 275 F.3d 981 (10th Cir. 2001)
United States v White, 244 F.3d 1199 (10th Cir. 2001)
Vargas v. City of Salinas, 205 P.3d 207, 215 n.8 (Cal. 2009)
Vermont v Keller, No. 1372-4-84 (Dist. Court, Vt. 1984)
Vermont v McCann, No. 2857-7-86 (Dist. Court, Vt. 1987), reprinted in 44 GUILD PRAC. 101 (1987)
Ward v Rock Against Racism, 491 U.S. 781 (1989)

Table of Legislation

International Treaties, Conventions and Other Documents

Council of Europe, The European Convention for the Protection for Human Rights and Fundamental Freedoms (Rome, 1950)

Council of Europe, Convention on Cybercrime (ETS no.185, Budapest, 2001)

Directive 2000/31/EC of the European Parliament and of the Council on certain legal aspects of information society services, in particular electronic commerce, in the Internal Market, OJ EL 178

Directive 2002/21/EC of the European Parliament and of the Council on a common regulatory framework for electronic communications networks and services (Framework Directive) OJ L 108

Directive 2002/58/EC of the European Parliament and of the Council concerning the processing of personal data and the protection of privacy in the electronic communications sector (Directive on privacy and electronic communications) OJ L 201

EU Council Framework Decision 2005/222/JHA of 24 February 2005 on attacks against information systems, OJ L 69

Strafgesetzbuch (German Criminal Code)

United Kingdom

Anti-Terrorism, Crime and Security Act of 2001 (c. 24)

Coroners and Justice Act 2009 (c.25)

Computer Misuse Act 1990 (c.18)

Criminal Justice Act 2003 (c.44)

Criminal Law Act 1977 (c.45)

Digital Economy Act 2010 (c.24)

Electronic Commerce (EC Directive) Regulations of 2002, No. 2013

Human Rights Act 1998 (c.42)

Magistrates' Courts Act 1980 (c.43)

Police and Justice Act 2006 (c.48)
Prevention of Terrorism Act 2005 (c.2)
Public Order Act 1986 (c.8)
Terrorism Act 2000 (c.11)
Terrorism Act 2006 (c.11)
The Terrorism Act 2000 (Remedial) Order 2011, No.631

United States

Acts of Terrorism Transcending National Boundaries,
18 U.S.C. Part I Chapter 113B, Section 2332b
Animal Enterprise Terrorism Act,
18 U.S.C. Part I, Chapter 3, Section 43
Application of Guidelines in Imposing a Sentence,
18 U.S.C. Chapter 227 Subchapter A. Section 3553(b)
Fraud and Related Activity in Connection with Access Devices,
18 U.S.C. Part I, Chapter 47 Section 1029
Fraud and Related Activity in Connection with Computers,
18 U.S.C. Part I, Chapter 47 Section 1030
Homeland Security Act of 2002,
116 Stat. 2135,
Homicide,
18 U.S.C. Chapter 51, Section 1111
Identity Theft Enforcement and Restitution Act 2008,
Title II, 122 Stat. 3560
Intelligence Reform and Terrorism Prevention Act of 2004,
118 Stat. 3638
Manslaughter,
18 U.S.C. Chapter 51, Section 1112
Model Penal Code (American Law Institute, 1968)
United States Constitution, Amendment I – Freedom of Religion, Press, Expression
Uniting and Strengthening America by Providing Appropriate Tools Required to Intercept and Obstruct Terrorism Act of 2001 – USAPA) 115 Stat. 272

Secondary Sources

Anonymous Works and Arithmetic Names

———, 'Immunizing the Internet, Or: How I Learned to Stop Worrying and Love the Worm' (2006) 119 Harvard Law Review 2442

0100101110101101.org, 'Copies' (*0100101110101101.org,* 1999–2000) http://0100101110101101.org/copies/, accessed 31 July 2017

———, 'The K Thing: Story of an Infamous Online Performance' (*0100101110101101.org,* 2001) http://0100101110101101.org/the-k-thing, accessed 31 July 2017

———, '0100101110101101.Org Projects' (*0100101110101101.org,* 2011) http://www.0100101110101101.org/projects.html, accessed 31 July 2017

———, 'Contagious Paranoia 0100101110101101.org Spreads a New Computer Virus' (*0100101110101101.org,* 2011) http://0100101110101101.org/biennale-py/, accessed 31 July 2017

2600 Magazine, 'Press Release – 2600 Magazine Condemns Denial of Service Attacks' (*2600 Magazine,* 10 December 2010) https://dear2600.wordpress.com/2010/12/10/press-release-2600-magazine-condemns-denial-of-service-attacks/, accessed 16 October 2017

4chan http://www.4chan.org/, accessed 25 June 2017

A

Aas K F, *Globalization & Crime* (Sage, London 2007)

Abbas M, 'Economic Crisis Could Widen Inequality – Report' (*Reuters,* 10 October 2010) http://uk.reuters.com/article/idUKTRE6992CY20101010, accessed 24 October 2017

Adler F, 'Socioeconomic Factors Influencing Jury Verdicts' (1973) 3 New York University Review of Law and Social Change 1

Adler J, *The Urgings of Conscience: A Theory of Punishment* (Temple University Press, Philadelphia 1992)

Agamben G, *Means without End: Notes on Politics* (University of Minnesota Press, Minneapolis 2000)

Akester P, 'Copyright and the P2P Challenge' (2005) 27 European Intellectual Property Review 576

Alexander L, 'Lesser Evils: A Closer Look at the Paradigmatic Justification' (2005) 24 Law and Philosophy 611

Alexander L, Kessler K F, and Morse S J, *Crime and Culpability: A Theory of Criminal Law* (Cambridge University Press, Cambridge 2009)

All Party Internet Group (APIG), 'Revision of the Computer Misuse Act': Report on an Inquiry by the All Party Internet Group (2004) http://www.cullen-international.com/cullen/multi/national/uk/laws/cmareport.pdf, accessed 14 August 2013

Allan G, 'Responding to Cybercrime: A Delicate Blend of the Orthodox and the Alternative' (2005) New Zealand Law Review 149

Allnutt L, 'Old-School Hacker Oxblood Ruffin Discusses Anonymous and the Future of Hacktivism' (*Tangled Web*, 08 June 2011) http://www.rferl.org/content/hacker_oxblood_ruffin_discusses_anonymous_and_the_future_of_hacktivism/24228166.html, accessed 20 September 2011

Alschuler A, 'Implementing the Criminal Defendant's Right to Trial: Alternatives to the Plea Bargaining System' (1983) 50 University of Chicago Law Review 931

Alton S R, 'In the Wake of Thoreau: Four Modern Legal Philosophers and the Theory of Non-Violent Civil Disobedience' (1993) 24 Loyola University Law Journal 39

Amnesty International, 'Undermining Freedom of Expression in China: The Role of Yahoo!, Microsoft and Google' (*Amnesty International*, 2006) https://www.amnesty.org/en/documents/POL30/026/2006/en/, accessed 20 May 2017

Anderson N, 'Germany Adopts "Anti-Hacker" Law; Critics Say It Breeds Insecurity' (*ArsTechnica*, 28 May 2008) http://arstechnica.com/security/news/2007/05/germany-adopts-anti-hacker-law-critics-say-it-breeds-insecurity.ars, accessed 20 May 2017

Androulakis N, *Penal Law: General Part* (P.N. Sakkoulas, Athens 2000)

Anonymous, 'Teenage Hacker Admits Scientology Cyber-Attack USA v. Guzner – Information' (*Secretdox*, 18 October 2008) http://secretdox.wordpress.com/2008/10/18/usa-v-guzner-plea-agreement-for-defendant-dmitriy-guzner/, accessed 20 May 2011

———, 'Anonymous – Code of Conduct' (*YouTube*, 21 December 2010) https://www.youtube.com/watch?v=-063clxiB8I, accessed 16 February 2013

———, 'Anonymous Press Release: Open Letter from Anonymous to the UK Government' (*Anonops*, 27 January 2011) https://www.indymedia.org.uk/en/2011/01/472905.html, accessed 10 November 2017

———, 'Anonymous Is Not Unanimous' (*Pastebin*, 17 August 2011) http://pastebin.com/4vprKdXH, accessed 20 December 2011

Anonymous Interviewer, 'Fragmented Plurality: An Interview with Gabriella Coleman' (*The Breaking Time,* 14 April 2011) http://thebreakingtime.typepad.com/the_breaking_time/2011/04/an-enormous-plurality-an-interview-with-gabriella-coleman.html, accessed 20 May 2017

Arendt H, *Crises of the Republic* (4th edn, Harvest Books, San Diego 1972)

Aronowitz S and Gautney H (eds), *Implicating Empire: Globalization and Resistance in the 21st Century World Order* (Basic Books, New York 2003)

Arthur C, 'Inside 'Anonymous': Tales from within the Group Taking Aim at Amazon and Mastercard' (*The Guardian Technology Blog*, 13 December 2010) http://www.guardian.co.uk/technology/blog/2010/dec/13/hacking-wikileaks, accessed 19 December 2017

———, 'Lulzsec: What They Did, Who They Were and How They Were Caught' (*The Guardian Technology Blog,* 16 May 2013) http://www.guardian.co.uk/technology/2013/may/16/lulzsec-hacking-fbi-jail, accessed 20 June 2017

Ashford W, 'Infosec 2013: Cyber Crime Challenges Law Enforcement' (*Computer Weekly,* 25 April 2013) http://www.computerweekly.com/news/2240182575/Infosec-2013-Cyber-crime-challenges-law-enforcement, accessed 20 June 2017

Ashworth A, *Sentencing and Penal Policy* (Weidenfeld and Nicolson, London 1983)

———, 'Some Doubts About Restorative Justice' (1993) 4 Criminal Law Forum 277

———, 'Is the Criminal Law a Lost Cause?' (2000) 116 Law Quarterly Review 225

Ashworth A and Player E, 'Sentencing, Equal Treatment and the Impact of Sanctions' in Ashworth A and Wasik M (eds), *Fundamentals of Sentencing Theory* (Clarendon Press, Oxford 1998)

Aspen Institute, 'ASF 2011 Cyber-Security' (Aspen Security Forum Proceedings, *YouTube,* 29 July 2011) http://www.youtube.com/watch?v=yoWkAVXmSs0, accessed 31 July 2013

Astier S, 'Ethical Regulation of the Internet: The Challenges of Global Governance' (2005) 71 International Review of Administrative Sciences 133

Ayres I and Braithwaite J, *Responsive Regulation: Transcending the Deregulation Debate* (Oxford University Press, New York 1995)

B

Badiou A, *Metapolitics* (Jason Barker tr, Verso, London 2005)

Baggini J, 'England Riots: Are Harsh Sentences for Offenders Justified?' (*The Guardian*, 17 August 2011) http://www.guardian.co.uk/uk/2011/aug/17/england-riots-harsh-sentences-justified, accessed 08 September 2011

Bainbridge D I, *Introduction to Information Technology Law* (6th edn, Pearson Education Limited, Essex 2007)
Baldwin R, *Rules and Government* (Clarendon Press, Oxford 1995)
Baldwin R and Black J, 'Really Responsive Regulation' (2008) 71 The Modern Law Review 59
Ball J, 'By Criminalising Online Dissent We Put Democracy in Peril' (*The Guardian,* 01 August 2011) http://www.guardian.co.uk/commentisfree/2011/aug/01/online-dissent-democracy-hacking, accessed 21 September 2017
Ballard T, 'Newsmakers: Italian Artist Couple Eva and Franco Mattes' (*Blouinartinfo,* 03 June 2016) http://www.blouinartinfo.com/news/story/1414857/newsmakers-italian-artist-couple-eva-and-franco-mattes, accessed 31 July 2017
Barbwise M, 'Google Scanning – Is It Legal?' (*H-Online,* 20 February 2008) http://www.h-online.com/security/features/Google-scanning-is-it-legal-746155.html, accessed 29 October 2017
Bauman Z, *Modernity and Ambivalence* (Polity Press, Cambridge 1991)
Bazelon D L, Choi Y J, and Conaty J F, 'Computer Crimes' (2006) 43 American Criminal Law Review 259
Bazzichelli T, *Networking: The Net as Artwork* (*Digital Aesthetics Research Center,* Aarhus University, Aarhus 2008)
BBC, 'The Cyber Raiders Hitting Estonia' (*BBC,* 17 May 2007) http://news.bbc.co.uk/1/hi/world/europe/6665195.stm, accessed 24 October 2010
———, 'Email and Web Use "to Be Monitored" under New Laws' (*BBC,* 01 April 2012) http://www.bbc.co.uk/news/uk-politics-17576745, accessed 15 April 2012
———, 'The Pirate Bay Must Be Blocked by UK ISPs, Court Rules' (*BBC,* 30 April 2012) http://www.bbc.co.uk/news/technology-17894176, accessed 29 May 2012
———, 'Dutch Court Bans Pirate Party Links to the Pirate Bay' (*BBC,* 10 May 2012) http://www.bbc.co.uk/news/technology-18016819, accessed 29 May 2012
———, 'Gary McKinnon Extradition to US Blocked by Theresa May' (*BBC,* 16 October 2012) http://www.bbc.co.uk/news/uk-19957138, accessed 10 November 2012
———, 'Anonymous Hackers "Cost Paypal £3.5m"' (*BBC,* 22 November 2012) http://www.bbc.co.uk/news/uk-20449474, accessed 24 November 2012
Beale S S, 'What's Law Got to Do with It? The Political, Social, Psychological and Non-Legal Factors Influencing the Development of (Federal) Criminal Law' (1997) 1 Buffalo Criminal Law Review 23

———, 'The News Media's Influence on Criminal Justice Policy: How Market-Driven News Promotes Punitiveness' (2006) 48 William & Mary Law Review 397

Bedau H A, 'Civil Disobedience and Personal Responsibility for Injustice' (1970) 54 The Monist 517

———, 'Civil Disobedience in Focus: Introduction' in Bedau H A (ed), *Civil Disobedience in Focus* (Routledge, London 2002)

Benkler Y, *The Wealth of Networks: How Social Production Transforms Markets and Freedom* (Yale University Press, London 2006)

———, 'Free Irresponsible, Press: Wikileaks and the Battle over the Soul of the Networked Fourth Estate' 46 Harvard Civil Rights-Civil Liberties Law Review, 311

Bentham J, 'Introduction to the Principles of Morals and Legislation' in Alan Ryan (ed), *John Stuart Mill and Jeremy Bentham: Utilitarianism and Other Essays* (Penguin Group, London 1824)

Biancuzzi F, 'Achtung! New German Laws on Cybercrime' (*Security Focus*, 10 July 2007) http://www.securityfocus.com/columnists/448, accessed 20 May 2017

Bickel A M, 'Civil Disobedience and the Duty to Obey' (1973) 8 Gonzaga Law Review 199

Biegel S, *Beyond Our Control?: Confronting the Limits of Our Legal System in the Age of Cyberspace* (The MIT Press, London 2003)

Bix B, *Jurisprudence: Theory and Context* (5th edn, Thomson Reuters (Legal) Limited, London 2009)

Black J, 'Constitutionalising Self-Regulation' (1996) 59 The Modern Law Review 24

———, 'Decentring Regulation: Understanding the Role of Regulation and Self Regulation in a "Post-Regulatory" World' (2001) 54 Current Legal Problems 103

———, 'Critical Reflections on Regulation' (2002) 27 Australian Journal of Legal Philosophy 1

———, 'Proceduralisation and Polycentric Regulation' (2005) Especial 1 RevistaDIREITOGV http://direitogv.fgv.br/sites/direitogv.fgv.br/files/rdgv_esp01_p099_130.pdf, accessed 16 December 2012

Black T, 'Hacktivism: The Poison Gas of Cyberspace' (*Spiked-Online,* 14 December 2010) http://www.spiked-online.com/newsite/article/10001#.Wl3fMq5l9hE, accessed 14 December 2017

Blackstone W T, 'Civil Disobedience: Is It Justified?' (1969) 3 Georgia Law Review 679

Bliss J and Blum J, 'Holder Says U.S. Probes Wikileaks-Related Web Attacks' (*Bloomberg,* 09 December 2010) http://www.bloomberg.com/news/2010-12-09/holder-says-u-s-is-looking-into-wikileaks-tied-cyber-attacks.html, accessed 16 January 2011

Borradori G, *Philosophy in a Time of Terror: Dialogues with Jürgen Habermas and Jacques Derrida* (University of Chicago Press, Chicago 2003)

Bowling B, Marks A, and Murphy C C, 'Crime Control Technologies: Towards an Analytical Framework and Research Agenda', in Brownsword R and Yeung K (eds), *Regulating Technologies: Legal Futures, Regulatory Frames and Technological Fixes* (Hart Publishing, Oxford 2008)

Boyd C, 'Estonia Open Politics to the Web' (news.bbc.co.uk, 07 May 2004) http://news.bbc.co.uk/1/hi/technology/3690661.stm, accessed 24 October 2010

———, 'Profile: Gary Mckinnon' (*BBC,* 30 July 2008) http://news.bbc.co.uk/1/hi/technology/4715612.stm, accessed 30 May 2012

Boyd L, 'The Yes Men and Activism in the Information Age' (MA Thesis, Louisiana State University and Agricultural and Mechanical College 2005)

Braithwaite J, 'Rules and Principles: A Theory of Legal Certainty' (2002) 27 Australian Journal of Legal Philosophy 47

———, *Restorative Justice and Responsive Regulation* (Oxford University Press, Oxford 2002)

Braun S et al., 'Secret to Prism Program: Even Bigger Data Seizure' (*Associated Press,* 15 June 2013) https://www.yahoo.com/news/secret-prism-program-even-bigger-140403980.html, accessed 21 June 2017

Brenner S W, 'At Light Speed: Attribution and Response to Cybercrime/Terrorism/Warfare' (2007) 97 Journal of Criminal Law & Criminology 379

———, *Cybercrime: Criminal Threats from Cyberspace* (Praeger Publishers, Oxford 2010)

Brody S R, 'The Effectiveness of Sentencing: A Review of the Literature' (Home Office Research Study No. 35, Home Office Research Unit, London 1976)

Brown Jr S M, 'Civil Disobedience' (1961) 58 The Journal of Philosophy 669

Brownlee K, 'The Communicative Aspects of Civil Disobedience and Lawful Punishment' (2006) 1 Criminal Law and Philosophy Journal 179

———, 'Justifying Punishment: A Response to Douglas Husak' (2008) 2 Criminal Law and Philosophy 123

———, 'Civil Disobedience' (*Stanford Encyclopedia of Philosophy*, 23 December 2009) http://www.illc.uva.nl/~seop/entries/civil-disobedience/, accessed 12 August 2017

Buckland B S, Schreier F and Winkler T H, 'Democratic Governance Challenges of Cyber Security' (DCAF Horizon 2015 Working Paper No. 1, *Geneva Security Forum,* 2012) http://www.cpahq.org/CPAHQ/CMDownload.aspx?ContentKey=d0b04bfb-f36f-444c-94ba-16331ce13e88&ContentItemKey=363dbd1e-a7f4-481c-ab4e-985b841b1f8b, accessed 15 May 2017

Burris S, Kempa M, and Shearing C, 'Changes in Governance: A Cross-Disciplinary Review of Current Scholarship' (2008) 41 Akron Law Review 1

Burstein P, 'The Impact of Public Opinion on Public Policy: A Review and an Agenda' (2003) 56 Political Research Quarterly 29

C

Cabinet Office, *The UK Cyber Security Strategy: Protecting and Promoting the UK in a Digital World* (London 2011) https://www.gov.uk/government/uploads/system/uploads/attachment_data/file/60961/uk-cyber-security-strategy-final.pdf, accessed 03 August 2013

Cabinet Office, National Security and Intelligence, HM Treasury, and The Rt Hon Philip Hammond MP, '*National Cyber Security Strategy 2016 to 2021*' (London 2016) https://www.gov.uk/government/publications/national-cyber-security-strategy-2016-to-2021, accessed 01 August 2017

Cahill M, 'Punishment Decisions at Conviction: Recognizing the Jury as Fault-Finder' (2005) University of Chicago Legal Forum 91

Calabrese A, 'Virtual Nonviolence? Civil Disobedience and Political Violence in the Information Age' (2004) 6 info www.emeraldinsight.com/1463-6697.htm, accessed 15 June 2010

Calkins M M, 'They Shoot Trojan Horses, Don't They-an Economic Analysis of Anti-Hacking Regulatory Models' (2000) 89 Georgia Law Journal 171

Callinicos A, 'The Anti-Capitalist Movement after Genoa and New York', in Arownowitz S and Gautney H (eds), *Implicating Empire: Globalization and Resistance in the 21st Century World Order* (New York, Basic Books 2003)

Carroll/Fletcher Gallery, 'Eva and Franco Mattes – Abuse Standards Violation' *Carroll / Fletcher*. http://www.carrollfletcher.com/exhibitions/55/overview/, accessed 29 July 2016

Cashell B et al., 'CRS Report for Congress: The Economic Impact of Cyber-Attacks' (2004).

Cassim F, 'Formulating Specialised Legislation to Address the Growing Spectre of Cybercrime: A Comparative Study' (2009) 12 Potchefstroom Electronic Law Journal/Potchefstroomse Elektroniese Regsblad 35

Castells M, *Information Age, Economy, Society and Culture* (Blackwell, Oxford 1996)

———, 'Informationalism, Networks, and the Network Society: A Theoretical Blueprint' in Castells M (ed), *The Network Society: A Cross Cultural Perspective* (Edward Elgar Publishing Limited, Cheltenham 2004)

———, *Communication Power* (Oxford University Press, Oxford 2009)

Castle N, 'Internet Art and Radicalism in the Digital Culture Industry' (2000) http://www.lulu.com/items/volume_1/89000/89324/2/preview/netart_preview.pdf, accessed 16 June 2017

Castronova E, *Synthetic Worlds: The Business and Culture of Online Games* (University of Chicago Press, Chicago 2005)

Cavallaro J L, 'The Demise of the Political Necessity Defense: Indirect Civil Disobedience and United States v. Schoon' (1993) 81 California Law Review 351

Centre for the Protection of National Infrastructure, 'The National Infrastructure' (undated) http://www.cpni.gov.uk/about/cni/, accessed 20 June 2013

Choi B H, 'The Grokster Dead-End' (2005) 19 Harvard Journal of Law & Technology 393

Christensen H S, 'Political Activities on the Internet: Slacktivism or Political Participation by Other Means?' (2011) 16 First Monday http://firstmonday.org/htbin/cgiwrap/bin/ojs/index.php/fm/article/view/3336/2767, accessed 17 December 2012

Christie G C, 'Lawful Departures from Legal Rules: "Jury Nullification" and Legitimated Disobedience' (1974) 62 California Law Review 1289

Christopher R L, 'The Prosecutor's Dilemma: Bargains and Punishments' (2003) 72 Fordham Law Review 93

CISCO, 'Combating Botnets Using the Cisco Asa Botnet Traffic Filter' (*CISCO White Paper,* 2009) http://www.cisco.com/en/US/prod/collateral/vpndevc/ps6032/ps6094/ps6120/white_paper_c11-532091.html, accessed 26 February 2017

Clark B, 'Anonymous' #OpTrump Isn't a 'War,' It's a Nail in the Coffin of the Encryption Debate' (*The Next Web*, 15 March 2016) http://thenextweb.com/opinion/2016/03/15/anonymous-declares-war-on-donald-trump-again-with-optrump/, accessed 31 July 2017

Clarkson C M V, Keating H M, and Cunningham S R, *Criminal Law: Text and Materials* (7th edn, Thomson Reuters, London 2010)

Clinton A C, 'Taming the Hydra: Prosecutorial Discretion under the Acceptance of Responsibility Provision of the US Sentencing Guidelines' (2012) 79 The University of Chicago Law Review 1467

Cody J A, 'Derailing the Digitally Depraved: An International Law and Economics Approach to Combating Cybercrime & Cyberterrorism' (2002) 11 MSU DCL Journal of International Law 231

Cohan J A, 'Civil Disobedience and the Necessity Defense' (2007) 6 Pierce Law Review 111

Cohen A, 'Case Study: The Supreme Court and Corporate Free Speech' (*Time,* 07 July 2010) http://www.time.com/time/nation/article/0,8599,2001844,00.html, accessed 21 December 2012

Cohen C, 'Civil Disobedience and the Law' (1966) 21 Rutgers Law Review 1

Cohen S, *Folk Devils and Moral Panics* (Paladin, St Albans 1973)

Colby C P, 'Civil Disobedience: A Case for Separate Treatment' (1968) 14 Wayne Law Review 1165

Coleman G E, 'Anonymous: From the Lulz to Collective Action' (*The New Everyday*, 06 April 2011) http://mediacommons.futureofthebook.org/tne/pieces/anonymous-lulz-collective-action, accessed 21 September 2017

Colon M, 'RSA Conference 2012: Hacktivism Forcing Organizations to Look Inward' (*SC Magazine*, 29 February 2012) http://www.scmagazine.com/rsa-conference-2012-hacktivism-forcing-organizations-to-look-inward/article/230051/, accessed 10 November 2012

Columbia Law Review Association, 'Sentencing in Cases of Civil Disobedience' (1968) 68 Columbia Law Review 1508

Council on Crime and Justice, *The Collateral Effects of Incarceration on Fathers, Families, and Communities* (Research Demonstration Advocacy, 2006) https://static.prisonpolicy.org/scans/ccj/CEI%20FINAL%2003312006.pdf, accessed 15 February 2017

Couts A, 'US Gov't Ramps up Anti-Anonymous Rhetoric, Warns of Power Grid Take-Down' (*Digital Trends,* 12 February 2012) http://www.digitaltrends.com/web/us-govt-ramps-up-anti-anonymous-rhetoric-warns-of-power-grid-take-down/, accessed 20 June 2013

Crawford A, 'Policing and Security as 'Club Goods': The New Enclosures', in Wood J and Dupont B (eds), *Democracy, Society and the Governance of Security* (Cambridge University Press, Cambridge 2006)

Crenshaw A, 'Crude, Inconsistent Threat: Understanding Anonymous' (*Irongeek,* 2011) http://www.irongeek.com/i.php?page=security/understanding-anonymous, accessed 21 September 2017

Criminal Justice Alliance, 'Crowded Out: The Impact of Prison Overcrowding on Rehabilitation' (*The Criminal Justice Alliance,* 2012) http://www.criminaljusticealliance.org/wp-content/.../Crowded_Out_CriminalJusticeAlliance.pdf, accessed 20 June 2017

Critical Art Ensemble, *Electronic Disturbance* (Autonomedia, New York 1993) http://www.critical-art.net/books.html, accessed 31 July 2016

———, *Electronic Civil Disobedience and Other Unpopular Ideas* (Autonomedia, New York 1996) http://www.critical-art.net/books.html, accessed 31 July 2016

———, *Digital Resistance* (Autonomedia, New York 2001) http://www.critical-art.net/books.html, accessed 31 July 2016

———, *Disturbances, 2012*, http://critical-art.net/?page_id=309, accessed 18 July 2017

Cross F B, 'Decisionmaking in the US Circuit Courts of Appeals' (2003) 91 California Law Review 1475

CrossTalk, 'From Hacktivism to Wikiwarfare' (*RT,* uploaded 17th December 2010) http://www.youtube.com/watch?v=mFJa9RHAfOk, accessed 17 December 2017

Crown Prosecution Service, 'Appeals: Judicial Review of Prosecutorial Decisions' (2009) http://www.cps.gov.uk/legal/a_to_c/appeals_judicial_review_of_prosecution_decisions/, accessed 24 November 2012

Crown Prosecution Service, 'The Code for Crown Prosecutors' (2010) http://www.cps.gov.uk/publications/code_for_crown_prosecutors/, accessed 15 February 2013

Cullen F, Fisher B, and Applegate B, 'Public Opinion About Punishment and Corrections' (2000) 27 Crime and Justice 1

D

Dagger R J, *Civic Virtues: Rights, Citizenship, and Republican Liberalism* (Oxford University Press, New York 1997)

Dampier P, '300,000 Protest Verizon-Google Net Neutrality Pact' (stopthecap.com, 10 August 2010) http://stopthecap.com/2010/08/10/300000-protest-verizon-google-net-neutrality-pact/, accessed 31 May 2012

Danidou Y and Schafer B, 'In Law We Trust? Trusted Computing and Legal Responsibility for Internet Security' (2009) Emerging Challenges for Security, Privacy and Trust 399

Davies H and Holdcroft D, *Jurisprudence: Text and Commentary* (Butterworths & Co Ltd, London 1991)

Davis A J, *Arbitrary Justice: The Power of the American Prosecutor* (Oxford University Press, Oxford 2007)

Davis M, 'How to Make the Punishment Fit the Crime' (1983) 93 Ethics 726

De Silva S and Weedon F, 'A Future Less Certain for the Digital Economy Act?' (2011) 17 Computer and Telecommunications Law Review 149

De Villiers M, 'Distributed Denial of Service: Law, Technology & Policy' (2007) University of New South Wales Faculty of Law Research Series, Paper 7, 1

Decker C, 'Cyber Crime 2.0: An Argument to Update the United States Criminal Code to Reflect the Changing Nature of Cyber Crime' (2007) 81 South California Law Review 959

DeForrest M E, 'Civil Disobedience: Its Nature and Role in the American Legal Landscape' (1998) 33 Gonzaga Law Review 653

Denning D E, 'Hacktivism: An Emerging Threat to Diplomacy' (2000) 77 Foreign Service Journal 43

———, 'Activism, Hacktivism, and Cyberterrorism: The Internet as a Tool for Influencing Foreign Policy', in Arquila J and Ronfeldt D (eds), *Networks and Netwars: The Future of Terror, Crime, and Militancy* (RAND Corporation 2001)

Devine D J et al., 'Jury Decision Making: 45 Years of Empirical Research on Deliberating Groups' (2000) 7 Psychology, Public Policy and Law 622

Dictionary.com, 'Protest' (2012) http://dictionary.reference.com/browse/protest, accessed 25 January 1013

DJNZ and The Action Tool Development Group of the Electrohippies Collective, 'Client-Side Distributed Denial-of-Service: Valid Campaign Tactic or Terrorist Act?' (2001) 34 Leonardo 269

Dominguez R, 'Electronic Civil Disobedience in Solidarity with Greek Anarchists' (*thing.net*, 2008) http://post.thing.net/node/2457, accessed 19 December 2017

———, 'Electronic Disobedience Post-9/11' (2008) 22 Third Text 661

———, 'Electronic Civil Disobedience' (*thing.net*, undated) http://www.thing.net/~rdom/ecd/ecd.html, accessed 16 January 2017

Dotan Y, 'Should Prosecutorial Discretion Enjoy Special Treatment in Judicial Review?: A Comparative Analysis of the Law in England and Israel' (1997) 3 Public Law 513

Dotcom K, 'Prism: Concerns over Government Tyranny Are Legitimate' (*The Guardian,* 13 June 2013) http://www.guardian.co.uk/commentisfree/2013/jun/13/prism-utah-data-center-surveillance, accessed 21 June 2013

Dowland P et al., 'Computer Crime and Abuse: A Survey of Public Attitudes and Awareness' (1999) 18 Computers & Security 715

Doyle C, *Cybercrime: An Overview of the Federal Computer Fraud and Abuse Statute and Related Federal Criminal Laws* (Congressional Research Service, Report for Congress, DIANE Publishing, 2011)

Duff A, *Punishment, Communication, and Community* (Oxford University Press, Oxford 2001)

Dutton W H et al., *Freedom of Connection, Freedom of Expression: The Changing Legal and Regulatory Ecology Shaping the Internet* (UNESCO, Oxford 2010)

Dworkin R, 'The Model of Rules' (1967) 35 University of Chicago Law Review 14
———, *Taking Rights Seriously* (2nd edn, Harvard University Press, Cambridge, MA 1978)
———, *A Matter of Principle* (Harvard University Press, Cambridge, MA 1985)

E

Earl J and Beyer J L, 'The Dynamics of Backlash Online: Anonymous and the Battle for WikiLeaks' (2014) 37 Intersectionality and Social Change 207–33.
Eatwell R, 'Community Cohesion and Cumulative Extremism in Contemporary Britain' (2006) 77 The Political Quarterly, 204
Electronic Disturbance Theater and Comrades, E-Graffiti in Solidarity with the Zapatistas – May.24.2014. http://www.thing.net/~rdom/ZapatistasMayo24/, accessed 5 July 2016.
Electronic Frontier Foundation, 'Letter to Governor Pataki' (*Electronic Frontier Foundation,* 12 March 2003) https://w2.eff.org/Privacy/TIA/20030314_letter_to_pataki.php, accessed 12 July 2017
Ely A N, 'Prosecutorial Discretion as an Ethical Necessity: The Ashcroft Memorandum's Curtailment of the Prosecutor's Duty to Seek Justice' (2004) 90 Cornell Law Review 237
Engle E, 'The Rights' Orchestra: Proportionality, Balancing, and Viking' (2011) New England Journal of International Law and Comparative Law http://papers.ssrn.com/sol3/papers.cfm?abstract_id=1704503, accessed 31 January 2012
EpidemiC, 'Antimafia: The Action Sharing' (EpidemiC.ws, 2002) http://epidemic.ws/antimafia/action.php?lng=en, accessed 20 September 2011
Epstein D, 'The Duality of Information Policy Debates: The Case of the Internet Governance Forum' (DPhil, Cornell University 2012) http://core.kmi.open.ac.uk/display/6103666, accessed 13 June 2013
Epstein R A, 'Cybertrespass' (2003) 70 The University of Chicago Law Review, Centennial Tribute Essays 73
Eriksson J and Giacomello G, 'The Information Revolution, Security, and International Relations:(Ir) Relevant Theory?' (2006) 27 International Political Science Review 221
European Data Protection Supervisor, 'Opinion of the European Data Protection Supervisor: On Net Neutrality, Traffic Management and the Protection of Privacy and Personal Data' (*EDPS*, Brussels 2007) http://www.edps.europa.eu/EDPSWEB/webdav/site/mySite/shared/Documents/Consultation/Opinions/2011/11-10-07_Net_neutrality_EN.pdf, accessed 13 May 2017

European Digital Rights, 'Frankfurt Appellate Court Says Online Demonstration Is Not Coercion' (*European Digital Rights*, 07 June 2006) https://edri.org/edrigramnumber4-11demonstration/, accessed 20 May 2011

F

Fafinski S, 'The Security Ramifications of the Police and Justice Act 2006' (2007) Network Security 8

———, 'Computer Misuse: The Implications of the Police and Justice Act 2006' (2008) 72 Journal of Criminal Law 53

Fafinski S, Dutton W H, and Margetts H, 'Mapping and Measuring Cybercrime' (2010) OII Forum Discussion Paper No 18

Farivar C, 'NY Judge Compels Twitter to Reveal User's Data' (*ArsTechnica*, 02 July 2012) http://arstechnica.com/tech-policy/2012/07/ny-judge-compels-twitter-to-reveal-user-data/, accessed 02 September 2012

Farrell D, 'Paying the Penalty: Justifiable Civil Disobedience and the Problem of Punishment' (1977) 6 Philosophy & Public Affairs 165

Federal Communications Commission, 'Preserving the Open Internet – Broadband Industry Practices' (Federal Communications Commission Report, 2010)

Feinberg J, '*Harm to Others: The Moral Limits of the Criminal Law, Vol. 1*' (Oxford University Press, Oxford 1984)

Fiedler S, 'The Right to Rebel: Social Movements and Civil Disobedience' (2009) 1 Cosmopolitan Civil Societies Journal 42

Finklea K and Theohary C, 'CRS Report for Congress: Cybercrime: Conceptual Issues for Congress and U.S. Law Enforcement' (*Congressional Research Service*, 2013) http://www.fas.org/sgp/crs/misc/R42547.pdf, accessed 04 May 2013

Finman T and Macaulay S, 'Freedom to Dissent: The Vietnam Protests and the Words of Public Officials' (1966) Wisconsin Law Review 632

Finnis J, *Natural Law and Natural Rights* (Oxford University Press, Oxford 2011)

Fitzpatrick A, 'WikiLeaks Wins Battle against Visa, Mastercard' (*Mashable*, 12 July 2012) http://mashable.com/2012/07/12/wikileaks-wins-battle-against-visa-mastercard/, accessed 10 June 2013

Fletcher G P, *Basic Concepts of Criminal Law* (Oxford University Press, New York 1998)

Forte D M, 'Is "Virtual" Activism Not "Real" Activism' (*Cyberspace Ethnography: Political Activism and the Internet Blog*, 29 January 2010) http://webography.wordpress.com/2010/01/29/is-virtual-activism-not-real-activism/, accessed 20 May 2011

Foucault M, 'Prison Talk' in Gordon C (ed), *Power/Knowledge* (Brighton Harvester 1980)

———, *The Will to Knowledge: The History of Sexuality* (Penguin, London 1998)

Fox L, 'From Hacktivists to Spammers: Is Anonymous Failing?' (newsjunkiepost.com, 12 December 2010) http://newsjunkiepost.com/2010/12/12/from-hacktivists-to-spammers-is-anonymous-failing/, accessed 28 September 2011

Freeman J, 'Real Democracy Problem in Administrative Law' in Dyzenhaus D (ed), *Recrafting the Rule of Law* (Hart Publishing, Oxford 1999)

Froomkin M, 'Habermas@ Discourse. Net: Toward a Critical Theory of Cyberspace' (2003) 116 Harvard Law Review 749

Frydman B and Rorive I, 'Regulating Internet Content through Intermediaries in Europe and the USA' (2002) 23 Zeitschrift für Rechtssoziologie 41

Fuchs C, *Internet and Society: Social Theory in the Information Age* (Routledge, New York 2008)

Fuller L, *The Morality of Law* (Revised edn, Yale University Press, New Haven 1969)

Furnham A, McClelland A, and Baxter E D, 'The Allocation of a Scarce Correctional Resource: Deciding Who Is Eligible for an Electronic Monitoring Program' (2010) 40 Journal of Applied Social Psychology 1606

G

Gallagher S, 'High Orbits and Slowlorises: Understanding the Anonymous Attack Tools' (*Ars Technica*, 16 February 2012) http://arstechnica.com/business/news/2012/02/high-orbits-and-slowlorises-understanding-the-anonymous-attack-tools.ars accessed 10 January 2017

Gardbaum S, 'The Horizontal Effect of Constitutional Rights' (2003) 102 Michigan Law Review 387

Gardiner M E, 'Wild Publics and Grotesque Symposiums: Habermas and Bakhtin on Dialogue, Everyday Life and the Public Sphere' (2004) 52 The Sociological Review 28

Gardner J, 'Crime: In Proportion and in Perspective', in Ashworth A and Wasik M (eds), *Fundamentals of Sentencing Theory* (Clarendon Press, Oxford 1998)

Garland D, *The Culture of Control: Crime and Social Order in Contemporary Society* (Oxford University Press, Oxford 2001)

Gillett G, 'A World without Internet: A New Framework for Analyzing a Supervised Release Condition That Restricts Computer and Internet Access' (2010) 79 Fordham Law Review 217

Gilroy A A, 'CRS Report for Congress: Net Neutrality: Background and Issues' (Congress Research Service, 2008) http://www.fas.org/sgp/crs/misc/RS22444.pdf, accessed 13 June 2013

Global Research, 'U.S. Social Inequality Income Gap Hits Record High' (*Market Oracle*, 29 September 2010) http://www.marketoracle.co.uk/Article23088.html, accessed 24 October 2017

Goldsmith J and Wu T, *Who Controls the Internet? Illusions of a Borderless World* (Oxford University Press, Oxford 2006)

Goldsmith J L, 'Against Cyberanarchy' (1998) 65 The University of Chicago Law Review 1199

Goldstein E R, 'Digitally Incorrect' (*The Chronicle Review*, 03 October 2010) http://chronicle.com/article/Digitally-Incorrect/124649/, accessed 12 August 2017

Goldstein N, 'Steubenville's Tangled Web of Injustice' (*The Guardian*, 12 June 2013) http://www.guardian.co.uk/commentisfree/2013/jun/12/steubenville-tangled-web-injustice, accessed 21 June 2013

Goode L, 'Anonymous and the Political Ethos of Hacktivism' (January 2, 2015) 13/1 Popular Communication 74–86. doi:https://doi.org/10.1080/15405702.2014.978000.79

Graber C B, 'Internet Creativity, Communicative Freedom and a Constitutional Rights Theory Response to "Code Is Law"' (Lucerne i-call, The Research Centre for International Communications and Art Law, University of Lucerne, Working Paper 03, 2010)

Granick J, 'Faking It: Calculating Loss in Computer Crime Sentencing' (2005) 2 I/S: A Journal of Law and Policy 207

Green N and Halliday J, 'Twitter Unmasks Anonymous British User in Landmark Legal Battle' (*The Guardian*, 29 May 2011) http://www.guardian.co.uk/technology/2011/may/29/twitter-anonymous-user-legal-battle, accessed 02 September 2017

Greenawalt K, 'A Contextual Approach to Disobedience' (1970) 70 Columbia Law Review 48

———, *Conflicts of Law and Morality* (Oxford University Press, New York 1989)

Greene S and O'Brien C O, 'Exceeding Authorized Access in the Workplace: Prosecuting Disloyal Conduct under the Computer Fraud and Abuse Act' (2013) 50 American Business Law Journal 1

Greenpeace, 'Bhopal Protests Move Online' (*Greenpeace*, 10 March 2003) http://www.greenpeace.org/international/en/news/features/bhopal-protests-move-online/, accessed 24 October 2010

Griffin J G H, 'The "Secret Path" of Grokster and Corley: Avoiding Liability for Copyright Infringement' (2005) 10 Communications Law 147

Griffith M, *Sophocles: Antigone* (Cambridge University Press, Cambridge 1999)
Gross H, *A Theory of Criminal Justice* (Oxford University Press, Oxford 1979)
Gross S R et al., Exonerations in the United States 1989–2003, (2005) 95/2 Journal of Criminal Law and Criminology 523
Grossman J, 'Social Backgrounds and Judicial Decision-Making' (1966) 79 Harvard Law Review 1551

H

Habermas J, 'Civil Disobedience: Litmus Test for the Democratic Constitutional State' (1985) 30 Berkeley Journal of Sociology 95
———, *Between Facts and Norms: Contributions to a Discourse Theory of Law and Democracy* (William Rehg tr, Polity, Cambridge 1996)
Habermas J and Calhoun M, 'Right and Violence: A German Trauma' (1985) 1 Cultural Critique 125
Habib J, 'Cyber Crime and Punishment: Filtering out Internet Felons' (2003) 14 Fordham Intellectual Property Media & Entertainment Law Journal 1051
Hacktivismo, 'cDc Releases Goolag Scanner' (*Hacktivismo*, 20 February 2008) http://www.hacktivismo.com/news/ accessed 29/07/2010, accessed 22 December 2017
———, 'Hacktivismo Projects' (*Hacktivismo*, undated) http://www.hacktivismo.com/projects/index.php, accessed 01 December 2017
———, 'About Hacktivismo' (*Hacktivismo,* undated) http://www.hacktivismo.com/about/index.php, accessed 20 September 2017
Haksar V, 'Civil Disobedience and Non-Cooperation' in Bedau H (ed), *Civil Disobedience in Focus* (Routledge, London 2002)
———, 'The Right to Civil Disobedience' (2003) 41 Osgoode Hall Law Journal
Hall R, 'Legal Toleration of Civil Disobedience' (1971) 81 Ethics 128
Halliday J, 'Anonymous Hackers Jailed for Cyber Attacks' (*The Guardian*, 24 January 2013) http://www.guardian.co.uk/technology/2013/jan/24/anonymous-hackers-jailed-cyber-attacks, accessed 18 June 2013
Hampson N, 'Hacktivism: A New Breed of Protest in a Networked World' (2012) 35 Boston College International & Comparative Law Review 511
Hampton J, 'The Moral Education Theory of Punishment' (1984) 13 Philosophy & Public Affairs 208
Haney C, 'The Psychological Impact of Incarceration: Implications for Postprison Adjustment' in Travis J and Waul M (eds), *Prisoners Once Removed: The Impact of Incarceration and Reentry on Children, Families, and Communities* (Urban Institute Press 2003)

Hardt M and Negri A, *Empire* (4th edn, Harvard University Press, Cambridge, MA 2001)
Hart H L A, 'Are There Any Natural Rights?' (1955) 64 The Philosophical Review 175
———, *Punishment and Responsibility: Essays in the Philosophy of Law* (Oxford University Press, Oxford 1968)
Herring J, *Criminal Law* (3rd edn, Palgrave Macmillan, Hampshire 2002)
Herwig J, 'Anonymous: Peering Behind the Mask' (*The Guardian,* 11 May 2011) http://www.guardian.co.uk/technology/2011/may/11/anonymous-behind-the-mask, accessed 21 September 2011
Hess D and Martin B, 'Repression, Backfire, and the Theory of Transformative Events' (2006) 11/2 Mobilization: An International Quarterly 249–267.
Heymann L, 'Inducement as Contributory Copyright Infringement: Metro-Goldwyn-Mayer Studios Inc. v. Grokster, Ltd' (2006) 37 International Review of Intellectual Property and Competition Law 31
Himma K E, 'Hacking as Politically Motivated Digital Civil Disobedience: Is Hacktivism Morally Justified?' (2005) http://papers.ssrn.com/sol3/papers.cfm?abstract_id=799545#, accessed 19 June 2013
Hintz A, 'Deconstructing Multi-Stakeholderism: The Discourses and Realities of Global Governance at the World Summit on the Information Society (WSIS)' (Central European University, Budapest 2007)
Hintz A and Milan S, 'At the Margins of Internet Governance: Grassroots Tech Groups and Communication Policy' (2009) 5 International Journal of Media & Cultural Politics 23
Hobbes T, *Leviathan* (1651) http://oregonstate.edu/instruct/phl302/texts/hobbes/leviathan-contents.html, accessed 20 June 2013
Hofmann J, 'Multi-Stakeholderism in Internet Governance: Putting a Fiction into Practice' (2016) 1/1 Journal of Cyber Policy 1
Holland B, 'The Failure of the Rule of Law in Cyberspace? Reorienting the Normative Debate on Borders and Territorial Sovereignty (Draft)' (2005) 24 Journal of Computer and Information Law
Holloway W and Jefferson T, 'The Risk Society in an Age of Anxiety: Situating Fear of Crime' (1997) 48 The British Journal of Sociology 255
Holmes Jr O W, *The Common Law* (Paulo J. S. Pereira and Diego M. Beltran (eds), University of Toronto Law School Typographical Society, Toronto 2011)
Home Office, 'Electronic Monitoring on Bail for Adults – Procedures' (Home Office Circular 25, London 2006)
Home Office, Serious Crime Act 2015 Fact Sheet: Overview of the Act (2015) https://www.gov.uk/government/uploads/system/uploads/attachment_data/file/415943/Serious_Crime_Act_Overview.pdf, accessed 19 July 2017

Honderich T, *Punishment: The Supposed Justifications Revisited* (Pluto Press, London 2006)
Honig B, 'Rawls on Politics and Punishment' (1993) 46 Political Research Quarterly 99
Hough M and Roberts J V, 'Sentencing Trends in Britain: Public Knowledge and Public Opinion' (1999) 1 Punishment & Society 11
House of Lords Select Committee on Science and Technology, 'Science and Technology – Fifth Report' (London, 2007) http://www.publications.parliament.uk/pa/ld200607/ldselect/ldsctech/165/16502.htm, accessed 20 May 2013
Hudson B, *Justice in the Risk Society: Challenging and Re-Affirming Justice in Late Modernity* (Sage, London 2003)
Husak D N, *Overcriminalization: The Limits of the Criminal Law* (Oxford University Press, Oxford 2008)
Hyne D, 'Examining the Legal Challenges to the Restriction of Computer Access as a Term of Probation or Supervised Release' (2002) 28 New England Journal on Criminal & Civil Confinement 215

I

International Telecommunication Union ICT Applications and Cybersecurity Division, 'Understanding Cybercrime: A Guide for Developing Countries' (*International Telecommunication Union*, 2009) http://www.itu.int/ITU-D/cyb/cybersecurity/docs/itu-understanding-cybercrime-guide.pdf, accessed 26 January 2013

J

Jansen R S, 'Populist Mobilization: A New Theoretical Approach to Populism' (2011) 29 Sociological Theory 75
Jarrett M et al., 'Prosecuting Computer Crimes' (Criminal Division Computer Crime and Intellectual Property Section Criminal Division, Department of Justice, Washington DC undated) http://www.justice.gov/criminal/cybercrime/docs/ccmanual.pdf, accessed 20 May 2017
Johnson B and Youm H, 'Commercial Speech and Free Expression: The United States and Europe Compared' (2008) 2 Journal of International Media & Entertainment Law 159
Johnson D and Post D, 'Law and Borders-the Rise of Law in Cyberspace' (1995) 48 Stanford Law Review 1367

Jordan T, *Activism!: Direct Action, Hacktivism and the Future of Society* (Reaktion Books, London 2002)

———, *Hacking: Digital Media and Technological Determinism* (Polity, Cambridge 2008)

Jordan T and Taylor P A, *Hacktivism and Cyberwars: Rebels with a Cause?* (Routledge, London 2004)

Juergen Habermas and Martha Calhoun, 'Right and Violence: A German Trauma' (1985) 1 Cultural Critique 125

Juris J S, 'Networked Social Movements: Global Movements for Global Justice', in Castells M (ed), *The Network Society: A Cross-Cultural Perspective* (Edward Elgar Publishing Ltd, Cheltenham 2004)

K

Kahn D, 'Social Intermediaries: Creating a More Responsible Web through Portable Identity, Cross-Web Reputation, and Code-Backed Norms' (2010) 11 Columbia Science & Technology Law Review 176

Karagiannopoulos V, 'The Role of the Internet in Political Struggles: Some Conclusions from Iran and Egypt' (2012) 34 New Political Science 151

———, 'China and the Internet: Expanding on Lessig's Regulation Nightmares' (2012) 9 SCRIPTed 150

Karnow C, 'Launch on Warning: Aggressive Defense of Computer Systems' (2004) 7 Yale Journal of Law & Technology 87

Katz B J, 'Civil Disobedience and the First Amendment' (1985) 32 UCLA Law Review 904

Kavada A, 'The Internet and Decentralized Architectures' in Karatzogianni A (ed), *Cyberconflicts and Global Politics* (Routledge, London 2009)

Kellner M M, 'Democracy and Civil Disobedience' (1975) 37 The Journal of Politics 899

Kelly M G E, *The Political Philosophy of Michel Foucault* (Taylor & Francis e-Library, 2009)

Kemshall H, *Understanding Risk in Criminal Justice* (Mike McGuire (ed), Open University Press, Maidenhead 2003)

Kendrick K, 'The Tipping Point: Prison Overcrowding Nationally, in West Virginia, and Recommendations for Reform' (2011) 113 West Virginia Law Review 585

Kerr O S, 'Cybercrime's Scope: Interpreting Access and Authorization in Computer Misuse Statutes' (2003) 78 New York University Law Review 1596

———, 'Vagueness Challenges to the Computer Fraud and Abuse Act' (2010) 94 Minnesota Law Review

———, 'United States v. Auernheimer, and Why I Am Representing Auernheimer Pro Bono on Appeal Before the Third Circuit' (*The Volokh Conspiracy*, 21 March 2013) http://volokh.com/2013/03/21/united-states-v-auernheimer-and-why-i-am-representing-auernheimer-pro-bono-on-appeal-before-the-third-circuit/, accessed 31 August 2017

Kesan J P and Rajiv S C, 'Deconstructing Code' (2003–4) 6 Yale Journal of Law & Technology 277

Kesan J P and Majuca R, 'Optimal Hackback' (2010) 84 Chicago-Kent Law Review 831

Kierkegaard S M, 'Here Comes the 'Cybernators'!' (2006) 22 Computer Law & Security Report 381

Kiss J, 'The Pirate Bay Trial: Guilty Verdict' (*The Guardian,* 17 April 2009) http://www.guardian.co.uk/technology/2009/apr/17/the-pirate-bay-trial-guilty-verdict, accessed 22 January 2013

Kizza J M, *Ethical and Social Issues in the Information Age* (Springer-Verlag, New York 2010)

Klang M, 'A Critical Look at the Regulation of Computer Viruses' (2003) 11 International Journal of Law and Information Technology 162

———, 'Civil Disobedience Online' (2004) 2 Info, Communications and Ethics in Society 75

———, 'Disruptive Technology: Effects of Technology Regulation on Democracy' (DPhil, Goeteborg University 2006)

Klein A G, 'Vigilante Media: Unveiling Anonymous and the Hacktivist Persona in the Global Press' (2015) 82/3 Communication Monographs, http://nca.tandfonline.com/doi/abs/10.1080/03637751.2015.1030682, accessed 13 July 2017

Klein N, *No Logo: Taking Aim at the Brand Bullies* (Flamingo, London 2001)

———, *The Shock Doctrine* (Penguin Books, London 2007)

Kleinig J, *Ethics and Criminal Justice: An Introduction* (Cambridge University Press, Cambridge 2008)

Knafo S, 'Occupy Wall Street and Anonymous: Turning a Fledgling Movement into a Meme' (huffingtonpost.com, 20 October 2011) http://www.huffingtonpost.com/2011/10/20/occupy-wall-street-anonymous-connection_n_1021665.html, accessed 01 December 2017

Knappenberger B, 'We Are Legion: The Story of the Hacktivists' (*YouTube*, 19 June 2013) https://www.youtube.com/watch?v=ELcAEwJdTeQ, accessed 02 August 2013

Koops B-J, 'Criteria for Normative Technology: The Acceptability of 'Code as Law' in Light of Democratic and Constitutional Values' in Brownsword R and Yeung K (eds), *Regulating Technologies Legal Futures, Regulatory Frames and Technological Fixes* (Hart Publishing, Oxford 2008)

Kramer M and Lombardi F, 'New Top State Judge: Abolish Grand Juries & Let Us Decide' (*New York Daily News,* New York 1985)

Krauss R, 'The Theory of Prosecutorial Discretion in Federal Law: Origins and Developments' (2009) 6 Seton Hall Circuit Review 1

Kravets D, 'Virtual Sit-Ins Doom Online Animal Rights Activists' (*ThreatLevel Blog*, 16 October 2009) http://www.wired.com/threatlevel/2009/10/animals/, accessed 20 May 2017

———, 'Guilty Plea in "Anonymous" DDoS Scientology Attack' (*ThreatLevel Blog,* 26 January 2010) http://www.wired.com/threatlevel/2010/01/guilty-plea-in-scientology-ddos-attack/, accessed 20 May 2017

———, 'Analysis: FCC Comcast Order is Open Invitation to Internet Filtering' (*Threat Level Blog,* 20 August 2012) http://www.wired.com/threatlevel/2008/08/analysis-fcc-co/, accessed 23 June 2013

———, 'Appeals Court Reverses Hacker/Troll "weev" Conviction and Sentence [Updated]' (*Ars Technica*, 11 April 2014) https://arstechnica.com/tech-policy/2014/04/appeals-court-reverses-hackertroll-weev-conviction-and-sentence/, accessed 31 July 2017

Krygier M, 'Ethical Positivism and the Liberalism of Fear' (1999) 24 Australian Journal of Legal Philosophy 65

Kumar M, 'Anonymous Hit Egyptian Government Websites as #Opegypt' (*The Hacker News*, 09 December 2012)

L

La Rue F, 'Report of the Special Rapporteur on the Promotion and Protection of the Right to Freedom of Opinion and Expression. Vi. Conclusions and Recommendations' (*United Nations General Assembly,* 16 May 2011) http://www2.ohchr.org/english/bodies/hrcouncil/docs/17session/a.hrc.17.27_en.pdf, accessed 14 February 2013

Ladeur K-H, 'Prozedurale Rationalitaet – Steigerung der Legitimationsfaehigkeit oder der Leistungfaehigkeit des Rechtssystems?' 7 Zeitschrift fuer Rechtssoziologie 265

Laidlaw E, '*Regulating Speech in Cyberspace*' (Cambridge University Press, Cambridge 2015)

Lambek B D, 'Necessity and International Law: Arguments for the Legality of Civil Disobedience' (1987) 5 Yale Law & Policy Review 472

Lane J and Dominguez R, 'Digital Zapatistas' (2003) 47 TDR 129

Law Commission, 'Computer Misuse' (Hansard Report No.186, 1989)

Lazos G, *Informatics and Crime* (Nomiki Vivliothiki, Athens 2000)

Lee M et al., 'Electronic Commerce, Hackers, and the Search for Legitimacy: A Regulatory Proposal' (1999) 14 Berkeley Technology Law Journal 839

LeGrande J L, 'Nonviolent Civil Disobedience and Police Enforcement Policy' (1967) 58 The Journal of Criminal Law, Criminology, and Police Science 393

Lemley M A, 'Place and Cyberspace' (2003) 91 California Law Review, 521. http://scholarship.law.berkeley.edu/californialawreview/vol91/iss2/5, accessed 31 July 2017

Lessig L, *Code and Other Laws of Cyberspace* (Basic Books, New York 1999)

———, *Code v.2.0* (Basic Books, New York 2006)

———, 'Prosecutor as Bully' (*Lessig Blog, v2*, 12 January 2013) http://lessig.tumblr.com/post/40347463044/prosecutor-as-bully, accessed 20 June 2013

Levy P A, 'Responding to Prosecutors Seeking to Identify Anonymous Bloggers – Google and Other ISP's Could Learn from the Mainstream Media' (*Consumer Law and Policy Blog*, 17 November 2010) http://pubcit.typepad.com/clpblog/2010/11/responding-to-prosecutors-seeking-to-identify-anonymous-bloggers-google-and-other-isps-could-learn-f.html, accessed 23 November 2012

Levy S, *Hackers: Heroes of the Computer Revolution* (Bantam Doubleday Dell, New York 1984)

Leyden J, 'Webroot Guesstimates Inflate UK Spyware Problem' (*The Register*, 20 October 2005) http://www.theregister.co.uk/2005/10/20/webroot_uk_spyware_guesstimates/, accessed 21 April 2012

———, 'Techwatch Weathers DDoS Extortion Attacks' (*The Register*, 30 January 2009) http://www.theregister.co.uk/2009/01/30/techwatch_ddos/, accessed 26 October 2017

———, 'Iranian Hacktivists Hand-Crank Ddos Attack' (*The Register*, 22 June 2009) http://www.theregister.co.uk/2009/06/22/iranian_hactivism/, accessed 20 October 2017

———, 'Spanish Police Cuff Three Anonymous Hack Suspects' (*The Register*, 10 June 2011) http://www.theregister.co.uk/2011/06/10/spain_anonymous_arrests/, accessed 21 September 2017

———, 'Anonymous Unsheathes New, Potent Attack Weapon' (*The Register*, 04 August 2011) http://www.theregister.co.uk/2011/08/04/anon_develops_loic_ddos_alternative/, accessed 11 September 2011

Lievrouw L A, 'Oppositional and Activist New Media: Remediation, Reconfiguration, Participation' (*Proceedings of the Ninth Participatory Design Conference*, Trento 2006) https://dl.acm.org/citation.cfm?id=1147279, accessed 03 August 2017

Lippman M, 'Civil Disobedience: The Dictates of Conscience Versus the Rule of Law' (1986) 26 Washburn Law Journal 233

Lippman M R, *Contemporary Criminal Law: Concepts, Cases, and Controversies* (Sage, London 2010)

Lloyd I J, *Information Technology Law* (6th edn, Oxford University Press, Oxford 2011)

Loader I and Walker N, *Civilizing Security* (Cambridge University Press, Cambridge 2007)

Loesch M C, 'Motive Testimony and a Civil Disobedience Justification' (1990) 5 Notre Dame Journal of Law, Ethics & Public Policy 1069

Lofgren Z and Wyden R, 'Introducing Aaron's Law, a Desperately needed Reform of the Computer Fraud and Abuse Act' (*Wired*, 20 June 2013) http://www.wired.com/opinion/2013/06/aarons-law-is-finally-here/, accessed 21 June 2013

Logan C C, 'Liberty or Safety: Implications of the USA Patriot Act and the UK's Anti-Terror Laws on Freedom of Expression and Free Exercise of Religion' (2006) 37 Seton Hall Law Review 863

Long M C, 'Anonymous' Hacker Brags on Twitter and Gets Caught' (Adweek, 17 April 2012) http://www.adweek.com/digital/hacker-brags-on-twitter/, accessed 31 July 2017

Loren L P, 'Deterring Abuse of the Copyright Takedown Regime by Taking Misrepresentation Claims Seriously' (2011) 46 Wake Forest Law Review 745

Lovink G and Rossiter N, 'Dawn of the Organised Networks' (2005) 5 Fibreculture Journal http://five.fibreculturejournal.org/fcj-029-dawn-of-the-organised-networks/, accessed 15 February 2013

Lucas, D, 'Exclusive: The Legendary #Anonymous Paypal 14 Speak Out Post-Sentencing' (*The Cryptosphere*, 31 October 2014) https://thecryptosphere.com/2014/10/31/exclusive-the-anonymous-paypal-14-speak-out-post-sentencing/, accessed 24 July 2017

Lucchi N, 'Access to Network Services and Protection of Constitutional Rights: Recognizing the Essential Role of Internet Access for the Freedom of Expression' (2011) 19 Cardozo Journal of International and Comparative Law 646

Lupton D, *Risk* (Taylor and Francis E-Library, 2005)

M

MacDonald M, Greifinger R, and Kane D, 'The Impact of Overcrowding' (2012) 8 International Journal of Prisoner Health
MacKinnon R, *Consent of the Networked: The Worldwide Struggle for Internet Freedom* (Basic Books, New York 2012)
Majone G, 'Regulatory Legitimacy' in Richardson J (ed), *Regulating Europe* (Routledge, London 1996)
Malik S, 'Cyber Crime "Threatens UK Stockmarket, Pensions and Businesses"' (*The Guardian*, 02 March 2011) http://www.guardian.co.uk/uk/2011/mar/02/cyber-crime-threat-uk, accessed 29 September 2011
Mann R and Belzley S, 'The Promise of Internet Intermediary Liability' (2005) 47 William & Mary Law Review 239
Mansfield-Devine S, 'Anonymous: Serious Threat or Mere Annoyance?' (2011) Network Security 4
Markovits D, 'Democratic Disobedience' (2005) 114 The Yale Law Journal 1897
Masnick M, 'Why Didn't Google or Comcast Protect the Identity of Anonymous Church Blogger Who Was Outed?' (*Techdirt*, 18 November 2010) http://www.techdirt.com/articles/20101118/05102511923/why-didn-t-google-or-comcast-protect-the-identity-of-anonymous-church-blogger-who-was-outed.shtml, accessed 02 September 2017
McCullagh D, 'Renewed Push to Give Obama an Internet "Kill Switch"' (*TechTalk*, 24 January 2011) http://www.cbsnews.com/8301-501465_162-20029302-501465.html, accessed 01 June 2012
McGoogan, C, 'British Hacker Lauri Love to Be Extradited to the US for "Accessing Government Computers"' (*The Telegraph*, 16 September 2016) http://www.telegraph.co.uk/technology/2016/09/16/british-hacker-lauri-love-to-be-extradited-to-the-us-for-access/, accessed 31 July 2017
McGuire M, *Hypercrime: The New Geometry of Harm* (Routledge Cavendish, Oxford 2007)
McIntyre TJ and Scott C, 'Internet Filtering: Rhetoric, Legitimacy, Accountability and Responsibility' in Brownsword R and Yeung K (eds), *Regulating Technologies: Legal Futures, Regulatory Frames and Technological Fixes* (Hart Publishing, Oxford 2008)
McLeod I, *Legal Theory* (2nd edn, Palgrave Macmillan, New York 2003)
McNamee J, 'The Slide from "Self-Regulation" to Corporate Censorship' (*European Digital Rights,* Brussels 2011) http://www.edri.org/files/EDRI_selfreg_final_20110124.pdf, accessed 15 February 2013

Mead D, *The New Law of Peaceful Protest: Rights and Regulation in the Human Rights Act Era* (Hart Publishing, Oxford 2010)

Meikle G, 'Electronic Civil Disobedience and Symbolic Power' in Karatzogianni A (ed), *Cyberconflicts and Global Politics* (Routledge, London 2009)

Melilli K J, 'Prosecutorial Discretion in an Adversary System' (1992) Brigham Youth University Law Review 669

Mezzofiore G, 'Anonymous Targets Facebook, IBM, Intel and AT&T in Operation Defense Phase II' (*IBTimes*, 13 April 2012) http://www.ibtimes.co.uk/articles/327682/20120413/cispa-operation-defense-anonymous-pledges-attack-intel.htm, accessed 21 June 2013

Mill J S, *Utilitarianism* (Original Edition 1879, The Floating Press 2009)

Mills E, 'Wikileaks Fans Should Think before They Botnet' (*CNet*, 10 December 2010) http://news.cnet.com/8301-27080_3-20025373-245.html, accessed 28 September 2011

———, 'Anonymous to Target Iran with DoS Attack' (*CNet*, 29 April 2011) http://news.cnet.com/8301-27080_3-20058700-245.html, accessed 21 June 2013

———, 'Anonymous Exposes Info of Alleged Pepper Spray Cop' (*CNet*, 26 September 2011) http://news.cnet.com/8301-27080_3-20111813-245/anonymous-exposes-info-of-alleged-pepper-spray-cop/, accessed 15 August 2012

Mills S, *Foucault* (Routledge, London 2003)

Milone M G, 'Hactivism: Securing the National Infrastructure' (2002) 58 The Business Lawyer 383

Mintz H, '"Anonymous" Defendants Appear in San Jose Federal Court in Paypal Cyberattack Case' (*Mercury News*, 01 September 2011) http://sip-trunking.tmcnet.com/news/2011/09/01/5747845.htm, accessed 01 September 2017

Moitra S D, 'Developing Policies for Cybercrime-Some Empirical Issues' (2005) 13 European Journal of Crime, Criminal Law & Criminal Justice 435

Morgan B and Yeung K, *An Introduction to Law and Regulation: Text and Materials* (Cambridge University Press, Cambridge 2007)

Morozov E, 'In Defense of DDoS' (*Slate Magazine*, 13 December 2010) http://www.slate.com/id/2277786/, accessed 20 May 2011

———, *The Net Delusion: The Dark Side of Internet Freedom* (Public Affairs, New York 2011)

Morreal J, 'The Justifiability of Violent Civil Disobedience' in Bedau H (ed), *Civil Disobedience in Focus* (Routledge, London 1976)

Mueller M, Mathiason J, and Klein H, 'The Internet and Global Governance Principles and Norms for a New Regime' (2007) 13 Global Governance 237

Mueller M, 'IGF 2015: Running in Place' (2015) http://www.internetgovernance.org/2015/11/16/igf-2015-running-in-place/, accessed 17 December 2017

Murray A D, *The Regulation of Cyberspace: Control in the Online Environment* (Routledge, London 2007)
Musiani F, 'The Internet Bill of Rights Project: The Challenge of Reconciliation between Natural Freedoms and Needs for Regulation' (Fourth Annual GigaNet Symposium, Sharm-el-Sheikh, Egypt, 2009)
Myers H, 'Anonymous Anarchist Action Hacktivist Group Founded' (*libcom.org*, 10 March 2011) http://libcom.org/news/anonymous-anarchist-action-hacktivist-group-founded-10032011, accessed 22 September 2017

N

Netanel N W, 'Cyberspace Self-Governance: A Skeptical View from Liberal Democratic Theory' (2000) 88 California Law Review 395
Newman A, 'Hacker Group Takes on Fed, IMF, "Global Banking Cartel"' (*The New American*, 15 March 2011) http://www.thenewamerican.com/tech/computers/item/7213-hacker-group-takes-on-fed-imf-global-banking-cartel, accessed 12 August 2011
Nicolson D, 'Ideology and the South African Judicial Process-Lessons from the Past' (1992) 8 South Africa Journal on Human Rights 50
Nicolson D and Webb J S, *Professional Legal Ethics: Critical Interrogations* (Oxford University Press, Oxford 1999)
Noga K E, 'Securitizing Copyrights: An Answer to the Sonny Bono Copyright Term Extension Act' (2007) 9 Tulane Journal of Technology & Intellectual Property 1
Norrie A, *Crime, Reason and History: A Critical Introduction to Criminal Law* (Butterworths Tolley, London 2001)
Nunziato D C, 'The Death of the Public Forum in Cyberspace' (2005) 20 Berkeley Technology Law Journal 1115

O

O'Neill F J, 'Symbolic Speech' (1975) 43 Fordham Law Review 590
Ohm P, 'The Myth of the Superuser: Fear, Risk, and Harm Online' (2008) 41 University of California Davis Law Review 1327
Oliver P E, 'Bringing the Crowd Back In: The Non-organizational Elements of Social Movements' (1989) 11 Research in Social Movements, Conflict and Change 1

Omidyar P, 'WikiLeaks, Press Freedom and Free Expression in the Digital Age' (*Huffington Post*, 2 February 2014) http://www.huffingtonpost.com/pierre-omidyar/wikileaks-press-freedom-a_b_4380738.html, accessed 31 July 2017

Organisation for Economic Co-Operation and Development (OECD), *The Economic and Social Role of Internet Intermediaries* (OECD, 2010) http://www.oecd.org/internet/ieconomy/44949023.pdf, accessed 23 February 2013

Out-Law, 'UK Law Makes Hacking an Act of Terrorism' (*Out-Law*, 21 February 2001) http://www.out-law.com/default.aspx?page=1409, accessed 20 May 2017

———, 'Commission Proposes New EU Cybercrime Law' (*The Register*, 11 October 2010) http://www.theregister.co.uk/2010/10/11/eu_new_cybercrime_law/print.html, accessed 10 November 2017

Owen T, 'Cyber-Violence: Towards a Predictive Model, Drawing upon Genetics, Psychology and Neuroscience.' 9/1 International Journal of Criminology and Sociological Theory 1–11

P

Packer H L, *The Limits of the Criminal Sanction* (Stanford University Press, Stanford 1968)

Page B I and Shapiro R Y, 'Effects of Public Opinion on Policy' (1983) 77 The American Political Science Review 175

Palfrey J, 'Four Phases of Internet Regulation' (2010) 77/3 Social Research 981

Parker C, *Just Lawyers: Regulation and Access to Justice* (Oxford University Press, Oxford 1999)

Parnell B-A, 'Brit Mastermind of Anonymous Paypal Attack Gets 18 Months' Porridge' (*The Register*, 24 January 2013) http://www.theregister.co.uk/2013/01/24/uk_anonymous_hackers_sentencing_payback/, accessed 26 January 2013

Pasquale F, 'Trusting (and Verifying) Online Intermediaries' Policing' in Szoka B and Marcus A (eds), *The Next Digital Decade: Essays on the Future of the Internet* (Techfreedom, Washington DC 2010)

Perritt Jr H H, 'Towards a Hybrid Regulatory Scheme for the Internet' (2001) The University of Chicago Legal Forum 215

Philips M, 'The Justification of Punishment and the Justification of Political Authority' (1986) 5 Law and Philosophy 393

Pickerill J, 'Radical Politics on the Net' (2006) 59 Parliamentary Affairs 266

Pickett B L, 'Foucault and the Politics of Resistance' (1996) 28 Polity 445

Podgor E S, 'Cybercrime: Discretionary Jurisdiction' (2009) 47 University of Louisville Law Review 727

Posner R A, *Not a Suicide Pact: The Constitution in a Time of National Emergency* (Oxford University Press, Oxford 2006)

Post D, 'Anarchy, State and the Internet' (1995) 3 Journal of Online Law http://papers.ssrn.com/sol3/papers.cfm?abstract_id=943456, accessed 18 December 2012

Poullet Y, 'How to Regulate Internet: New Paradigms for Internet Governance Self-Regulation: Value and Limits' (2001) 20 Cahiers du Centre de Recherches Informatique et Droit 79

Power P F, 'Civil Disobedience as Functional Opposition' (1972) 34 The Journal of Politics 37

Q

Quint P E, *Civil Disobedience and the German Courts: The Pershing Missile Protests in Comparative Perspective* (Taylor and Francis e-Library, 2007)

R

Raghavan T M, 'In Fear of Cyberterrorism: An Analysis of the Congressional Response' (2003) Journal of Law Technology & Policy 297

Raley R, *Tactical Media* (University of Minnesota Press, Minneapolis 2009)

Ranum M J, *The Myth of Homeland Security* (Wiley Publishing Inc, Indiana 2004)

Rawlinson K, 'Inside Anonymous: The "Hacktivists" in Their Own Words' (*The Independent,* 21 September 2011) https://whyweprotest.net/threads/inside-anonymous-the-hacktivists-in-their-own-words.89494/, accessed 21 September 2017

———, 'Activists Warned to Watch What They Say as Social Media Monitoring Becomes "Next Big Thing in Law Enforcement"' (*The Independent*, 01 October 2012) http://www.independent.co.uk/news/uk/crime/activists-warned-to-watch-what-they-say-as-social-media-monitoring-becomes-next-big-thing-in-law-enforcement-8191977.html, accessed 06 October 2017

Rawls J, 'Justice as Fairness: Political Not Metaphysical' (1985) 14 Philosophy and Public Affairs 223

———, *The Theory of Justice* (Harvard University Press, Cambridge 1999)

———, *The Law of the Peoples; with the Idea of Public Reason Revisited* (Harvard University Press, London 2000)

Raz J, *The Authority of Law: Essays on Law and Morality* (Oxford University Press, Oxford 1979)

Real D L and Honourable Irwin J F, 'Unconscious Influences on Judicial Decision-Making: The Illusion of Objectivity' (2010) 43 McGeorge Law Review

Reardon M, 'Verizon Sued for Alleged NSA Cooperation' (*CNet*, 15 May 2006) http://news.cnet.com/Verizon-sued-for-alleged-NSA-cooperation/2100-1036_3-6072483.html, accessed 29 May 2012

Reed C, *Making Laws for Cyberspace* (Oxford University Press, Oxford 2012) 17–26

Reidenberg J R, 'Governing Networks and Rule-Making in Cyberspace' (1996) 45 Emory Law Journal 911

———, 'Lex Informatica: The Formulation of Information Policy Rules through Technology' (1997) 76 Texas Law Review 533

———, 'States and Internet Enforcement' (2004) 1 University of Ottawa Law & Technology Journal 216

———, 'Technology and Internet Jurisdiction' (2004) 153 University of Pennsylvania Law Review 1951

Reynolds G, 'Ham Sandwich Nation: Due Process When Everything Is a Crime' (Legal Studies Research Paper No. 206, University of Tennessee 2013) http://ssrn.com/abstract=2203713, accessed 20 June 2013

Rheingold H, *The Virtual Community: Homesteading on the Electronic Frontier* (The MIT Press, Cambridge, MA 2000)

Ribeiro J, 'Winsconsin Man Sentenced for Participating in Anonymous DDoS' (*PCWorld*, 2 December 2013) http://www.pcworld.com/article/2068600/wisconsin-man-sentenced-for-participating-in-anonymous-ddos.html, accessed 31 July 2017

Rietjens B, 'Give and Ye Shall Receive! The Copyright Implications of Bittorrent' (2005) 2 SCRIPT-ed 108

Roberts J V, 'Sentencing Guidelines and Judicial Discretion' (2011) 51 British Journal of Criminology 997

Roberts J V and Hough M, 'Sentencing Riot-Related Offending: Where Do the Public Stand?' (2013) 53 British Journal of Criminology 1

Robinson P H, 'Why Does the Criminal Law Care What the Layperson Thinks Is Just? Coercive Versus Normative Crime Control' (2000) 86 Virginia Law Review 1839

Robinson P H and Dubber M D, 'An Introduction to the Model Penal Code' (2007) 10 New Criminal Law Review 319
Rosenzweig P, 'Overcriminalization: An Agenda for Change' (2004) 54 American University Law Review 809
Rousseau J-J, *The Social Contract* (The Penguin Group, London 2004)
Ruffin O, 'Hacktivism: From Here to There' (*cDc Communications,* 06 March 2004) http://www.cultdeadcow.com/cDc_files/cDc-0384.html, accessed 20 September 2017

S

Salamon L (ed), *The Tools of Government: A Guide to the New Governance* (Oxford University Press, Oxford 2002)
Salter M and Mason J, *Writing Law Dissertations: An Introduction and Guide to the Conduct of Legal Research* (Longman Publishing Group, London 2007)
Samuel A W, 'Hacktivism and the Future of Political Participation' (DPhil Thesis, Harvard University 2004)
Sankin A, 'Anonymous' BART Police Attack: Hackers Expose Cops' Personal Information' (*Huffington Post*, 17 August 2011) http://www.huffingtonpost.com/2011/08/17/anonymous-bart-police-attack-personal-information_n_929627.html, accessed 31 July 2017
Schesser S D, 'A New Domain for Public Speech: Opening Public Spaces Online' (2006) 94 California Law Review 1791
Schjølberg S, '*ITU Global Cybersecurity Agenda [GCA]*' (High Level Experts Group [HLEG] Global Strategic Report, International Telecommunications Union, Geneva 2008) http://www.itu.int/osg/csd/cybersecurity/gca/docs/Report_of_the_Chairman_of_HLEG_to_ITU_SG_03_sept_08.pdf, accessed 15 February 2013
Schlesinger S R, 'Civil Disobedience: The Problem of Selective Obedience to Law' (1976) 3 Hastings Constitutional Law Quarterly 947
Schopp R F, *Justification Defenses and Just Convictions* (Cambridge University Press, Cambridge 1998)
Schor E, 'Telecoms Granted Immunity in US Wiretapping Probe' (*The Guardian,* 20 June 2008) http://www.guardian.co.uk/world/2008/jun/20/georgebush.usa, accessed 21 June 2013
Schwarz A M, 'Civil Disobedience' (1970) 16 McGill Law Journal 542
Scott C, 'Accountability in the Regulatory State' (2000) 27 Journal of Law and Society 38

Segall L, 'Anonymous Strikes Back after Feds Shut Down Piracy Hub Megaupload' (*CNN Money*, 20 January 2012) http://money.cnn.com/2012/01/19/technology/megaupload_shutdown/index.htm, accessed 20 July 2013.

Seid R A, 'A Requiem for O'Brien: On the Nature of Symbolic Speech' (1992) 23 Cumberland Law Review 563

Sentencing Guidelines Council, 'Overarching Principles: Seriousness' (2004) http://sentencingcouncil.judiciary.gov.uk/docs/web_seriousness_guideline.pdf, accessed 15 February 2013

———, 'Magistrate's Court Sentencing Guidelines: Definitive Guideline' (2012) http://sentencingcouncil.judiciary.gov.uk/docs/MCSG_Update9_October_2012.pdf, accessed 21 June 2013

Shane D, 'Think Tank Calls for "Geneva Convention" on Cyber War' (*Information Age*, 04 February 2011) http://www.information-age.com/technology/security/1599193/think-tank-calls-for-'geneva-convention'-on-cyber-war, accessed 10 November 2012

Shapiro I (ed), *Two Treatises of Government and a Letter Concerning Toleration* (Yale University Press, London 2003)

Shapiro M, *Who Guards the Guardians? Judicial Control of Administration* (University of Georgia Press, Athens 1988)

Shearing C, 'Reflections on the Refusal to Acknowledge Private Governments' in Jennifer Wood and Benoit Dupont (eds), *Democracy, Society and the Governance of Security* (Cambridge University Press, Cambridge 2006) 11–32

Shearing C and Wood J, 'Nodal Governance, Democracy, and the New 'Denizens'' (2003) 30 Journal of Law and Society 400

Sherman L W, 'Defiance, Deterrence, and Irrelevance: A Theory of the Criminal Sanction' (1993) 30 Journal of Research in Crime and Delinquency 445

Shore M, Du Y, and Zeadally S, 'A Public-Private Partnership Model for National Cybersecurity' (2011) 3 Policy and Internet 1

Simon B, 'Illegal Knowledge: Strategies for New Media Activism: Dialogue with Ricardo Dominguez and Geert Lovink' in Bousquet M and Wills K (eds), *The Politics of Information: The Electronic Mediation of Social Change* (Altx Press 2003)

Simon J, *Governing through Crime* (Oxford University Press, Oxford 2007)

Simmonds N E, *Central Issues in Jurisprudence* (3rd edn, Sweet and Maxwell Ltd, London 2008)

Singel R, 'Dutch Arrest Teen for Pro-Wikileaks Attack on Visa and Mastercard Websites' (*Threat Level*, 09 December 2010) http://www.wired.com/threatlevel/2010/12/wikileaks_anonymous_arrests/#seealsoaff033736dd3e21e1f35daab3a12f8f9, accessed 12 August 2011

Sinrod E and Reilly W, 'Cyber-Crimes: A Practical Approach to the Application of Federal Computer Crime Laws' (2000) 16 Santa Clara Computer & High Tech Law Journal 177

Skibell R, 'Cybercrime and Misdemeanors: A Reevaluation of the Computer Fraud and Abuse Act' (2003) 18 Berkeley Technology Law Journal 909

Smith B P, 'Hacking, Poaching, and Counterattacking: Digital Counterstrikes and the Contours of Self-Help' (2005) 1 Journal of Law Economy & Policy 171

Smith G and Reilly R J, 'Alleged 'Paypal 14' Hackers Seek Deal to Stay Out of Prison after Nearly 2 Years in Limbo' (*Huffington Post,* 18 May 2013) http://www.huffingtonpost.com/2013/05/18/paypal-14-hackers_n_3281768.html, accessed 20 May 2013

Smith M B E, 'Is There a Prima Facie Obligation to Obey the Law?' (1973) 82 The Yale Law Journal 950

Smith W, 'Civil Disobedience and Social Power: Reflections on Habermas' (2008) 7 Contemporary Political Theory 72

Somaiya R, 'Activists Say Web Assault for Assange Is Expanding' (*New York Times,* 10 December 2010) http://www.nytimes.com/2010/12/11/world/europe/11anonymous.html?_r=4, accessed 16 January 2017

Sommer P, 'Criminalising Hacking Tools' (2006) 3 Digital Investigation 68

Sophos, 'Security Threat Report 2012' (*Sophos,* 2012) https://www.sophos.com/en-us/press-office/press-releases/2012/01/security-threat-report-2012.aspx, accessed 30 August 2017

Spamhaus.org, 'Spamhaus Botnet Controller List', https://www.spamhaus.org/bcl/, accessed 31 July 2017

Stalbaum B, 'Why I Made a Formal Statement to the UCSD Police' (*Walking Tools,* 21 July 2010) http://www.walkingtools.net/?p=489, accessed 26 October 2017

Stein A R, 'Parochialism and Pluralism in Cyberspace Regulation' (2004) 153 University of Pennsylvania Law Review 2003

Storing H J, 'The Case against Civil Disobedience' in Bedau H A (ed), *Civil Disobedience in Focus* (Routledge, London 2002)

Strong E W, 'Justification of Juridical Punishment' (1969) 79 Ethics 187

Sunstein C R, *Laws of Fear: Beyond the Precautionary Principle* (Cambridge University Press, Cambridge 2005)

———, *Republic.Com 2.0* (Princeton University Press, Princeton 2007)

Swire P, 'No Cop on the Beat: Underenforcement in E-Commerce and Cybercrime' (2009) 7 Journal on Telecommunications & High Technology Law 107

T

Tang L and Yang P, 'Symbolic Power and the Internet: The Power of a 'Horse'' (2011) 33 Media Culture Society 675

Taylor P A, *Hackers: Crime in the Digital Sublime* (Routledge, London 1999)

Techdirt, 'The Internet Strikes Back: Anonymous Takes Down Doj.Gov, RIAA, MPAA Sites to Protest Megaupload Seizure' (*Techdirt,* 19 January 2012) http://www.techdirt.com/articles/20120119/14494917475/internet-strikes-back-anonymous-takes-down-dojgov-riaa-mpaa-sites-to-protest-megaupload-seizure.shtml, accessed 19 November 2017

Terban S, 'Anonymous and Their Alleged Propagandist Barrett Brown' (*Infosec Island,* 10 March 2011) https://www.infosecisland.com/blogview/12441-Anonymous-and-Their-Alleged-Propagandist-Barrett-Brown.html, accessed 28 September 2017

Terranova T, *Network Culture: Politics for the Information Age* (Pluto Press, London 2004)

Teubner G, 'Juridification: Concepts, Aspects, Limits, Solutions' in Teubner G (ed), *Juridification of Social Spheres: A Comparative Analysis in the Areas of Labour, Corporate, Antitrust and Social Welfare Law* (De Gruyter, Berlin 1987)

———, *Law as an Autopoietic System* (Blackwell, Oxford 1993)

The Economist, 'Cyberwar: War in the Fifth Domain' (*The Economist*, 3rd July 2010) 25–27

The Electrohippies Collective, 'Cyberlaw UK: Civil Rights and Protest on the Internet' *(iwar.org,* 2000) http://www.iwar.org.uk/hackers/resources/electrohippies-collective/comm-2000-12.pdf, accessed 15 February 2013

The Smoking Gun, 'Judge Lifts Twitter Ban on "Anonymous" 14' (*The Smoking Gun*, 19 March 2012) http://www.thesmokinggun.com/documents/judge-lifts-anonymous-twitter-ban-145792, accessed 30 August 2017

Thomassen L, 'Within the Limits of Deliberative Reason Alone: Habermas, Civil Disobedience and Constitutional Democracy' (2007) 6 European Journal of Political Theory 200

Thompson T, 'Terrorizing the Technological Neighborhood Watch: The Alienation and Deterrence of the White Hats under the CFAA' (2008) 36 Florida State University Law Review 537

Tice M, 'Civil Disobedience: A Study of Law and Its Relation to Society' (1968) 13 South Dakota Law Review 356

Tiefenbrun S, 'Civil Disobedience and the US Constitution' (2003) 32 Southwestern University Law Review 677

Tierney T A, 'Civil Disobedience as the Lesser Evil' (1988) 59 University of Colorado Law Review 961

Tilley N, 'Thinking About Crime Prevention Performance Indicators' in Laylock G (ed), *Police Research Group Crime Detection and Prevention Series* (Home Office Police Research Group, London 1995)

TorrentFreak, 'Copyright Holders Punish Themselves with Crazy DMCA Takedowns' (*Torrentfreak*, 25 May 2012) http://torrentfreak.com/copyright-holders-punish-themselves-with-crazy-dmca-takedowns-120525/, accessed 29 May 2017

———, 'Copyright Trolls Slammed in UK House of Lords' (*TorrentFreak*, June 16, 2016) https://torrentfreak.com/copyright-trolls-slammed-in-uk-house-of-lords-160616/, accessed 31 July 2017

Travis J and Waul M, *Prisoners Once Removed: The Impact of Incarceration and Reentry on Children, Families, and Communities* (Urban Institute Press, Washington DC 2003)

Tremlett G and Agencies In Istanbul, 'Turkish Arrests Intensify Global War between Hacker Activists and Police' (*The Guardian*, 13 June 2011) http://www.guardian.co.uk/technology/2011/jun/13/turkish-arrests-global-war-hackers-police, accessed 21 September 2017

Trimegisto, 'History of Anonymous Hacktivism' (*The Trembling Uterus Blog*, 26 January 2011) http://tremblinguterus.blogspot.com/2011/01/history-of-anonymous-hacktivism.html, accessed 28 September 2017

Tunick M, 'Hegel on Justified Disobedience' (1998) 26 Political Theory 514

U

United States Department of Homeland Security, 'National Infrastructure Protection Plan: Information Technology Sector' (undated) https://www.dhs.gov/xlibrary/assets/nipp_it.pdf, accessed 30 August 2017

———, 'What Is Critical Infrastructure?' (undated) http://www.dhs.gov/what-critical-infrastructure, accessed 20 June 2013

United States Department of Justice, 'United States Attorney's Manual' (1997) http://www.justice.gov/usao/eousa/foia_reading_room/usam/, accessed 21 June 2017

United States Senate, 'The National Information Infrastructure Protection Act of 1995' (1996) (Report 104-357)

United States Sentencing Commission, '2011 Federal Sentencing Guidelines Manual' (2011) http://www.ussc.gov/Guidelines/2011_Guidelines/Manual_PDF/index.cfm, accessed 21 June 2013

———, 'Guidelines Manual 2016' (2016) https://www.ussc.gov/guidelines/2016-guidelines-manual, accessed 31 July 2017

Urbas G, 'Criminalising Computer Misconduct: Some Legal and Philosophical Concerns' (2006) 14 Asia Pacific Law Review 95

Urbelis A, 'Toward a More Equitable Prosecution of Cybercrime: Concerning Hackers, Criminals, and the National Security' (2004) 29 Vermont Law Review 975

V

Vamos N, 'Please Don't Call It "Plea Bargaining"' (2009) 617 Criminal Law Review 617

van Kokswijk J, *Social Control in Online Society–Advantages of Self-Regulation on the Internet* (International Conference on Cyberworlds, Singapore 2010)

Vegh S, 'Classifying Forms of Online Activism: The Case of Cyberprotests against the World Bank' in McCaughey M and Ayers M D (eds), *Cyberactivism: Online Activism in Theory and Practice* (Routledge, London 2003)

Verizon, '2011 Was the Year of the "Hacktivist" According to the "Verizon 2012 Data Breach Investigations Report"' (*Verizon*, 2012) http://newscenter.verizon.com/press-releases/verizon/2012/2011-was-the-year-of-the.html, accessed 10 November 2017

Vidanage H, 'Rivalry in Cyberspace and Virtual Contours of a New Conflict Zone: The Sri Lankan Case' in Karatzogianni A (ed), *Cyberconflicts and Global Politics* (Routledge, London 2009)

Vijayan J, '"Anonymous" Arrests Tied to Paypal DDoS Attacks, FBI Says' (*ComputerWorld*, 20 July 2011) http://www.computerworld.com.au/article/394256/_anonymous_arrests_tied_paypal_ddos_attacks_fbi_says/, accessed 10 November 2017

Vikas S N, '"Anonymous" Operation India Removed from Facebook and Twitter' (*TheNextWeb*, 12 June 2011) http://thenextweb.com/in/2011/06/12/anonymous-operation-india-removed-from-facebook-and-twitter/, accessed 30 August 2017

Violet Blue, 'Anonymous Attacks Child Porn Websites and Publish User Names' (*ZDnet Blog*, 21 October 2011) http://www.zdnet.com/blog/violetblue/anonymous-attacks-child-porn-websites-and-publish-user-names/757, accessed 19 February 2017

Virilio P, *The Information Bomb* (Verso Books, New York 2005)
von Hirsch A, *Censure and Sanctions* (Oxford University Press, Oxford 1996)
———, 'Proportionate Sentences: A Desert Perspective' in Ashworth A and von Hirsch A (eds), *Principled Sentencing: Theory and Policy* (Oxford Hart Publishing 1998)
———, 'Seriousness and Severity' in von Hirsch A (ed), *Censure and Sanctions* (Oxford University Press, Oxford 2003)
von Hirsch A et al. (eds), *Restorative Justice and Criminal Justice: Competing or Reconcilable Paradigms?* (Hart Publishing, Oxford 2003)

W

Walden I, *Computer Crimes and Digital Investigations* (Oxford University Press, New York 2007)
Walker C, 'Cyber-Terrorism: Legal Principle and Law in the United Kingdom' (2005) 110 Penn State Law Review 625
———, 'Clamping Down on Terrorism in the United Kingdom' (2006) 4 Journal of International Criminal Justice 1137
Walker N, 'Legislating the Transcendental: Von Hirsch's Proportionality' (1992) 51 The Cambridge Law Journal 530
Walker S, *Taming the System: The Control of Discretion in Criminal Justice, 1950–1990* (Oxford University Press, Oxford 1993)
Walker-Osborn C and McLeod B, 'Getting Tough on Cyber Crime' (1 June 2015) 57/2 ITNOW 32–33. doi:https://doi.org/10.1093/itnow/bwv042
Wall D, *Cybercrime: The Transformation of Crime in the Information Age* (Polity Press, Cambridge 2007)
Walton R, 'The Computer Misuse Act' (2006) 11 Information Security Technical Report 39
Warner G, 'Internet Anarchy: Anonymous Crowds Flex Their Muscles' (*CyberCrime and Doing Time Blog*, 13 December 2010) http://garwarner.blogspot.com/2010/12/internet-anarchy-anonymous-crowds-flex.html, accessed 13 August 2017
Watkins M, Bradshaw T, and Menn J, 'Global Police Moves against "Hacktivists"' (*The Financial Times*, 27 January 2011) http://www.ft.com/cms/s/0/db6f5ab0-2a34-11e0-b906-00144feab49a.html#axzz1YaNDtzCj, accessed 21 September 2017
Watts S, 'Former Lulzsec Hacker Jake Davis on His Motivations' (*BBC*, 16 May 2013) http://www.bbc.co.uk/news/technology-22526021, accessed 18 May 2013

Webster F, *Theories of the Information Society* (3rd edn, Routledge, London 2006)

West J L, 'Is Injustice Relevant? Narrative and Blameworthiness in Protester Trials' (2013) Vermont Law School Research Paper No. 11–13 (86/1 Temple Law Review, 107–48) http://ssrn.com/abstract=2247518, accessed 17 May 2013

Whitehead J W, 'Civil Disobedience and Operation Rescue: A Historical and Theoretical Analysis' (1991) 48 Washington & Lee Law Review 77

Wikipedia, 'Netizen' http://en.wikipedia.org/wiki/Netizen, accessed 25 June 2012

———, 'World Wide Web' http://en.wikipedia.org/wiki/World_Wide_Web, accessed 29 May 2012

———, 'List of Mergers and Acquisitions by Microsoft' http://en.wikipedia.org/wiki/List_of_mergers_and_acquisitions_by_Microsoft, accessed 29 May 2012

———, 'IP Address' http://en.wikipedia.org/wiki/IP_address#cite_note-rfc760-0, accessed 29 May 2012

———, 'Mafiaboy' http://en.wikipedia.org/wiki/MafiaBoy, accessed 11 March 2011

———, 'Internet Society (ISOC)' http://en.wikipedia.org/wiki/Internet_Society, accessed 15 June 2012

———, 'Right to Internet Access' http://en.wikipedia.org/wiki/Right_to_Internet_access, accessed 16 November 2011

Wilson C, 'Botnets, Cybercrime, and Cyberterrorism: Vulnerabilities and Policy Issues for Congress' (Library of Congress, Congressional Research Service, Washington DC 2008)

Williams J, 'Ninth Circuit Panel Backs Away From Dangerous Password Sharing Decision—But Creates Even More Confusion About the CFAA' (*Electronic Frontier Foundation*, 15 July 2016) https://www.eff.org/deeplinks/2016/07/ninth-circuit-panel-backs-away-dangerous-password-sharing-decision-creates-even, accessed 31 July 2017

Winston S, '"Don't Be Evil": Uncovering the Implications of Google Search' (2011) 7 Dalhousie Journal of Interdisciplinary Management 1

Wittgenstein L, *Philosophical Investigations* (G.E.M. Anscombe, tr, 2nd ed, Blackwell, Oxford 1958)

Wolff J, 'Interview: Howard Schmidt' (*MSNBC,* 21 December 2010) http://www.newsweek.com/2010/12/21/interview-with-cyber-security-czar-howard-schmidt.html, accessed 18 January 2017

Wolff M A, 'Evidence-Based Judicial Discretion: Promoting Public Safety through State Sentencing Reform' (2008) 83 New York University Law Review 1389

Wood J, 'Research and Innovation in the Field of Security: A Nodal Governance View' in Wood J and Dupont B (eds), *Democracy, Society and the Governance of Security* (Cambridge University Press, Cambridge 2006)

Wood J, Shearing C, and Froestad J, 'Restorative Justice and Nodal Governance' (2011) 35 International Journal of Comparative and Applied Criminal Justice 1

Woozley A D, 'Civil Disobedience and Punishment' (1976) 86 Ethics 323

Worley B, 'Facebook: Another Privacy Scandal' (*ABCNews*, 19 October 2010) http://abcnews.go.com/GMA/Consumer/facebook-privacy-scandal-facebooks-watergate/story?id=11912201#.T8dLoJLoU4k, accessed 31 May 2017.

Worthy J and Fanning M, 'Denial-of-Service: Plugging the Legal Loopholes?' (2007) 23 Computer Law & Security Report 194

Wright E O, *The Politics of Punishment: A Critical Analysis of Prisons in America* (National Criminal Justice Reference Service Library Collection Harper & Row Publishers, New York 1973)

Wu T, 'When Code Isn't Law' (2003) 89 Virginian Law Review 103

Wu T and Yoo C, 'Keeping the Internet Neutral?: Tim Wu and Christopher Yoo Debate' (2007) 59 Federal Communications Law Journal 575

Y

Yar M, *Cybercrime and Society* (Sage, London 2006)

———, 'Public Perceptions and Public Opinion About Internet Crime' in Jewkes Y and Yar M (eds), *Handbook of Internet Crime* (Willand Publishing, Devon 2010)

Yeung K, 'Towards an Understanding of Regulation by Design' in Brownsword R and Yeung K (eds), *Regulating Technologies: Legal Futures, Regulatory Frames and Technological Fixes* (Hart Publishing, Oxford 2008)

Z

Zandt D, 'Are the Cyber Battles with the Enemies of Wikileaks the New Civil Disobedience?' (*Alternet*, 13 December 2010) http://www.alternet.org/story/149183/are_the_cyber_battles_with_the_enemies_of_wikileaks_the_new_civil_disobedience, accessed 28 September 2017

Zavrsnik A, 'Cybercrime Definitional Challenges and Criminological Particularities' (2008) 2 Masaryk University Journal of Law & Technology 1

Zedner L, 'Too Much Security?' (2003) 31 International Journal of the Sociology of Law 155

———, *Criminal Justice* (Oxford University Press, Oxford 2004)

———, 'Securing Liberty in the Face of Terror: Reflections from Criminal Justice' (2005) 32 Journal of Law and Society 507

———, 'Pre-Crime and Post-Criminology?' (2007) 11 Theoretical Criminology 261

———, *Security* (Routledge, New York 2009)

Zeidy D, 'Facebook Just REVERSED Ban Against Anonymous Group That Has Been Targeting ISIS' (*MintPress News*, 18 March 2015) http://www.mintpressnews.com/facebook-just-reversed-ban-against-anonymous-group-that-has-been-targeting-isis/203449/, accessed 31 July 2017

Zetter K, 'Hackers Release 1 Million Apple Device IDs Allegedly Stolen from FBI Laptop' (*Wired*, 09 April 2012) http://www.wired.com/threat-level/2012/09/hackers-release-1-million-apple-device-ids-allegedly-stolen-from-fbi-laptop/, accessed 08 September 2012

Zhang C, 'Regulation of the Internet-New Laws and New Paradigms' (2006) 17 Journal of Law, Information & Science 53

Zittrain J, *The Future of the Internet and How to Stop It* (Yale University Press, Virginia 2008)

Zizek S, 'Shoplifters of the World Unite' (*London Review of Books*, 19 August 2011) http://www.lrb.co.uk/2011/08/19/slavoj-zizek/shoplifters-of-the-world-unite, accessed 24 August 2017

Zlotnick D M, 'The War within the War on Crime: The Congressional Assault on Judicial Sentencing Discretion' (2004) 57 South Methodist University Law Review 211

Index[1]

[1] Note: Page numbers followed by 'n' refer to notes.

V. Karagiannopoulos, *Living With Hacktivism*, Palgrave Studies in Cybercrime and Cybersecurity, https://doi.org/10.1007/978-3-319-71758-6

S

The manufacturer's authorised representative in the EU is Springer
Nature Customer Service Centre GmbH, Europaplatz 3, 69115 Heidelberg,
Germany. If you have any concerns regarding our products, please
contact ProductSafety@springernature.com

Printed and bound by CPI Group (UK) Ltd, Croydon, CR0 4YY
05/10/2026
02228140-0009